KING SCUM
The Life and Crimes of Tony Felloni
Dublin's Heroin Boss

Includes new & updated material

KING SCUM

The Life and Crimes of Tony Felloni
Dublin's Heroin Boss

Includes new & updated material

PAUL REYNOLDS

Gill & Macmillan

Gill & Macmillan Ltd
Hume Avenue, Park West, Dublin 12
with associated companies throughout the world
www.gillmacmillan.ie

© Paul Reynolds, 1998, 2004
ISBN-13: 978 07171 3748 0
ISBN-10: 0 7171 3741 8
Design and print origination by Andy Gilsenan and Carole Lynch
Printed and bound by Nørhaven Paperback A/S, Denmark

This book is typeset in Goudy 10 on 12 point.

*The paper used in this book comes from the wood pulp of
managed forests. For every tree felled, at least one tree is
planted, thereby renewing natural resources.*

A CIP catalogue record for this book is available
from the British Library.

9 8 7 6 5

Contents

Acknowledgments

The nature of a book like this is such that you cannot publicly acknowledge and thank all those who've helped you the most. But it goes without saying that I am eternally grateful to all the Gardaí, the prison officials, the court officers, the lawyers, the people of the north inner city, the community workers, the drug counsellors, the criminal associates, and those in the Departments of Justice, Education, Defence and the Revenue Commissioners without whom this book would not have been possible. You know who you are.

I am also grateful for the help and encouragement I received from, among others, the indefatigable Paul Williams of the *Sunday World*; Pádraig Yeates and Seán Flynn of *The Irish Times*; Eamon Kennedy and Ed Mulhall at RTÉ; Tomás Mac Ruairí at the courts; Michael, Fergal, D, Gabrielle and Angela at Gill & Macmillan; Anne, Maria, Lena and Ann Felloni; Conor McDonnell and Eoin McCullough; Gregory O'Connor and the staff at the National Archives; and the staff at the Gilbert Library and RTÉ's News and References Libraries.

Finally, I would like to thank my family and friends for all their 'rapport and support'—Teasie, John-Willy, Gerry, Tina, Kevin, Karen, John, Carola, Marcus, Fergal, Kevin, Sean, Mick, Ian and Judy.

THE FELLONI FAMILY TREE

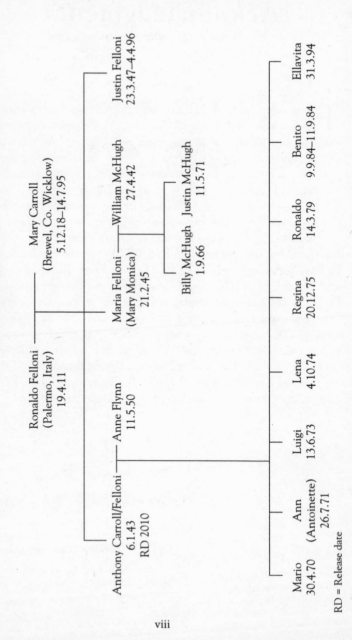

Ronaldo Felloni
(Palermo, Italy)
19.4.11

Mary Carroll
(Brewel, Co. Wicklow)
5.12.18–14.7.95

Anthony Carroll/Felloni
6.1.43
RD 2010

Anne Flynn
11.5.50

Maria Felloni
(Mary Monica)
21.2.45

William McHugh
27.4.42

Justin Felloni
23.3.47–4.4.96

Billy McHugh
1.9.66

Justin McHugh
11.5.71

Mario
30.4.70

Ann
(Antoinette)
26.7.71

Luigi
13.6.73

Lena
4.10.74

Regina
20.12.75

Ronaldo
14.3.79

Benito
9.9.84–11.9.84

Ellavita
31.3.94

RD = Release date

viii

Tony Felloni's Criminal Record

All courts refer to Dublin except where otherwise stated.

Date / Court / Charge / Sentence

1. 20/11/1959 / Children's Court / Taking a scooter / Bound over for twelve months

2. 9/12/1959 / Children's Court / Housebreaking and larceny / Two years in St Conleth's Reformatory, Daingean

3. 8/8/1960 / District Court / Larceny from a shop / £2 fine

4. 14/5/1963 / District Court / Malicious damage / One month prison and £16 10s compensation

5. 14/2/1964 / Circuit Criminal Court / Conspiracy to steal, demanding money with menaces, blackmail and larceny / Three years' penal servitude

6. 11/4/1967 / Circuit Court / Car theft / Three months

7. 6/7/1967 / Circuit Court / Receiving stolen goods / One year

8. 26/8/1968 / District Court / Housebreaking and larceny / Six months

9. 17/10/1968 / Circuit Court / Office-breaking with two counts of breaking into shops / Fifteen months

10. 1/11/1968 / District Court / Housebreaking and larceny / Eight months

11. 4/11/1968 / District Court / Larceny from a person / Three months

12. 26/9/1969 / District Court / Loitering with intent (two counts) / Three months

13. 23/9/1970 / Bray District Court / Two counts of possession of contraband spirits / Fourteen days each count, total four weeks

14. 5/11/1970 / District Court / Loitering with intent / Three months

15. 28/1/1971 / District Court / Possession of housebreaking implements by night / Three months

16. 2/11/1971 District Court / Carried in motor car without owner's consent and loitering / Six months and three months—nine months total

17. 8/2/1972 / Circuit Court / Breaking and entering / Six months

18. 14/2/1972 / District Court / Breaking and entering / Nine months

19. 26/11/1973 / District Court / Driving without insurance / Three months

20. 29/1/1974 / Circuit Court / Driving without insurance / Six months

21. 4/10/1974 / District Court / Possession of housebreaking implements / Twelve months (suspended)

22. 4/12/1974 / Circuit Court / Assault on police officer / Three months

23. 28/2/1975 / Mullingar District Court / Assault / Probation Act

24. 12/11/1975 / Templemore District Court / Taking possession of motor vehicle without owner's consent / Six months

25. 29/1/1976 / Circuit Court / Driving without licence/insurance (two counts) / Six months on first, £2 fine or seven days on second, disqualified for one year (increased to fifteen on appeal)

26. 28/1/1977 / Circuit Court / Assault on Garda / Six months (suspended), £50, bound over for six years

27. 9/6/1977 / District Court / Common assault / Six months

28. 17/2/1978 / District Court / Unlawful assault on wife / Six months

29. 13/6/1978 / District Court / Unlawful assault on wife / Six months

30. 24/7/1978 / Central Criminal Court / Trespassing with intent to steal / Three years

31. 30/11/1981 / Kingston Crown Court, Surrey, England / Conspiracy to supply drugs / Four years

32. 2/7/1986 / Circuit Court / Possession and supply of heroin / Ten years

33. 20/6/1996 / Circuit Court / Possession and supply of heroin / Twenty years

Introduction

Heroin dealing is not an exact science. Heroin in bulk is difficult to price, it depends on who is buying the drug and how much of it they want. As in any other market, prices fluctuate, but because of the craving heroin creates among addicts, prices rocket if the supply falls off. Following the murder of Bernard 'Verb' Sugg in Dublin in the summer of 2003, there was a severe shortage of heroin. Sugg handled much of the supply for the so-called 'Westies' criminal gang and for three weeks the capital's drug addicts found it extremely difficult to score. They had to pay more than twice as much for a hit—€50 for a €20 bag. The last time there was such a shortage was in 1994. There is at present a glut of the drug on the streets of Dublin; consequently prices are low.

Heroin is weighed in ounces and grams and divided up into street deals or 'Q's. It is then sold on to addicts. A Q contains enough heroin for one fix, i.e. one injection or one smoke. Heroin suppliers will make between eight and fourteen Qs out of every gram of heroin depending on the purity level, which on the streets varies between 15 and 20 per cent. The greater the purity, the more expensive the Q. One of the most common ways in Dublin to divide heroin into Qs is to use a small white plastic McDonald's spoon.

When Tony Felloni was selling heroin, a level teaspoon made a £10 bag; a heaped teaspoon sold for around £20. A heroin supplier sold the drug in batches to his street dealers. There were between seven and twenty Qs in a batch depending on who was supplying and who was selling. Chronic addicts working for particular suppliers could sell batches of twenty Qs at a time, but addicts likely to run off with the supplier's heroin would only be trusted to sell a batch of seven at a time. Street dealers could in turn sell heroin at different levels of purity. Those selling £20 20- or 30-per-cent pure bags got a reputation for 'good gear', but those selling £10 bags were also popular with poor junkies or young heroin smokers who may only recently have developed a habit.

In the 1990s nearly all the capital's street dealers were themselves drug addicts, selling to feed their own habits. They worked on a percentage basis. In the case of a batch of fifteen £10 deals, the dealer usually sold ten for the supplier and gave him £100. He kept the remaining five for himself. He could then sell the £50 worth but he was more likely to shoot it into his own veins. Five Qs might have got a new smoker through the day but it wouldn't have lasted a chronic junkie to lunchtime.

Today in 2004, the business on the street has been somewhat simplified although the street dealers are still all addicts. Suppliers no longer hand out to their dealer addicts pre-prepared batches of heroin containing individual Qs. They sell them what is known as an 'eight' or a 'half-eight', either of which is still referred to as a batch, and let the addicts themselves divide up the drug into the Qs or fixes. In the square mile around the offices of Dublin City Council, which includes parts of Dame Street, Thomas Street and the Merchant's Quay Drugs Project, there could be as many as fifty pusher addicts selling heroin in any one day.

An eight is about 3.4 grams of heroin, but street dealers usually buy half-eights (around 1.7 grams) and make up about twenty individual Qs or street deals from them. They pay €240 for an eight, €125 for a half-eight. Each of the twenty deals they make from the half-eight sells for €20 a bag. There are now only standardised €20 bags for sale on the streets of Dublin. The days of the £10 bag are over. The profit on the retail sale of a half-eight after it has been converted into street deals could be up to €275, but pusher addicts sell to feed their habits. They usually make up ten bags of individual fixes to sell from what they buy, then shoot up the rest.

The prices and measurements may have changed, but much of the drug dealing on the street and the type of people who operate there remain the same. There are drug addicts in Dublin today who do nothing else but sell heroin and shoot up their own percentage. Some sell as many as nine or ten batches—€4,000 of heroin every day. As soon as they return to their supplier having sold one batch, he'll have another for them. These pusher addicts are usually feeding two habits: the heroin they keep is split between themselves and their girlfriends.

Street dealers carry their batches of heroin around in their mouths. Less than the size of a marble, the deals are packed individually in cellophane and lumped together in the corner of a plastic bag. All the Qs inside the batch are knotted, as is the batch itself to ensure it doesn't leak. It is carried under the tongue and swallowed if the pusher is attacked by other addicts or stopped and searched by a Garda. Once the danger has passed the pusher has a cigarette, a glass of milk or something to make himself sick. In the same way that a cow regurgitates grass to chew the cud, the Dublin junkie is able to vomit back up an entire batch of heroin soon after swallowing it. He'll wipe it down and sell it off.

A Garda body search is a mere inconvenience but detention poses a more difficult problem. If a pusher is held for longer than two hours the drugs will have entered his system and are harder to throw up. The heroin now has to be passed. Once this has happened, junkies have no compunction about picking through their own faeces to recover their drugs. The Gardaí have special toilets for drug dealers to use while in custody which enables them to retrieve, for prosecution purposes, the cleansed and disinfected package of drugs once it has been passed. There is now legislation enabling the Gardaí to hold for up to seven days suspected dealers, couriers and mules, who smuggle drugs by stuffing or swallowing them.

Some pusher addicts can carry a batch of heroin up their nose by dividing up the Qs and putting seven or eight into each nostril. They also store it in their backsides and some can even conceal five or six street deals in the foreskins of their penises. When the time comes for them to sell the heroin, the nod is given and the junkies gather round the dealer in a bunch. The money is handed over, the Qs are passed out, the dealing is done in less than a minute and the dealer is gone to his supplier with the money.

This is the world in which Tony Felloni operated. He was one of the country's biggest heroin dealers in the 1980s and 1990s. He was, however, unique in that he tried to control every aspect of the business. In the morning he could be directly involved in the importation of hundreds of thousands of pounds worth of the drug while in the evening he was personally selling £10 and £20 bags to desperately sick junkies at the door of his parents' Corporation flat. He lodged thousands of pounds in bank accounts in Dublin, Liverpool and Belfast yet he refused to hand over fixes to addicts who came to him £1 short. The man operated both at the very top and the very bottom of the Dublin heroin market and it ultimately precipitated his downfall.

Felloni's meanness and small-mindedness appear to have arisen from his origins as a petty thief. He started stealing as a juvenile, before moving on to blackmail, burglary and drugs. His progression through life mirrors that of most criminals. It didn't matter what the illegal commodity was, Felloni was prepared to trade in it. He was the small-time nasty who spent most of his life locked up for his crimes. It didn't discourage him, and it never rehabilitated him. For more than thirty-five years, Felloni regularly broke the law. He was caught and convicted thirty-three times but there is no doubt that he got away with a lot more.

But to dismiss him as Tony Baloney is to miss the point. Felloni is the local criminal that clogs up the system, costs the state a fortune and inflicts misery on those around him. He has destroyed lives and devastated communities. Always quick to jump up and down demanding his own civil rights, he has not hesitated in violating those of others. Felloni has used and abused the criminal justice system to the best of his ability. He has secured bail and committed more crime while on it. He has bargained for the minimum prison term for the maximum number of crimes and received concurrent sentences in the courts; in his first twenty years as a criminal he never received a sentence longer than three years. He has had cases moved from one court to another in the hope of securing more lenient sentences. Using the best lawyers—paid for not by him but by the taxpayer on free legal aid—he has fought cases, appealed convictions and challenged the Constitution.

Tony Felloni was a criminal who picked out and preyed on the weakest, the poorest and the most vulnerable, a thug who beat up his wife. He has attacked with knives and sticks but was considered a coward by other criminals. He didn't even have much of the warped sense of morality that goes with the underworld. With no sense of personal or social responsibility, the man was amoral and appears unrepentant.

There was no romance about Felloni. He wasn't even the anti-hero. He was and perhaps still is the archetypal criminal. There is someone like him in every city in the world. He is still alive, there is no martyrdom, no hero worship for him in death, and I couldn't find one person who had a good word to say about him.

His mother, Mary Felloni, is buried in a place called, somewhat ironically, Crookstown. It is a mark of the character of Tony Felloni that as her eldest son and with all his money, he never bought a headstone for her grave. It is also a mark of the man that he neglected his children. His six adult children are heroin addicts and have spent much of their lives in jail.

The eldest, Mario, is a heroin addict at the second stage of HIV. Luigi is also a heroin addict; his addiction is so severe that he can't avoid getting caught again with the drug once released from prison. Ronaldo, the youngest, is also a chronic and chaotic drug user who resorts to robbing handbags and holding up tourists to feed his habit.

Tony's daughters have fared no better. The eldest, Ann, has lost her children because of her heroin habit and associated criminal activity. They are now in care. Lena and Regina, both mothers with children, are also heroin addicts who have been sent to jail. Regina worked closely with her father in the drug business. And Tony isn't around to see his youngest daughter grow up: Ellavita was born in 1994.

Portlaoise Prison is the country's most secure jail. Guarded by the army, it is reserved for paramilitary prisoners, hardened criminals and those involved in organised crime. Here in a cell in E Block, on a landing holding some of the country's most serious criminals, Tony Felloni is serving the longest sentence ever handed down for drug dealing in Ireland. This is his story, though he may not like it. This is the story of 'King Scum'.

1 'Dippers, Lifters and Mitchers' 1911–69

The octogenarian Sicilian Ronaldo Felloni ended his days in a ward at the James Connolly Memorial Hospital in Blanchardstown, Dublin. He was transferred there from a room overlooking the sea in a nursing home in Bray, Co. Wicklow. He grew tired and wheezy in his later years and was bedridden and hard of hearing. His memory was a little hazy but he remained sharp and bright to the end. He died in a geriatric unit cared for by nurses but with none of his family around him.

Ronaldo was born on 19 April 1911 in Palermo, the capital of Sicily. The family later moved to Parma on the Italian mainland. His father, Giuseppe, and his mother, Rosa, had five children, all boys, one of whom, Giovanni, died in the Second World War. Ronaldo was the eldest. Giuseppe was a terrazzo floor worker. A skilled tradesman, he laid ornate marble floors in churches and created intricate mosaics with paints and coloured tiles in the homes of wealthy Italians. But Parma was a relatively poor city between the wars and there was no shortage of terrazzo craftsmen. Giuseppe was unable to find enough work to support his wife and family so they emigrated to Scotland.

One of his sons, Giulio, remained in Scotland, while the other three, Ronaldo, Angelo and Adolphus, moved to Belfast, arriving in Ireland on 6 April 1935. Ronaldo had by now learned his father's trade and as a terrazzo floor worker he tried with his brothers to set up a business in the city. The business failed and while Angelo remained a terrazzo floor worker, Adolphus opened a café in Belfast. Ronaldo left and moved to Dublin. He lived in a flat in Capel Street in the city centre and that was when he met the woman he would live with for the rest of his life.

Mary Carroll was born on 5 December 1918 in Brewel, a townland near Colbinstown on the Kildare–Wicklow border. The eldest daughter of Patrick Carroll and Josephine Moore, she had two sisters and three brothers. She had a sallow complexion and dark eyes and the first time he saw her Ronaldo was convinced she was of Italian origin. She worked as a waitress in a city centre hotel.

Ronaldo and Mary began going out together and when she got pregnant they moved in to one of the Corporation flats in North Cumberland Street in the north inner city, across the road from where the Social Welfare office is today. They were a pretty unusual couple around Dublin in the forties; they never married. They still stayed together for over fifty years until Mary died in 1995 and Ronaldo was moved into a nursing home. They had three children together, Tony, Mary Monica—or Maria as she's known—and Justin.

Tony Felloni was born in Holles Street Maternity Hospital in Dublin on 6 January 1943. His father's name was not written on his birth certificate, as was the case for the children of unmarried parents. In Catholic Ireland of the period there was a stigma attached to children born out of wedlock. Their mothers were labelled as fallen women and many were forced to give their children away. But Mary held on to her first-born and Ronaldo stood by his girlfriend. Tony was given his mother's surname; under 'Ainm' on his birth certificate, Anthony Carroll was recorded. His sister, Maria, was born two years later but when Justin was born on 23 March 1947, he was given the surname Felloni. Ronaldo's name and occupation were duly recognised in law.

Ronaldo found work as a terrazzo floor worker at Verso's, one of the biggest ceramic tiling companies in Dublin. Although based in Gardiner Street in the north inner city, Verso's tradesmen worked all over the country. The company was responsible for the mosaic pillars at University College, Dublin, and for mosaic tiling in both the Redemptorist College in Galway and the Imperial Hotel in Cork. Ronaldo worked on the terrazzo staircase in Mount Carmel Hospital in Dublin but he spent much of his thirty years with Verso's outside the city.

Tony Felloni's father was a highly skilled and well-paid tradesman, earning more than most carpenters, plumbers or electricians. He was a small, quiet man, but one whom people knew not to cross. He had a long face and a distinctive white beard, so the children in the flats called him Santa Claus. He wore a waistcoat and jacket over a jumper, and with his trademark black beret he looked like a figure from the French resistance. His daughter christened him 'Dan Joe' after a character called the Dan Joe in a film she saw about a Mexican revolutionary. The name stuck, and his grandchildren still call him Dan Joe today.

Mary gave up her job although she still earned money on the side from knitting. She made and sold hats, flags and scarves outside Croke Park. Years later she knitted a jumper for a Garda who was on so many search parties that he was a regular visitor to her home. She was a polite, hard-working woman, who usually invited people—including Gardaí—in to the flat and made them tea. But Mary Felloni was also a rogue. She had a reputation for being a moneylender and in later years she became Tony Felloni's banker. She not only deposited and withdrew cash from his accounts for him, she turned up at District and Circuit Criminal Court hearings with the money to bail him out.

Mary always doted on her eldest child. His childhood home was as normal as any and more comfortable than most. His father worked, his mother was a housewife and the children didn't go hungry. The family lived in the flat at 18 North Cumberland Street, although Tony spent some of his childhood in his mother's homeplace. He went to the local national school in Marlborough Street, but started 'mitching' (playing truant) and getting into trouble from early on. He had a criminal record by the time he was sixteen, and was convicted twice in three weeks in the Children's Court in 1959 for stealing a scooter and breaking into houses. On 9 December he was given the maximum sentence of two years for larceny and burglary and sent to the only boys' reformatory in the country, St Conleth's, in Daingean, Co. Offaly.

The Oblate fathers ran the reformatory in Daingean and took in boys aged twelve to sixteen. The law forbade them to detain anyone older than nineteen, and the longest a juvenile could be sent there for was two years. The vast majority of its children came from the poorer areas of Dublin: Ballyfermot, Finglas, Cabra, Coolock and the inner city. The children sent to the industrial schools such as

3

Letterfrack in Connemara were younger than those at Daingean and could be kept there a lot longer.

The daily routine in the reformatory proved a major culture shock for Tony Felloni. Daingean was strict, austere and lonely and the boys there had no mothers to dote over them. His day began at 7.30 a.m. with mass and breakfast, followed by school from 9.00 a.m. until 3.00 p.m. Then there was a variety of jobs open to him. He could either work in the kitchen or on the farm, or learn a trade such as cobbling or metalwork. In the evening there was homework and he was allowed play with the other boys only after that was done. Bedtime was at 10.00 p.m.

The reformatory at Daingean was used to detain some of the most serious young offenders who came before the courts and Tony Felloni was in good criminal company there. Among the more notable scholars to graduate from the midlands academy were Martin Cahill, the notorious Dublin criminal who was known as 'The General', and Larry Dunne, the biggest single heroin supplier in Dublin in the early 1980s, whose business Tony took over after Larry was sent to jail in 1985.

The General later referred to the priests in Daingean as 'the mad monks from down the bog', and accused them of corrupting him. Tony Felloni also said he had been unhappy as a child in Daingean. Dr Brian McCaffrey, an Eastern Health Board consultant psychiatrist, interviewed him for a court report before he was jailed for twenty years. At fifty-three years of age Felloni still blamed some of his reformatory experiences for the way he ended up. 'His experiences there were quite disturbing,' the court was told on the day he was sentenced, 'and had a significant effect on his future.' The court was not specifically told what those experiences were.

The school in Daingean closed in 1972 and the Oblate fathers moved to Ard Mhuire in Lusk, in north county Dublin. Most of the records of Tony Felloni's time there were lost in the move, but even though it is nearly forty years ago, there are still priests and teachers alive today whose memories of him are quite different to his own. They remember Anthony Carroll as a sly and devious teenager.

Felloni actually began his career in drug sales in the reformatory. He pretended he was seriously ill in the residence hall one day, and while the doctor called in to examine him could find nothing wrong, he wasn't prepared to take any chances and had Tony brought to Tullamore Hospital.

The charming delinquent was a big hit with the nurses. He was handsome, polite, well spoken and popular. They felt sorry for him and he was given more freedom around the wards than was the norm. He got on so well with the nurses on night duty that one evening he was able to get away from them long enough to rob the hospital pharmacy. Tony knew what he was looking for, tablets and medicines, and he headed back to his bed with Anadins, paracetamol and cough bottles hidden in his pyjamas.

The next morning the theft was discovered, an investigation began and he was quickly apprehended. Relieved of his booty and unceremoniously discharged from hospital, he was sent back to the reformatory, but the priests and teachers there knew him better. They searched him again and found tablets hidden in his shoes and trousers. He had planned to hold on to his supply of drugs until visiting Sunday, when he could sell or barter them with the other boys for cash, food parcels or cigarettes.

Tony tried to escape from Daingean a number of times but he was always caught out on the country roads and brought back. The priests, however, became so concerned about security that they bought a Great Dane. The dog was tame and wouldn't bite the children but it was supposed to bark every time any of the boys tried to make a run for it. Far from thwarting Tony's escape attempts, the animal became an unwitting accomplice. Tony made friends with it and was able to make it stand still for long enough to allow him climb up on its back and scramble over the wall.

When Tony finally came out of Daingean his father hoped he would settle down and go straight. He came back to Dublin to live with his parents and Ronaldo succeeded in getting an apprenticeship for him at Verso's. He had hoped to be able to pass on to his son the same skills that his own father had handed on to him. But Tony had other ideas and decided to pursue a different career. The Felloni tradition of Italian craftsmanship through the generations died out with Ronaldo's retirement.

Tony had a penchant for crime and so did the woman he met in the mid-sixties who later became his wife. Born in the Coombe Hospital on 11 May 1950, Anne Maria Flynn was the second eldest in a family of fourteen children. One of her seven brothers is the author and actor Mannix Flynn. Anne grew up in St Patrick's House flats off York Street in the south inner city and went to the nearby national school in Whitefriar Street. Her father had a job with Dublin Corporation. Her mother ran a fruit and vegetable stall in Camden Street.

Anne didn't stay long in school either, preferring a life of 'lifting, dipping and mitching'—stealing, pickpocketing and truanting. She secured her first conviction at twelve years of age. She had called around for her friend Martina Keogh one morning. Martina's mother was a big strong Kerry woman who did not like her daughter hanging around with Anne Flynn. She herself had to go out but to stop Martina getting out with Anne, she locked her clothes in the coalhouse and left her half-naked in the front room, warning her not to leave the flat. Martina was trapped, or so she thought until Anne arrived.

'I can't get out,' she told her friend, 'I haven't got a stitch to wear.' But Anne would not be beaten. She looked around the flat and found other clothes. She dressed Martina up in one of her mother's tops and her father's jackets. She then wrapped a big skirt around her twice and put a pair of her brother's football boots on her. The two of them then headed into town. Martina Keogh couldn't walk properly as she tried to keep the clothes from falling off her. She looked like an urchin. Anne dragged her into Dunne's Stores, where she dressed up in a skirt, top, sandals and socks that fitted her perfectly. The pair of them walked out the door.

It was a hot summer's day so they decided to go to the beach. But first they needed swimsuits so they went into Cassidy's department store on George's Street. The problem was there was only one left and that was on the 'display dummy', the mannequin in the window. Martina stood holding bits of arms and legs as Anne tried to get the swimsuit off the dummy. A shopper who asked them what they were doing was told to 'Fuck off out of it,' so it wasn't long before the two were caught. On 9 August 1962 the judge in the Dublin Juvenile Court applied the Probation Act after Anne Flynn was found guilty of theft. Her career of petty crime had officially begun.

Nine months later she was fined twenty shillings at the same court for obstructing a Garda, Jim 'Lugs' Branigan. Anne and her friends were in a chip shop in South William Street when they got into a row with the owner over the flavour of the chips. The girls complained that they wanted vinegar; the owner's wife came around the counter and tried to push them out of the shop. A scuffle began and 'Lugs', who was on his rounds at the time, spotted the commotion, stormed in and hauled them away.

Anne also claimed then to be a year older than she was and to this day there are two dates of birth on her criminal record.

As a wild young teenager Anne Flynn and her friends went 'on gur'. This involved staying out all night and sleeping rough. They slept around a small fire in the pram sheds in the flat complexes, in the buses parked away for the night, or in lanes under piles of clothes. They stole the clothes from their neighbours' washing lines and balconies, and stole the milk from the doorsteps in the morning. Sometimes the Gardaí would wake their mothers at 3.00 a.m. and 4.00 a.m. and bring them out to take their children home. The beatings they got never deterred them.

Anne started mitching at around nine years of age. Three years later a judge at the Children's Court in Dublin Castle told her that if she didn't go to school he would send her away. She ignored the order and was later committed to an approved school, St Anne's in Kilmacud. The nuns there ran a tight ship and all the girls were expected to pull their weight. 'The head penguin', as Anne christened her, 'was a tough woman.' Juveniles who were used to being out on the streets half the night were woken at 6.00 a.m. They then had to wash, clean their dormitories, make their beds and go to mass, all before breakfast. If the rooms weren't clean or the beds weren't properly made it all had to be done again. There was no television at the time and recreation after school consisted of sports, volleyball and badminton.

Anne did not enjoy life in Kilmacud and spent a lot of her school time in the corner or outside the door. Like her future husband in Daingean, she embarked on a number of failed escape attempts. On one occasion she and her best friend stole two half-crowns from the pocket of one of the workers at the school. They headed for town and spent the money before they were recaptured by the Gardaí and separated back at the school. Anne disliked the place so much that when the Children's Court decided to send her back there on 11 May

1965, her fifteenth birthday, she successfully appealed the decision. The sentence was altered to a £1 fine or fourteen days' detention in default of payment. She was learning how to use the law to her own advantage.

During her teens Anne did hold down a variety of jobs but only for short periods of time. She worked in a sewing factory in South William Street and another in Montague Street when she was fourteen years old. She also worked in a shop beside the old Green Cinema, and she packed jams on the production line in the Chivers Jam factory. She says she spent time as a cleaner in the College of Technology in Kevin Street and put laces into boots and shoes in the old Winstanley shoe factory up in Christchurch Hill. But Anne Flynn's talent in life did not appear to lie in gainful employment. Her skill as a thief always came to the fore—she even stole some of the jam from the Chivers factory.

A brilliant shoplifter, cool, confident and extremely professional, she dressed up to go out stealing in a variety of wigs and outfits. Sometimes she was a schoolgirl, other times a nurse, but her most successful disguise was as a nun. If she had learned one thing from her time in Kilmacud, it was the power of the church in 1960s Ireland. She saw how the sisters were revered and respected and as women of the cloth were above suspicion. It was a public perception which Anne exploited to the full.

By modern standards, it was an age of innocence. The department stores were less suspicious and would never doubt the bona fides of the clergy or the religious. The shop assistants were more open and trusting of their customers; to thieves like Anne Flynn they were simply more naive. The scams they operated seem juvenile now. The assistants would bring out trays of jewellery to show their customers, and when asked to bring something from the window, would leave the jewellery unattended. 'When the girls turned their backs we'd do the tills,' Anne recalled. 'We did a number of things.' Anne and friends would steal only one or two valuable pieces and leave the shop before the theft was discovered.

She worked at the time with a small team of thieves. One or two of the other women would shoplift with her while at least one man would watch their backs for Gardaí or store detectives. On one of their outings Anne stole a large sum of money from a woman's handbag in a department store in town. Realising just how much they had, the three of them—Anne, another woman and a man—got a taxi and headed for Ballyfermot, where one of the team lived.

Anne was so excited she just couldn't contain herself and started counting the money in the back of the taxi. In spite of half-hearted pleas from the other two she would not put the money away. The driver eyed them suspiciously through the rear-view mirror, and when he received a £5 tip, an extraordinary sum at the time, he reported them to the Gardaí. The money was recovered. They had stolen it from a woman who was about to spend it on a wooden leg. When asked why she didn't notice anyone suspicious beside her, she said the only person she remembered was 'a holy nun'.

All three were arrested and charged, but while Anne was released on bail the other woman was remanded in custody. Pregnant at the time, she went into labour in the prison and was taken to hospital. Guarded by prison officers, she was not supposed to have any visitors, but Anne Flynn succeeded in getting in. She could not convince her friend to escape, however, as the woman was not prepared to leave her newborn baby behind.

Anne and friends also travelled around the country and stole wherever they went. They would often sleep in a hay-barn if they could not find a room for the night. There were always rich pickings for thieves at festivals and fairs. She would go on shoplifting sprees to Cork and Galway, where they were even less aware of the danger of theft than they were in the capital. Anne simply had no fear. She would walk in to a department store and select what she wanted—jumpers, shirts, coats, whatever, put them all in a bag and walk out the door. She would also send postcards not only to her friends but to one of the judges who regularly put her away: 'Pickings is great, I'm in Cork,' she wrote to him.

Anne had a love-hate relationship with Judge Robert Ó hUadhaigh, before whom she often appeared in the Dublin District Court. Once, when she had been caught stealing a pile of underwear, he asked, 'Was one pair not enough for you?' 'I have a kidney complaint,' she answered him back. 'I'll fix your kidney complaint for you,' he told her and gave her twelve months in prison. Yet she remembers him with respect and affection: 'I liked him, he was an old gentleman. He let me off a few times.' She still threw a shoe at him in the court one day when she didn't like the sentence he handed down.

Woolworth's in Dublin was one of Anne's favourite hunting grounds. One of the times that she and her friend were caught shoplifting there, they were made to wait for the Gardaí in a small back room. After about half an hour they got tired of waiting and started shouting to be let out. When their cries were ignored they opened up the cardboard boxes stored in the room and found they were full of delph. The two girls began to laugh hysterically as they smashed hundreds of pounds worth of plates, cups and saucers. When the judge later asked them why they had done it they told him it was because they felt claustrophobic. 'I'll send you somewhere now where you'll feel claustrophobic again,' he replied.

Anne Flynn first met Tony Felloni at the Rainbow Café in O'Connell Street. A mutual friend who worked as a ticket tout at the time introduced them. 'I'd just never met the likes of him in my life,' she remembers. 'He had impeccable manners.' With his suits, tanned complexion and Italian good looks, Tony was the consummate continental playboy. He was very polished and charming, and he spoke well. He looked remarkably fit, healthy and well fed, but that was because, as Anne later discovered, he had just come out after spending two years in prison.

Anne was wearing a school uniform that day, not because she had just come from school but as one of her shoplifting disguises. Tony wanted to have a look in the schoolbag she carried to put the stuff into, and he asked her lots of questions about herself. She answered none of them, refused to let him look in the bag and later headed off to steal from the shops. Tony Felloni had, however, made an impression on her.

Tony and Anne began to see each other more often and they started working as shoplifters together. Tony was supposed to be the lookout. He would stand facing the large display windows with his back to the street, so he could see Gardaí approaching through the reflection in the glass. But Tony and Anne were no Bonnie and Clyde. The lookout was supposed to remain within a yard or two of the thieves to be able to step in quickly if something happened. The girls complained that Tony wasn't doing his job. He stayed too far back to keep an eye on them properly and if something went wrong he was usually first away. He preferred burglaries, larcenies, housebreaking and pickpocketing to shoplifting so the business partnership between himself and Anne dissolved. But the romantic one developed in spite of the fact that both of them continued to see other people.

Tony was initially going out with a woman who was one of Anne's accomplices and best friends in the 1960s. The woman had an aunt in London who worked in a pub off the Holloway Road and who got her a flat there over a block of shops. Tony Felloni and Anne Flynn spent a lot of time there. Tony was not much of a drinker, but Anne and friends lived it up in the local pubs. Anne moved between Dublin and London between 1964 and 1969. Tony, she says, followed her over there after they met in 1966, but came back and continued stealing in Dublin.

Anne says she made her first trip to Britain on her own when she was only fourteen years old. She was spotted, picked up by the police and ended up being put back on the boat to Ireland after spending a few weeks in the Stoneycraft Children's Home in Liverpool. But that did not discourage her from going back and she received her first British conviction the following year. She was caught stealing from a shop window and discharged by Chelsea Juvenile Court on condition that she stay out of trouble for a year.

There wasn't much chance of that. By the time she was fifteen she had already chalked up seven convictions in Ireland for assault, violence in a police station, unlawful possession, stealing and receiving stolen goods. Four months after her conviction in Chelsea she was up in court again in Dublin for assaulting a female Garda. Two months later she was again convicted of shoplifting and sent to prison for three months. The system was good to her, however, and the sentence was reduced to three weeks on appeal. By now Anne had had enough of Dublin for a while and she went back to London again.

London in the late sixties was the place to be. There was plenty of fun, money, drink and drugs and the Beatles were number one. This was a city of opportunity and Anne and her fellow thieves were more than willing to cash in. She recalls going down to the West End and stealing sixty or seventy dresses at a time. 'I went into a shop one day and walked out with the whole bar, the whole bar of dresses with

11

another girl.' They stole from most of the main department stores and they picked pockets and robbed handbags at as many of the major sporting and cultural events as they could get into—from the Chelsea Flower Show to the Grand National.

One year they dressed in their finery, with long skirts and wide-brimmed hats, for the Epsom Derby. They then stole a pass and bluffed their way into the VIP tent, where they sat drinking champagne and brandy with Oliver Reed. 'We couldn't rob him,' Anne's friend remembers, 'because he didn't carry any cash.' The drink was put on the actor's tab and he paid for it all at the end by credit card. It wasn't Anne's sole brush with fame in England. She also says she was on remand in Holloway Prison at the same time as the Moors murderer Myra Hindley: 'She was beaten up in the church by the other prisoners.'

Anne liked London much better than Tony did. The type of crime committed there suited her better. She had been caught fighting and stealing a number of times in England but she tended to have more luck in the courts there. Of the ten convictions recorded against her by the time she was eighteen years old, only one was in London.

Although Tony also moved back and forth between Dublin and London in the 1960s, his criminal activity remained rooted in Ireland. He was convicted twice in 1967, for stealing a car and receiving stolen goods, and four times the following year on a total of eight counts of stealing and breaking into houses and offices.

On one of those charges Tony was arrested along with another man on suspicion of robbery. Both were taken to the Bridewell Garda Station, which is connected to the Dublin District Court by an underground tunnel. He would be taken through it to be charged in court. Tony was as usual immaculately dressed as he waited in the station. He wore a shirt and tie and a suit, and had a new crombie coat on him. He didn't look like a prisoner at all.

It was coming up to 2.00 p.m., the time Gardaí change shifts, and Tony asked to go to the toilet. When he came out he went straight to the steel gate that separates the holding area from the main Garda station. 'I'm a solicitor,' he told the young Garda there, who did not know him, 'I've conducted my business with my client and I'm now ready to leave.' The Garda opened the gate and Tony Felloni walked out.

He didn't remain at large for long, however. The Gardaí were furious at the way he had made a fool of them. The other man was charged and released on bail and he met up with Tony to celebrate later that evening. The Gardaí received a tip-off from a porter at the North Star Hotel in Amiens Street that the two of them were having a private party with two young women in one of the rooms.

The following morning at four o'clock the door went in and Tony was hauled out of bed. He was made to dress in the corridor in front of the Gardaí. When he asked if he could go to the toilet before being taken away, the Gardaí looked at him to see if he was joking; when it transpired that he wasn't, the request was firmly refused. The young Garda who had inadvertently freed him the day before was later disciplined and fined thirty shillings.

On another occasion he was up before Judge Charles Conroy in the Circuit Criminal Court. Judge Conroy had a habit of taking notes throughout the proceedings in a minute book so that he could direct the jury at the end of the trial. The book was important to him because it helped him remember the details of a case.

One afternoon in the middle of the trial the judge came back from lunch and could not find his minute book. The tipstaff who was the judge's assistant went back into chambers to see if it was there. A full search was ordered but the book could not be found. The judge felt he had no option but to abort the trial and Tony Felloni walked free again. The minute book never turned up and it was never proved that Tony had taken it. He kept the book for a while as a souvenir.

Tony spent more than four of the first nine years of the 1960s in Mountjoy Jail. However, 1969 was the year he decided to get married, if not settle down, and Anne Flynn agreed to be his bride. The fact that Tony was still sleeping with his ex-lover, her best friend, had no bearing on his plans. His wife-to-be had a son from another relationship in London.

Gary Flynn was born on 5 February 1968. Anne was seventeen and she brought the baby home to Dublin for her mother and younger sister Evelyn to rear. Gary did not survive to manhood. He and another youth set off the alarm while trying to rob a jeweller's shop in the city centre in 1985. The Gardaí arrived and shouted at both men to come down from the roof. The other man got away, but Gary fell to his death trying to escape. He landed beside the funeral undertakers that was to bury him. He was seventeen years of age.

At this time concern was being expressed in the courts about Anne Flynn's mental health. When she appeared before the Circuit Criminal Court on 11 October 1968 she pleaded guilty to stealing £121.10 from a Mrs Bridget Mary Kennedy the previous September. Four other offences of larceny were taken into consideration and Anne was given six months. The judge, Hugh McGivern, recommended she serve the sentence in St Brendan's Mental Institution. Anne appealed the decision to the Court of Criminal Appeal, but this was rejected on 17 December.

By the time Anne Flynn agreed to marry Tony Felloni she was back in England and back in jail. In March of 1969 she had been convicted at Marlborough Street magistrates' court on two counts of stealing and one of assault occasioning actual bodily harm. Anne and her friend had gone into a hotel in London with an accomplice. They made their way on to the upper floors and started going through the rooms until they came across a wad of foreign currency. The women hid it in their underwear and moved on to the next room. However, the guest came back, discovered the theft and phoned the manager. He in turn sealed off the hotel and called in the police. The two women were caught; the man got away down a drainpipe.

The police knew they had an accomplice but Anne and her friend categorically denied it. They were charged, convicted and sent to prison. Anne got two terms of six months for two stealing offences and three months for assault, but the sentences ran concurrently and she was released in time for her wedding. Tony's lover was also released, in time to spend the night before the wedding with the bridegroom. The two women later found out they were both pregnant and both due at the same time. Nine months after that they were in the Rotunda Hospital across the corridor from one another, each giving birth to one of Tony Felloni's children.

Anne Flynn married Tony Felloni on Monday, 1 September 1969. The wedding took place in the Church of Saints Michael and John in Essex Quay in Dublin. Before the ceremony took place, however, the problem of the bridegroom's name had to be sorted out. He was known as Tony Felloni, but the name on his birth certificate was Anthony Carroll. Anne Flynn was not happy about this technical

14

difficulty. She wanted to know exactly who she was marrying. 'How come your name is Carroll if you're called Anthony Felloni?' she asked him.

She refused to marry him unless he changed his name in law to the name she had always known him by. Four days before the wedding, Tony went to the offices of Mr David Bell, a solicitor on Bachelor's Walk in Dublin. Anne remembers him as 'a very nice man'. Anthony Carroll walked in and half an hour later Anthony Felloni walked out. The deed was sworn on 4 September and is now registered on page 3762 of the Miscellaneous Deeds Roll for 19 September 1969. Tony's father paid for the name change as a wedding present.

There were around a hundred people at the couple's wedding reception in Barry's Hotel in Dublin. Most of them were friends of the Flynn family, who in traditional fashion paid for their daughter's wedding breakfast. 'He invited his two mistresses and a friend of his, his mother and her friend,' Anne says. 'His father didn't come to the wedding.' 'Dan Joe' did not approve of this union between the Fellonis and the Flynns. Anne says he told her a few weeks beforehand that she should not marry his son. On the day she did he was working in Galway. 'You can't tell a young person much cos they know it all,' Anne says. 'I think the man was trying to tell me he was a schizo, but he couldn't come out with it.'

The newly-weds did not manage to stay together for long. Circumstances, specifically criminal circumstances, quickly intervened. 'I thought we'd just settle down and have a family and be normal and all this shoplifting and robbing and infidelity would stop,' she says. 'It didn't.' Tony Felloni was back in Mountjoy Jail less than a month after he was married. He was convicted at the Dublin District Court on two counts of loitering with intent and on 26 September he was sentenced to three months in prison.

His new bride wasn't far behind him. She managed to stay out of prison for only six weeks after the wedding. On 15 October she was convicted on another serious assault charge, causing actual bodily harm to the victim. She was sent to prison for a year. Three weeks later at Cork District Court she got another six months' hard labour for two counts of larceny from the person, a souvenir of one of her trips to the provinces earlier that year.

It was while serving these sentences in Mountjoy that Anne discovered she was pregnant, and launched a campaign for her own release on compassionate grounds. Eight months later she went into labour and had to be rushed to the Rotunda Hospital. On 30 April 1970 Tony Felloni's wife gave birth to their first child, her second son, Mario. The Minister for Justice, Mícheál O Móráin, signed her petition papers and Anne was released from prison the next day.

Tony Felloni's relationship with his lover did not last long after their son was born. She walked away from him after he began to beat her up and she reared the child without him. Six years later Tony turned up in a pub on the day of their son's first Holy Communion. He offered the boy a half-crown, the equivalent of twelve and a half pence and worth about eighty pence today. His mother was highly insulted. 'I felt like shoving it back down his throat,' she says. Even to this day she does not refer to Tony Felloni by name. She simply calls him 'Scum!'

2 Young Girls and Blackmail 1963–64

One night in the late summer of 1963, a well-dressed, respectable-looking middle-aged man brought a young girl into Clontarf Garda Station on the north side of Dublin. He was a publican who owned a bar at the end of Dorset Street. The girl was fourteen years of age and came from Co. Kildare. She kept her head bowed and said nothing. She just stood there shamed and shaking, moving only to nod her head in agreement with what the older man told the Garda behind the desk.

He made a number of shocking allegations on the young girl's behalf. Her name was Maeve[1] and she had been working as a nanny in his home for the past few months, cooking, cleaning and looking after his four young children. Two weeks earlier, on Thursday, 8 August, Maeve had a day off. She went into town to meet her friend Carmel, who was two years older than her; she too was from the country and working in Dublin. They had arranged to meet in front of the GPO on O'Connell Street. As she was standing there waiting, Maeve noticed another young girl watching her.

The girl walked up to her. 'Excuse me, have you got the time?' she asked. 'It's eight o'clock,' Maeve replied. The girl seemed friendly. She started to chat. 'I'm waiting for someone,' she told her, 'but they haven't turned up. Are you waiting for anyone?' Maeve told her she was waiting for a friend. The two made small talk for a little while longer. 'My two friends haven't turned up,' the girl said. 'Would you like to come to a party?' Maeve was cautious at first. 'I don't know. I'll have to wait until my friend comes.'

When Carmel came along, Maeve told her the other girl had invited them to a party. 'What kind of party?' Carmel asked. 'An

17

engagement party,' the girl replied. She introduced herself to the two country girls. 'My name is Rosa,' she said. 'I am not Irish, I come from France and I am going home tomorrow.' She chatted some more and took down the girls' names, addresses and telephone numbers, 'so I can write to you', she said.

Just then a young man came out of the GPO, where he had been making phone calls. He was well dressed, in a two-piece suit with a white handkerchief in the left breast pocket. He was tanned and handsome, with his hair combed back in a quiff. Rosa introduced the two girls to her brother Anthoni. He was going to the party as well. All four walked across O'Connell Street, past Nelson's Pillar, down Talbot Street, left on to Gardiner Street and up to the big green door of number 6.

The house was a large red-bricked, stone-floored tenement building, cold, musty and dimly lit inside. It was divided into a number of separate flats, but all the occupants came and went through the front door. Anthoni, Rosa, Carmel and Maeve went into a flat on the ground floor. There were only two rooms, a kitchen and a bedroom. There was a man playing records in the kitchen. 'We have to go in here first,' Rosa told them, 'because we're being collected and brought to the party in a car.' Anthoni took their coats and bags and left them in the bedroom. Rosa excused herself, saying she was going to phone another girlfriend. Anthoni set to work.

Anthoni's real name was Tony Felloni. Rosa was his sister, Maria. The man playing records in the flat lived there with his mother—his name was Jimmy Goff. Tony got up and went into the bedroom. He called Maeve in. She laughed a little nervously. 'What do you want me to go in there for?' she shouted in at him. There was no reply at first. Then he called back, 'There's a television in here. We can watch it together.' A television was a rare thing in an Irish home in 1963. The young girl was curious and she walked in to the bedroom. Felloni immediately jumped up behind her, closed the door and locked them both in. 'There's no party,' he said. 'I have lots of time on my hands and if you don't do what I tell you, you won't get out.'

Maria had come back to the flat after supposedly making her phone call and was sitting at the record player with Carmel trying to have a conversation. But as soon as Maeve went into the room with

Tony, Maria jumped up. 'Do you mind if I turn up the music?' she asked Carmel. 'I like it good and loud.'

In the bedroom Maeve saw there were two beds and a press, but no television set. Felloni grabbed her and flung her down on the bed. She started to scream but Carmel could not hear her over the music. 'If you scream much more now, I'll choke you,' Felloni warned. He put his hands around Maeve's throat and she began to faint. He called for a cup of water, which Maria left in. He gave her a minute or two to drink it but if she thought her ordeal was over she was sadly mistaken.

Felloni had totally metamorphosed from a romantic charmer to a brutal monster. 'Get into bed,' he ordered. 'No!' she replied. 'Take off your clothes.' She refused again. He didn't tell her again. He pulled down her zip and ripped the dress off her. He then ordered her to take off the rest of her clothes, threatening to kick her if she didn't. She remained defiant so he tore her underwear off as well. Then he pushed her on to the bed and took off his own clothes.

Maeve was trapped and terrified. 'He got into bed and lay on top of me,' she said. 'He opened my legs and I then felt my legs and the bed wet.' 'I did not have intercourse with her,' Tony insisted. After an hour and a half he left the room and called in another man, 'Denis'. Denis lived upstairs in flat 6c. His real name was Charles Behan. According to him, 'Felloni came in and asked me to have a look. He asked me to strip but I did not.' Behan kept his clothes on all right but he took out his penis and clambered on top of Maeve. 'I caught a hold of her private part and felt it,' he said. 'I wet her private part.'

When Behan was finished Felloni came back into the bedroom. This time he had a camera with him. Maria and Carmel were still in the kitchen. 'What does he want the camera for?' Carmel asked. 'He wants to photograph a television programme,' Maria told her. Felloni started taking pictures of Maeve naked. He ordered her to open her legs for some of the shots. 'He made me get out of the bed I was lying in and lie on the second bed,' she said. He told her there was a film in the camera and he took about eight or nine photographs. 'If you ever go to the police,' he warned her, 'I'll send those photographs home.'

Maeve was allowed to put her clothes back on. Her dress was ripped at the zip down the back. Felloni called Maria back into the bedroom and she sewed it up. Tony Felloni took £1 10s from Maeve's handbag and another £1 from Carmel's. 'You'll have to pay for the photos I'm sending home,' he said.

Carmel was oblivious to all the activity in the bedroom, but when Maeve came out she did notice 'she looked kind of frightened'. Tony gave the girls their coats and handbags and he, Maria and Charlie Behan walked them to the bus stop at the end of Gardiner Street. When Maeve checked her handbag she saw there was no money in it. She hadn't realised that Felloni had stolen it all. 'What did you do with it?' she asked him. 'I took it,' he said. 'I will take so much of your wages every week.' He didn't say why. He didn't have to. They left the two girls at around 10.30 p.m.

Maeve was still in shock. She had been robbed and indecently assaulted but at fourteen years of age she still wasn't quite sure what had happened. Carmel checked for her own bus fare and discovered that she too had been robbed. The two girls were stranded with no money to get home. They went back to the flat at number 6, but when they knocked on the door an old woman answered. None of the other four was there.

The next day Felloni phoned Maeve at the house in Griffith Avenue where she lived and worked. 'I'm ringing from Whitehall,' he said. Whitehall is near Griffith Avenue and about three miles from Felloni's own home. 'Why did you go back to the flat?' he asked. She told him that Carmel wanted her money back and he hung up. He phoned again the following Thursday (15 August) and said he wanted to meet her outside Drumcondra cinema. 'If you give me £1,' he said, 'I'll give you the photos.'

They met at 7.30 p.m. He showed her a brown envelope with her name on it. 'These are the photographs,' he said, and asked her for the money. She offered to give him ten shillings there and then and the rest the following week. Felloni didn't like the offer. He pulled her handbag off her and took £1 out of it. He told her he wanted more money. Even when she said that she'd now paid for the photographs, he repeated that he wanted more. Then he tore up the envelope in front of her face and threw the pieces in the bin. Maeve got no photos that night.

At 9.15 p.m. the following Tuesday, Felloni phoned Maeve again. He told her he was coming around to the house for the money. When

Maeve protested he asked to speak to either the man or the woman of the house. 'They're out,' she said. 'I'm minding their children.' 'Are the children in bed?' he asked. 'Some of them are up doing their homework,' she told him. Ten minutes later there was a bang on the front door. Maeve looked out the window and saw the man who sexually assaulted her and the man who was playing records that night in the flat.

Tony Felloni and Jimmy Goff started hammering on the door demanding to be let in. Maeve was terrified. She watched them through the glass but didn't speak to them. She tried to reassure one of the children before attempting to get rid of them. Telling 'the little fellow' to answer the door, she went out and hid in the back garden. When the eight-year-old boy opened the door, Felloni and Goff ignored him and walked right in. Felloni went out to the garden and pushed Maeve back into the house. He shoved her into the hall and locked the crying, screaming children in the kitchen. Jimmy Goff stood by the front door.

Felloni demanded money for the photos. Maeve told him she had only ten shillings. She went to her room to get it but he followed her. She gave him the money but he searched for more. He looked in the wardrobe, found her handbag and stole another ten-shilling note from it. Then he went downstairs to use the phone, bringing her with him. 'I did not want to but he pulled me beside him,' she said. 'He locked the front door before he made the call.'

Maeve tried to frighten him off. 'The people of the house will be coming home,' she told him. But Felloni wasn't that easily rattled. 'I'll go out the back if they do,' he replied calmly. 'You'll have to pay for the photos,' he told her, but he wouldn't name his price. She offered him £5 but didn't say where she'd get it. By this time Felloni had had enough of the children screaming. He went into the kitchen, closing the door behind him, and stood in front of the four of them. They were aged between four and eight. He told them he'd kick them if they didn't shut up and he slapped two of them across the face.

Jimmy Goff left at this stage. Felloni came out and dragged Maeve into the sitting room. He drew the curtains, turned off the lights and ordered her to lie on the sofa. 'Pull up your skirt,' he told her. He then got on top of her. 'I felt my skirt and the sofa were wet,' she said. After that he got up and turned on the light. 'I'll ring you again,' he said. 'I

21

found a letter in your bedroom with your home address.' He had taken a letter Maeve's mother had written to her. She pleaded with him as he was leaving. 'I have no money,' she said. Felloni didn't care. 'I'm sending the photos home,' he replied and walked out the door.

Maeve could not afford to wait to hear from him again. Felloni had threatened, robbed, blackmailed and indecently assaulted her. But now the children were involved. It was only a matter of time before their parents, her employers, found out what happened. Distressed and petrified, she broke down and told them what had been tormenting her for the past twelve days. That was how she ended up one night in August frightened and humiliated in Clontarf Garda Station over thirty-five years ago.

Detective Sergeant Bernard McLoughlin happened to be on the desk that night. 'The Buller', as he was known, was based in Fitzgibbon Street station in the north inner city, but was on loan to Clontarf because the regular sergeant was on holidays. After the young girl told her story, 'The Buller' and two other Gardaí put her in a squad car and drove around the usual Dublin haunts. They were looking for Anthoni, the Frenchman, his sister Rosa, 'Denis', the other man who got on top of Maeve, or 'the man with no name', the man who had been playing the records in the flat and who arrived at her home with Felloni that night.

Maeve didn't know the city very well. She thought she had been brought to a flat on Moore Street, about half a mile away from Gardiner Street. The squad car drove in and around the Moore Street area for two hours, but Maeve saw no one she recognised. Similar trips over the next few days proved equally futile. The investigation was going nowhere.

Maeve's story troubled McLoughlin. He was still in Clontarf but he put the word around Fitzgibbon Street and the north inner city that he was anxious to find this elusive Frenchman. 'The Buller' was respected in the area. He had a good relationship with the community and good contacts with local small-time 'cons'. The scam with the country girls was known in the area and it wasn't long before he heard a whisper that refocused his investigation. He discovered the main suspect was not French. He was of Italian origin.

McLoughlin contacted Maeve again after he was tipped off about Felloni's scam, who he was working with and where it was based. This time he drove her to Lower Gardiner Street. She immediately recognised the street. He stopped the squad car near the Custom House end. The girl got out and looked across the road. She pointed to the big green door of number 6. McLoughlin brought her into the house and she showed him the ground floor flat where she was photographed naked. It was the beginning of the end of Tony Felloni's most lucrative but insidious venture so far.

The blackmailing operation was a milestone in Felloni's criminal career. He had moved from petty thief to perverted pimp. All his convictions up to then had been minor: two convictions in the Children's Court for housebreaking and stealing; two more in the District Court for stealing and malicious damage. He was only fined £2 for stealing from a shop and sentenced to a month in jail for damaging property. Tony's move into blackmail lost him the only legitimate job he ever had, as an apprentice at Verso's, and put him on the road to becoming a professional criminal. He has never done another honest day's work.

Ireland in the early 1960s had a relatively low crime rate. There were 6,401 Gardaí in the force in 1963, the lowest number for over a decade. They simply weren't needed. Most people were poor so there wasn't much to steal. There was the occasional murder, and the IRA did carry out the odd bank or post office robbery, but most of the crime was petty crime. There was no overcrowding, no revolving door and no system of temporary release in the country's prisons. Career criminals emigrated.

The country was becoming more urbanised and Dublin was the city of opportunity. Emigration slowed down and people who previously went abroad now flocked to the city in search of work. Young men and women found jobs as teachers or civil servants, nurses or nannies. The fresh-faced well-dressed city boy watched all this. He saw hundreds of young, innocent girls soak up the glamour of the shops and restaurants. He watched the pretty and naive get sucked in by the glitz of the dance halls, theatres and cinemas. Most had hopes of one day finding a husband and settling down. Tony saw how they spent their money and he worked out a plan to separate one from the other. His sister was used as a decoy, his friend provided the flat and his friend's friend could have a piece of anything that was left over.

Maria Felloni, or Deenie as she was also known, had a longer criminal record than her brother, despite being two years younger. She once had a job as a part-time waitress in a city centre restaurant, but her chosen career was burglary and larceny; she had five convictions for stealing and housebreaking. Two months after the blackmailing scam came to light she was sent to prison for three months, having been caught breaking into a factory. Two and a half weeks after the three months were up, she was back up in court to answer the blackmail and vice charges.

Jimmy Goff, at twenty-one, was a year older than Tony but they had known each other as children. He lived with his elderly widowed mother in the flat on Lower Gardiner Street, about five minutes from Felloni's home. His father had been dead for years. Goff had only one previous conviction. He had been caught stealing, but instead of sending him to prison, the judge let him off with a fine. He hadn't been in trouble since. Goff was a mechanic—in the garage they said he was a good worker—and he was his mother's only means of support.

Mrs Goff was a very religious woman. One of the ways Tony and Jimmy used to get her out of the flat was to give her small amounts of money and send her down to Our Lady of Lourdes church on Seán MacDermott Street. While they were indecently assaulting and photographing naked women, she was lighting candles and praying for their souls. She had no idea what was going on in her home.

Maria and Jimmy were both active and willing conspirators and they were often with Tony when he met the women. Sometimes Tony was Frank Murphy and the other two were his friends Christy and Susan. Tony targeted the women on different afternoons and evenings at various locations in and around O'Connell Street. Tuesday evening in Dublin was 'nurses' night'. Hundreds of girls, most of them from the country, came to the old Galway Arms dance hall near the present-day National Busworkers' Union offices in Parnell Square. There were also dances at the Metropole Ballroom beside the GPO, where Penney's is today. Tony wore a suit and shirt and sometimes a tie for the occasion. His confidence, charm and Mediterranean looks enabled him to chat up the women he selected.

He approached one 25-year-old woman, Angela, while she was making a phone call at the GPO. Tony was well-spoken, formal and polite. 'Who are you telephoning?' he asked her in the middle of the call before he talked her name, address and phone number out of her. Nineteen-year-old Deirdre was walking along D'Olier Street when Tony, Maria and Jimmy bumped into her and chatted her up. Joan, seventeen years old, met Felloni on a blind date on Aston Quay. 'I did not know him,' she said, 'but he told me what he'd be wearing and I recognised him by his clothes.'

Bridget was walking down O'Connell Street at about eight o'clock one evening when Felloni shouted over, 'Hello, darling.' When she smiled at him he trotted after her and asked where she was going. Bridget told him she was on her way to meet a friend at a dance. She gave him her name, address and telephone number and he said he'd give her a call. At eleven that night he was waiting outside the Savoy Cinema as she walked past. 'Did you enjoy the dance?' he asked. 'No,' she replied. 'I have to rush away now,' he said, 'but I'll give you a ring tomorrow night.' The trap was set. Bridget was sixteen years of age.

All the women were invited to a party. Either it was at the flat in Gardiner Street or they were meeting there beforehand. 'He told me there would be couples there,' Bridget said, 'but he had no girl so would I go with him.' When the women walked in to the flat, Jimmy Goff put on the records. Felloni took their coats and handbags. When they got them back their money was missing.

'They said I would not be going to the party for a while,' Deirdre remembered. 'I was sent into the bedroom.' Then Felloni's whole demeanour changed. He became threatening and abusive. 'Do you know why you've come to the flat?' he asked Joan. 'There will be no party. Take off your clothes.' When she refused, he told her that if she didn't take them off he and Goff would.

He told Nora he'd leave the room so she could take off her clothes. When he came back and saw she was still fully clothed he stayed until she stripped. 'The bedroom door was already locked,' she said. 'That was why I took my clothes off.' 'If you don't take your clothes off,' he said to Bridget, 'I'll take them off you. I did it before and I'll do it again.' He also told her there were more fellows coming and if she didn't hurry up he'd let them ride her. When she refused again he lost his temper. He put his fist up to her face and roared, 'Get stripped!'

If the women continued to refuse, Felloni and Goff became violent. Felloni ordered them into bed and pushed them in if they didn't go. 'No one will hear you if you scream,' he said to Deirdre. Goff slapped Joan when she wouldn't take off any more than her cardigan and frock. 'There were two bottles of Guinness stout and a bottle of Bulmer's cider in the room,' she said, 'I made a run to get away but he hit me with a stout bottle.' Felloni and Goff then jumped on her and ripped the rest of her clothes off.

The rest of the sessions were made up of sex, pornography and theft. The blackmail came later. 'Felloni tried to get on top of me, but did not succeed,' Joan remembered. 'He pulled me on top of him and put his hand on my private part.' 'He tried to ride me but I resisted,' Bridget said. '"Stop messing", he said, "I'll kill you if you don't."' He felt her and asked her if she was a virgin. When he left the room Behan came in. 'Are you wet?' he asked her before he got into bed. He tried to have sex with her but she kept pushing him off. 'She won't let me,' he shouted out to Goff in the kitchen.

At one stage Felloni was bringing so many girls back to the flat that one going in could meet another coming out. When Nora was brought into the bedroom she saw another girl naked in the bed and Behan walking around with his pants off. When she came in, the girl got up and got dressed. When he had finished with Bridget in bed, Felloni said, 'Stay there, I'm going out for another girl.' On his return he put his head around the door and asked the sixteen-year-old if she had missed him. Then he brought another girl into the bedroom and ordered her to strip. He gave Bridget back her clothes only when the other girl was naked.

Felloni and Goff took pictures of the women in a variety of poses. Goff told Joan to stand up on the bed and open her legs. He photographed her there and lying naked across the couch. He took pictures of Deirdre naked in the kitchen, giving her two records to hold and making her open her legs. He also took photos of her sitting naked in an armchair. Felloni took pictures of Nora naked in the bed. 'I want to take pictures of you in the nude,' he said to Bridget, just before he stripped and indecently assaulted her.

After the pornography, Felloni or Goff stole sums ranging from ten shillings to £2 from the women's coats and handbags. After some complained that they had no money to get home, they started leaving just enough for bus fares. The threats began in the house before the women were released. 'He told me if I did not pay he would send them [the photos] to my house or work,' Deirdre said. Tony usually gave the women a price for the pictures before he let them go, but he never stuck to it. Bridget was told the photos would cost her £7. It was £5 for Nora, but the £5 for Joan and Deirdre was later reduced in both cases to £3. Like all blackmailers, however, no matter how much he was paid it was never enough.

Felloni phoned Joan three times and threatened to send the photos to her parents down the country if he wasn't paid £3. She agreed to meet him on O'Connell Bridge. 'I had a good weekend,' he told her there, 'I'll only take £2.' He showed her an envelope but would not open it until he got the money. 'I gave him £1,' she said, 'but he put the envelope in his pocket and said he would not give it unless he got more money.' Felloni walked off, saying he'd ring her again.

'I agreed to pay the money,' Nora said, 'because I was afraid they would send home the photos.' She met Tony Felloni at the GPO because he had promised to hand over one picture. 'I have the photo in my pocket,' he said. 'Thirty shillings and I will give it to you.' But Nora was not going to be fooled. 'If you show me the photo first,' she said, 'I'll give you the money.' 'I have it in my other pocket,' he told her, but Nora didn't pay him. He tried again a few days later. He rang the shop where she worked, looking for £5. He threatened her but Nora refused to give in.

Felloni also failed to get money out of Deirdre or Bridget. When he phoned, Deirdre refused to meet him. 'He did not say anything to me when I told him,' she said. 'He did not say how much he wanted.' Tony told Bridget that the other girls made weekly payments for the photos and suggested she should do the same. She wouldn't agree to pay him anything. 'He said if I went to the police they would not believe me. They said they would show them [the photos] to the police and I would get three years.'

The scheme went on for at least eight months. It produced a steady income for Goff and Felloni. The men charmed and cajoled the women before terrorising and indecently assaulting them. Tony and Jimmy took the photographs and rifled through the women's clothes and handbags. Tony gathered as much personal information about them as he could from letters, payslips and personal notebooks, and he and Jimmy kept records in diaries of their names, addresses and telephone numbers.

Pleas of inability to pay were always ignored. No sum of money, no matter how small, was ever refused but no amount of money, no matter how large, was ever sufficient. None of the photos was ever returned to any of the girls; some later doubted that they had actually been photographed. The average weekly wage in 1963 was around £9, and £1 was the equivalent of £13 today. Some girls were handing over more than half their pay. Gardaí estimated that over 100 women between the ages of fourteen and thirty were trapped in Felloni's vice ring.

When the number of women at the flat in one day became too much for either Felloni or Goff to handle, they banged on the ceiling with the handle of a brush for their neighbour Behan to come downstairs. Behan later said he interfered with only two women in the bedroom.

But these were not the exploits of a Romeo or a Latin lover, as Tony Felloni liked to see himself. That fact was clearly illustrated by the pitiful sight of a fourteen-year-old girl standing in Clontarf Garda Station as the sickening story of indecent assault, abuse and blackmail unfolded. A week later 'The Buller' McLoughlin put in the door of 6 Lower Gardiner Street.

---

1. The names of the women have been changed to protect their identities.

3 A Despicable Conspiracy 1963–64

'No man can have this many girlfriends,' Barney McLoughlin thought as he turned page after page in Tony Felloni's diary. It was just after 4.00 p.m. on Thursday, 29 August 1963 and the Gardaí were searching 6 Lower Gardiner Street. McLoughlin looked in the two rooms and checked under the beds. He searched around the record player and in the presses in the bedroom and the kitchen. He found three diaries. One belonged to Jimmy Goff, the other two to Tony Felloni. He opened them up and counted the names. There were eighty women.

Felloni was the first to be arrested. Two Gardaí picked him up in St Patrick's Teacher Training College in Drumcondra, where the apprentice was working with his father. He was taken to Clontarf Garda Station. Within an hour he signed a statement. He said he started 'making appointments' with girls he met outside the GPO in January 1963. He admitted he brought them back to Goff's house and got money from them.

'During the past nine months myself and Jimmy had about ten girls in the flat,' he said. 'We took photographs of a number of them in the nude and some partly dressed. We got sums of money from nearly all of these girls. I told the girls that if they did not give me the money I would use the photographs to get money from them. In all I got about £7.'

Felloni also outlined his version of what happened three weeks before with fourteen-year-old Maeve and her sixteen-year-old friend Carmel. He admitted telling Maeve she would not get out of the flat if she didn't do what he told her. 'I was bluffing,' he claimed, 'but she did not know it.' 'I stripped and got in beside her,' he went on. 'I got on top of her. I did not have intercourse with her.' He also admitted meeting her in Drumcondra and taking £1 off her as well as phoning and calling in to the house where she worked. 'Before I left,' he said, 'I put my hand up under her clothes while she was lying on the couch.'

Two hours later Jimmy Goff was pulled in. He detailed incidents with other women over five months before. He said that he and Felloni had met two girls from Offaly in O'Connell Street on St Patrick's Day and brought them back to the flat. One was taken into the bedroom and stripped by Felloni. He also told the Gardaí that Tony and Maria had brought two other girls to the flat two weeks before his arrest. He left soon after but Tony, Maria and Charlie Behan stayed on. 'The next day,' he said, 'Maria Felloni gave me twelve shillings which was stolen from one of the girls' handbags.'

Goff admitted taking photographs of the girls naked. 'Tony met another girl at the GPO', he said, 'and took her to the flat. There was another girl there. I had her in the nude. I told the second girl to take off her clothes. I took photos of the two of them on the bed, between their legs. Tony had them in separate beds and he was in the nude. I saw him in the bed at different times with the two of them. I got eight shillings cash from them.' Goff also admitted terrorising Maeve, stealing money, and being with Felloni when some of the girls handed over money for the photos. Two weeks later the camera was found hidden in Tony's parents' home in North Cumberland Street.

McLoughlin drew up a list of the names in the diaries and set about visiting every one of the women. Two other Gardaí, a man and a woman, were assigned to the case with him. None of them had ever come across anything like this before. The female Garda was to help him interview the women but she felt embarrassed and awkward asking young country girls about what went on in 6 Lower Gardiner Street.

McLoughlin was not called 'The Buller' for nothing, however, and he felt he had to get the job done. He was sympathetic to the plight of the victims but he was also under pressure to prosecute the case. Not all the women were prepared to co-operate. If McLoughlin didn't get the answers he needed he became characteristically blunt. He asked two questions of those he believed were obstructing the investigation: 'Did you know Tony Felloni?' and 'Did he screw you?' Most of the women came clean about the affair once they were assured their identities would be protected. In some cases their employers had also to be interviewed, but in almost all instances the women's families were never told.

Some of the women denied all knowledge of the scam. Others became abusive to the Gardaí when asked to tell them what happened. McLoughlin remembers one extremely good-looking blonde woman from the west of Ireland who refused to say anything at all. When he arrived to interview her she ordered him out of the flat. She took particular exception to being asked whether or not she had had sex with Tony Felloni.

Charlie Behan was arrested on 4 September 1963, six days after Felloni and Goff. He admitted indecently assaulting two of the women. But Maria Felloni was made of sterner stuff. When she was pulled in on 27 September, Tony's eighteen-year-old sister 'Deenie' had 'Nothing to say.'

McLoughlin organised a series of identity parades. At 11.30 a.m. on 20 September Felloni, Goff and Behan were put into a line-up with ten other men. They picked their own positions. Goff stood third from the left, Behan seventh and Felloni second last in line. One by one, three of the women were brought in. First Deirdre, then Bridget, then Nora. Both Bridget and Nora identified all three men by putting their right hands on the men's right shoulders. Deirdre recognised only Felloni and Goff. Neither of them said anything during the procedure, but Behan complained, 'I only saw the last girl.' He was referring to Nora.

Three weeks later Maeve identified all three as they lined up at the Bridewell Garda Station with eight other men. Carmel was up next but before she came in, the three changed places. She still identified all of them. Then Joan came in and recognised Felloni and Goff. Behan wasn't at the flat when she was abused.

The same day Maria Felloni was also put in a line-up with eight other women. She stood in first place. Maeve didn't remember her, but Carmel walked up to her and put her hand on her shoulder. 'Nothing to say until present in court,' Maria said. Two weeks later Angela picked Felloni and Goff from a line-up of seven other men and Maria Felloni from six other women. Maria looked Angela straight in the eye. 'Where exactly did you meet me?' she asked her. 'Inside the GPO,' Angela replied. 'I know nothing about it,' Maria said later when she was charged. 'I was in Liverpool and the Isle of Man.'

Maria and Tony Felloni, Charlie Behan and Jimmy Goff originally faced a total of thirty-four charges. These included blackmail, robbery, demanding money with menaces, unlawful carnal knowledge and rape. The pre-trial procedure took six weeks. It involved questioning witnesses and taking down depositions from the women in longhand. Eight were originally prepared to testify. In the end seven of the women gave evidence in court.

Felloni and Goff were remanded in custody after they were arrested and charged. Goff remained in jail from the end of August until the trial began in February. Maria was serving her three-month sentence from October on the charges of larceny and breaking into a factory. Tony, however, was released on £500 bail and that's when he started trouble again.

At around 8.45 p.m. on Tuesday, 22 October, Nora was walking down O'Connell Street towards Parnell Square, on her way to the Gardiner Street Girls' Club. Tony Felloni walked by her; then he stopped, turned around and called back to her, 'Why don't you speak to me?' 'We're not supposed to speak,' she replied. The witnesses were not supposed to talk about the case before the trial, least of all to the main protagonist. But that didn't bother Tony Felloni; he had a lot he wanted to say to Nora. He walked towards the club with her and tried to get her to contradict one of the other women's evidence. 'He told me to speak against the girl in court,' Nora said. 'He said I was to say that what she told the court was wrong.'

Felloni then tried emotional blackmail. 'He told me that I was the only one that could speak for him,' Nora recalled. He asked her about her statement to the Gardaí and when he heard what she had said he got angry and told her it was wrong. 'If the police come and see us talking,' she said to him, 'you'll be ruined.' 'Don't worry about Sergeant McLoughlin,' Felloni replied. 'He went off duty at six but don't tell him I've been speaking to you.' Felloni then suggested an elopement. He asked Nora to go to England with him. She declined the offer.

The memories of the abuse came back to Nora as they walked past the flat on Gardiner Street. As they got closer to the club, Felloni brought her into a car park. 'I didn't want to go,' she said, 'but I did so because I was afraid.' He started molesting her again. 'He tried to put his private part into mine but he did not succeed. While I was there I kept my legs together because I was afraid.'

Felloni then used a gang of local youths to intimidate and frighten the twenty-year-old woman. 'He told them I was one of the girls that was up in court. He asked me opposite [in front of] them to say nothing about him in court.' When she eventually got away from him Nora was afraid the gang would be waiting outside the club for her. Before he let her go he asked her for money and he left her with a chilling warning: 'If you speak to the guards, you might as well kill yourself.'

This was not the only instance of Felloni interfering with a witness while out on bail. He phoned one of the women at work seeking to prevent her testifying against him. He didn't succeed. He even threatened the female Garda working on the case, saying he would see her down a dark lane some night. She paid no attention but Barney McLoughlin had had enough. Felloni knew where all the women lived and he was not going to be allowed to undermine the case. On 24 October 1963 McLoughlin went into Judge Walter Maloney's court to get a warrant for Tony Felloni's arrest.

The judge became alarmed when he read the sergeant's explanation for the warrant. 'Is this your signature?' he asked. 'Yes, your honour,' McLoughlin replied. 'And the facts are correct?' 'Yes, your honour.' 'Bring that man before me,' the judge ordered. Tony was picked up the next morning in Ranelagh, where he was waiting for a lift to take him to a job in Wicklow. His arrest was the last straw for Verso's and he was fired. He later failed at an appeal hearing to have Judge Maloney's decision overturned and he was kept in prison until the start of the trial.

'Why are there no women on the jury?'

It was the first day of Tony Felloni's trial on Wednesday, 5 February 1964. The state was proceeding with only thirteen charges of vice, blackmail, theft and conspiracy against Tony, Maria Felloni and Jimmy Goff. Not all charges related to each defendant. The two men were also accused of stealing money and other items, including a camera and a key, from the home of a Mr William Higgins, the employer of one of the women. The offences were said to have taken place in June, July and August of 1963. All three pleaded not guilty. Tony and Maria didn't have a solicitor. They couldn't find a solicitor in Dublin at the time who was prepared to take the case, and an English solicitor whom Tony's mother had found for him died of a heart attack on the plane on the way over. The Fellonis conducted their own defence. The first thing Tony wanted to know was why there was an all-male jury.

The irony of the question was not lost on the judge. Tony Felloni was facing charges that had arisen out of indecent incidents involving more than eighty women over eight months. Now here he was in the Dublin Circuit Criminal Court claiming to be concerned about equal rights for the opposite sex. Judge Hugh McGivern glared at him and treated the question with the contempt he felt it deserved. He ignored it.

The first witness was Angela, who at twenty-five was a lot older and a lot stronger than the other women. She told a familiar story of meeting Felloni for the first time at the GPO on Monday, 3 June 1963. He said his name was Frank Murphy. Five days later he phoned her at William Higgins's home on Clonskeagh Road, where she lived and worked. The Higginses had a shop which adjoined the house. She told him she couldn't come out as she was minding the children. Five minutes later he arrived on the doorstep.

It was about half past nine on Saturday evening when Felloni arrived. He had a look around, then sat for a while and waited until the phone rang. He took the call and said he was going out to see someone. A few minutes later he came back with Jimmy Goff and another man, and sent Angela out to the kitchen to make them a cup of tea. Bringing it in to the sitting room, she found the three lads already busy trying to rob the place. Goff was trying to open one of the children's money boxes with a knife. He looked up, saw her and told her to get him something to open it with. She refused and told him to put it down, but he stuffed it into his pocket. Then they asked her for money, cigarettes and the keys of the shop. When she told them she didn't have the keys, Felloni tried to open the door to the shop with a knife. 'Sit down on the sofa,' he ordered. 'No,' Angela replied, 'I'm going to call the guards.' When Goff heard that he got annoyed, telling her he would stick her with a knife if she did. The three of them decided it was time to go but they took with them a camera, the money box, a key for the house and a brand new coat. 'I'll phone you later,' Felloni said to Angela on his way out.

He rang her the next day. They met again at the GPO. Jimmy Goff was with him and they took her to the Gardiner Street flat. The record player was put on, but the music was not for romantic purposes. Felloni called her into the bedroom and told her to take off her clothes. She refused and he got angry and violent. 'He pulled me down on the bed and broke the zip on my skirt,' she remembered. 'He lay on top of me, he had his clothes off at the time. He then pulled down my panties. He put his private part into mine. He remained on top of me for about five minutes. Then he told me to get up and get out.'

That was the first time Angela said she saw Maria Felloni. She was sitting in the kitchen and Angela walked past her as she headed for the door. Felloni came after her and escorted her to the bus stop. When he left her she discovered ten shillings missing from her handbag, which she had left on a chair in the kitchen while she went to the toilet.

Nearly a week later Felloni called again and told her to meet him at Higgins's shop in Clonskeagh. Angela met him at around 9.30 p.m. She was anxious to get the stolen goods back from him. 'He told me he'd ring the Higginses and tell them about the articles they took from the house,' she said. She gave him £2. She didn't want her employer to find out that his house had been robbed and that she had inadvertently let the thieves in. 'He told me he'd give me the key and the money box back. I thought I would get the lost property back, that was my reason for giving him the money.' But Felloni didn't think like Angela and Felloni didn't keep his promises. There was still a lot more juice for him to squeeze out of this fruit.

The following night, Sunday, 16 June, she met him again. She gave him ten shillings but he still wouldn't give her the stolen goods. 'Jimmy Goff gave me a key but it was not the right one,' she said. 'Anthony Felloni took it and put it in his pocket.' A week later he called again and said he had the goods. When she went to meet him, however, he told her 'the other fella has it in another flat'. Angela had sex with Felloni in the cold, bare, dingy flat two more times after that while the music blared in the kitchen. 'The reason why I got into bed', she said, 'was that I was anxious to get Mr Higgins's property back.'

Tony Felloni, defending himself in court, had a few questions to ask. 'Did you have permission from your employer, Mr Higgins, to entertain your friends in the house?' 'I did not,' she replied. 'Did you not tell me yourself what time to call to the house at that evening?' he asked. She admitted that she had and that she had introduced him to the children as her first cousin. She also said she was 'doing a line' with Felloni. Sensing her discomfort, Felloni asked her to tell the court what rooms she brought him into. 'I brought Mr Felloni into the sitting room first,' she said, 'before allowing him into the bedroom.' 'And did you not try to pretend to the children that I had left the house before you put them to bed?' he asked her. 'No, I did not,' she replied firmly.

Tony's cross-examination then started to go off on a tangent. He rambled and his questioning became aimless and irrelevant. The judge began to get annoyed.

When he began to ask a series of other questions, which had already been dealt with in direct evidence, the judge admonished him from the bench. 'If you ask any more of these questions, I will put an end to your cross-examination,' he told him. Felloni had succeeded in showing that Angela had a relationship with him but that was a side issue. It had no bearing on whether or not he had stolen from the house.

Jimmy Goff was the only one of the accused legally represented in court. His barrister, Horace Porter, questioned Angela on his behalf. She agreed that it was 'a risky thing' to give her name and address to two men she didn't know. She was 'doing a line' with Tony Felloni, she said, but she was never friendly with Jimmy Goff. She had broken up with Felloni and now had a new boyfriend. She was engaged to be married and she wore her engagement ring throughout the hearing. Angela was allowed to step down after three hours in the witness box. Her employer was next to take the stand.

William Higgins told the court that a key, a flash camera worth between £8 and £10, and one of his children's money boxes were missing after the robbery. There was no money in the child's piggy bank, but the camera was of sentimental value, as it contained a film of one of his children on his first Communion day. 'It was quite a horrifying experience at the time because nothing like that ever happened then,' he said afterwards. He never got his property back and he changed the locks on the doors of his home.

The Gardaí were anxious to protect the victims because of the sensitive nature of the evidence. After an application by the state, the judge ordered that their names and addresses were not to be published. The case had already gained a certain notoriety and was front-page news in the *Evening Press*, the *Evening Herald* and *The Irish Times*.

The Archbishop of Dublin, John Charles McQuaid, was shocked by the case and privately encouraged the Gardaí to process it as expeditiously as possible. He was anxious the public should be made aware of as little promiscuous and pornographic information as possible. The ethical and moral ramifications of the case for Catholic Ireland deeply disturbed Dr McQuaid. The Minister for Justice, Charles Haughey, also took an interest in the proceedings.

Some of the women told the Gardaí they had been raped and indecently assaulted but the state never proceeded against Felloni or Goff on charges of rape. One of the original charges related to an allegation that one of the women had been raped on waste ground on Clonliffe Road near the archbishop's palace. In the case of another young woman, a fifteen-year-old from Donegal who alleged she had been raped, the state could not proceed because her parents' consent was needed. The Gardaí were not prepared to break the promise of confidentiality and anonymity they gave to all the women. To this day Barney McLoughlin still wonders why the case was not prosecuted as he thought it should have been. 'It was considered a terrible scandal at the time,' he recalled.

Perhaps that was why the case fascinated the public so much. It was a scandalous but salacious story. There was deceit, sex, pornography, robbery and blackmail. The victims were innocent and naive; the blackmailers were devious and heartless. This was the dark underbelly of holy Ireland. There were queues outside the Circuit Criminal Court in Green Street from early morning and the court was packed every day, with disappointed spectators being turned away. The jury and the Gardaí were worried about the growing level of interest in the case as it went on. People came in and out of the court constantly. Some men came simply to stand at the back and leer at the women.

The women began to get upset and on the fourth day of the trial, the jury had had enough. Immediately after lunch the foreman asked the judge to bar the public from the court. 'We suggest', he declared, 'that it would be better if there were less people in the court as the witnesses seem to be too embarrassed to answer the questions. With no one here they might be able to speak louder.'

The judge, however, felt he could not accede to the request. Judge McGivern said he could not keep the public out of the court, although he did order the Gardaí to stop people coming or going while a witness was giving evidence. 'I will restrict members of the public as far as possible,' he said, 'but I have no power to clear the court.'

The case continued. Maeve and Carmel told their stories. 'Why did you pay Mr Felloni the money?' the judge asked the fourteen-year-old when she finished giving her evidence. 'I wanted to stop him from sending the photographs home to my parents,' she replied. The case was not going well for the three defendants. The women were holding up well under the pressure of testifying. Tony was not having much success defending himself either. He only succeeded in getting Joan to admit that after the incident in the flat, she went for a long walk with him and didn't complain.

Felloni then tried to raise the spectre of Garda brutality. He put it to Sergeant Barney McLoughlin that he was beaten up by the Gardaí after his arrest. He claimed he was hit as he was being brought into Clontarf Garda Station. 'The Buller' strongly denied the allegation: 'I was immediately behind him and no blows were struck.' In the climate of the time and considering the charges he was facing, the jury was unlikely to be sympathetic to Felloni's claims.

He also claimed that during his detention he was denied access to a priest. McLoughlin agreed that Felloni had asked to see one. 'I did not get a priest as there are no facilities for Confession in the station,' he said. 'I did not say I wanted Confession,' Felloni snapped back. 'That was the impression which I got,' McLoughlin replied.

Maria Felloni also made allegations of brutality against the Gardaí. 'Did you not say to me that if I did not make a statement I would get what my brother got?' she said to McLoughlin. 'No,' he replied. 'I told you I had reason to believe you were responsible for bringing a number of girls to a flat in Gardiner Street where they were photographed naked and money was robbed from their handbags.'

On the fourth day of the trial Goff's barrister produced one of his client's diaries in court. 'This was not a kind of rogues' gallery of entries specially kept of victims,' he declared. Under cross-examination McLoughlin agreed the first six to eight pages might be found 'in any ordinary person's diary'. But the sergeant drew the court's attention to the names, addresses and telephone numbers of a number of women that appeared later on, pointing out that five entries in one of the diaries were particular references to girls present in court.

Some of the women told the judge that they did not believe any photographs were taken. 'There was no flash from the camera,' Joan said, 'and neither of the boys [Goff or Felloni] turned the film on between the shots.' Deirdre said she didn't notice any flash either while she was being photographed. No photographs were ever recovered but the Gardaí still believed that pictures were taken. They also suspected two other people, a professional photographer and a local businessman, of being involved, but there was no hard evidence to back this up.

The Fellonis produced character witnesses. A civil defence officer said he remembered Felloni and Goff taking part in a three-day exercise in the Glen of Imal between 1 and 3 June 1963. It was not clear how testimony confirming a three-day absence from Dublin served as a defence against crimes that took place over six months.

Maria Felloni claimed she was in the Isle of Man at the time the offences were committed. 'The police there put me on a boat because I had run out of money,' she told the court. A Mr John Walsh took the stand to swear evidence on her behalf. He said, in reply to a question from her, that he had met her in a bar the previous August. He agreed that he had written a note asking her to meet him the next night. Maria then produced the note and Mr Walsh agreed that this was indeed the note he had written.

The prosecution counsel Mr Peter O'Malley then stood up and asked John Walsh a few questions. Yes, Walsh agreed, he had met Maria Felloni within the last three days. Yes, he agreed, she had asked him to give evidence at the trial. No, he said, he had not written the note within the last three days in order to set up an alibi for her.

In conclusion, Goff's barrister, Horace Porter, pointed out that Jimmy had a job and supported his widowed mother. 'He can not', he said, 'be termed a waster.' Tony and Maria's mother, Mary Felloni, did not appear in court as a character witness for her children.

It took the jury just three and a quarter hours to reach its verdict and on Tuesday, 11 February 1964 all three were convicted. Tony Felloni was found guilty on six charges of theft and three of blackmail. Goff was found guilty of five theft and three blackmail charges. Maria was found guilty of two charges of theft and one of blackmail. They were cleared on one charge of blackmail. The judge directed that another charge be struck out and he adjourned sentencing for three days. 'This was not a very pleasant case to sit and listen to,' he said. 'I will consider how to deal with the defendants on Friday.'

'I find it very difficult to know just how to deal with you,' Judge Hugh McGivern said to Maria Felloni on 14 February, St Valentine's Day. 'I find it hard to understand whether or not you were under the influence of your brother. Certainly you acted in a ruthless fashion on a number of occasions and you encouraged those unfortunate girls to accompany Goff and your brother to the flat. You did nothing to protect them from the treatment they got there. In your favour you did not perjure yourself by going into the witness box, but you did bring another person here and allow him to go into the witness box and perjure himself on your behalf.' He sentenced Maria Felloni to a year in prison.

The judge then turned to Jimmy Goff. 'It is fortunate for you and the others', he said, 'that the charges before me do not cover the entire transactions because you could be up on a more serious charge, and I can assure you that yourself and Felloni would have gone from the public gaze for a long time.' The judge accepted that Goff was not quite as ruthless as Tony Felloni but pointed out that he had been prepared to join in with him and was 'a very active supporter' of his. Jimmy Goff was sent to prison for two years.

Unlike the other three, Charles Behan pleaded guilty to the charge against him, unlawful carnal knowledge. He was dealt with separately, given a nine-month suspended sentence and bound to the peace for two years.

The judge reserved his real ire for the brains behind the scam, Tony Felloni. 'A despicable conspiracy it was too,' he said. 'It is rather significant that the girls you and your partner attempted to extract money from were domestic servants, working in Dublin, away from the protection of their own homes.'

He went on:

The most serious case involved a fourteen-year-old girl who had been lured to the flat in Gardiner Street. On the day you brought her to the flat you stole from her handbag the sum of thirty shillings, probably all the money this young girl had. You robbed this girl of every penny she had in her handbag, and then you met her again and asked her for more money.

You took photographs of the girl in a compromising position and you threatened to send them to her home or the Gardaí. You told this young girl if you did so she would get two years [in prison]. I am satisfied that you not only threatened to send these photographs to her home and employers, but you played on her mind that she would get two years if the photographs were shown to the Gardaí.

The amount of money is small, but the mental torture that this young girl went through can only be imagined. You pursued a hapless girl with your determined efforts to extract money from her. That young girl had got to the stage where she had decided to go to England to escape.

Tony Felloni was sentenced to a total of three years' penal servitude. It was his longest prison sentence to date. He also received four sentences of two years, three of twelve months and two more of nine months, but they all ran concurrently. The imposition of penal servitude or hard labour had no bearing on how he served his time. There was no rock-breaking in Irish prisons in the 1960s. Penal servitude was a hangover from the colonial era. It replaced transportation in 1853 when the British stopped shipping Irish convicts off to Australia.

Felloni's blackmailing scheme was a darkly original and imaginative crime. It was simple for him and devastating for its victims. Even though it was one of his earliest criminal ventures, it is still remembered today by people on both sides of the criminal justice system. Gardaí and criminals alike were disgusted by it.

The crime speaks volumes about the type of man Tony Felloni was and is. It clearly shows what he was prepared to do to others to get money, and illustrates characteristics that would emerge again and again throughout his criminal career. For the first time he displayed a willingness and an ability to target and then prey on the weak and the vulnerable. He did so without ever showing any pity or remorse. In 1960s Ireland where the Catholic church remained all-powerful, where morality and virginity were sacrosanct and where so-called fallen women were shunned and condemned, Felloni's scam was particularly cruel.

Felloni served two years and three months in prison and was released in May 1966. He was entitled to a quarter remission on his sentence for good behaviour. When his term of imprisonment was coming to an end he asked the prison governor, John A. Furlong, if he could be let out the night before. It was a common request among prisoners at the time but Furlong rang Barney McLoughlin first. 'Don't release him even half an hour before he's supposed to get out,' McLoughlin told him. Felloni didn't get out until eight o'clock the following morning.

Thirty-five years on, Maria Felloni still maintains she was wrongly convicted of blackmailing the country girls in 1963. 'I had no solicitor, I got stitched up,' she says. 'I had nothing to do with it, I was in the Isle of Man.' Maria accepts she met two of the girls outside the GPO and asked them to go to a party with her brother Tony and his friend Jimmy, but she says she only did it because he gave her one shilling and sixpence which she needed to go to the skating rink. She also says she came back to the flat later that night, saw one of the girls crying, gave her a drink of water and sewed her dress up. But she insists her brother lied about her role in the affair. 'I was put forward for another girl and told to shut my mouth. They didn't even let me show the letters I had from the Isle of Man in court.'

Tony's sister has had no contact with her brother for years and will have nothing to do with him now. At fifty-three years of age, she has some health problems and lives in a one-bedroomed flat in sheltered accommodation in a town in Antrim. She has, she says, come to terms with her own belief that she was convicted of a crime she didn't commit. She has never sought to prove her innocence in the courts. 'You can't carry guilt for what you didn't do,' she says. 'I can go to my God with a clear conscience.'

On 31 July 1987, the day he retired from the Garda Síochána, Barney McLoughlin stood in front of a shredder. He had a bundle of files in his hand. Into the shredder went the file on Nurse Mamie, or

Marie, Caden, the infamous backstreet Dublin abortionist. Her activities in the 1950s came to light only after a Garda's sister died in her flat. Into the shredder too went the file on a gang of Scottish safe-breakers. They came over to Ireland with explosives to rob Walpole's furniture shop in Suffolk Street and ended by blowing the whole place up. And last into the shredder before he walked out the door went the file—with statements, letters and handwritten depositions—on the seedy little vice ring on Gardiner Street run by Tony Felloni.

4 George Best's Brother 1966–72

'I'll have to see me Missus,' Anthony Best told the lady, 'but we'll move in tomorrow at midday.' It was a real coup for the two elderly women who lived in a big house on Victoria Road in Rathgar in Dublin. They didn't know much about football but they had heard of George Best and they were delighted his brother was moving in.

The two women were sisters. They were both from England and both had served in the Women's Royal Air Force. One of them owned the house; the other took responsibility for running it. They earned their living by renting out part of it, divided into bedsits. They had advertised for a lodger and their agent, Gerald Gilber and Company, told them there were two gentlemen calling to see the accommodation first thing in the morning.

On 17 June 1968 Anthony Best knocked on the door. 'He was about twenty-two or twenty-four years of age, athletic build and very brown complexion,' the landlady remembered. 'He did not introduce his friend to me.' She showed him the room at the top of the house and Mr Best agreed to rent it for £5 5s a week. The next day he and his wife called around at noon. He introduced 'Josephine' to their new landlady and they all had a nice chat. 'I'm a professional footballer,' he told her. 'I'm expecting to sign for Drumcondra.' The following week he told her his wife had gone to Belfast with her sister. The landlady never saw Josephine again.

Anthony Best was a charming tenant. He listened politely to the ladies' stories about the war, life in the WRAF, the officers they knew and the young men who died. They told him there was a tradition in the airforce of leaving a glass turned upside down on the bar in the officers' mess if a pilot failed to return from a mission.

Anthony told them stories too, about his own life organising parties with his famous brother George and how the Belfast man enjoyed Manchester United.

During his second week there, two men called to the house in a taxi. 'Is Tony Best in?' one of them asked. 'I don't know what time he'll be in,' the landlady replied. Just then, as if on cue, Anthony came around the corner. The landlady left the door open and went into the living room. She could still hear Mr Best and another man heaving and wheezing their way down the hallway and up the stairs to his room. 'I got the impression they were carrying something heavy,' she said.

The next day the landlady went into his room and found four newspaper parcels lying on the floor by the wall, blocking her way. Her patience with Anthony was beginning to wear a bit thin. 'Will you remove those parcels to another part of the room?' she asked him later. He replied with a big smile and a twinkle in his eye, 'Certainly, I will.' She couldn't help liking the man. Once he was late with his rent but he did leave it on the hall table the following Tuesday morning.

Mr Best was out a lot although he phoned in for his messages. He told the ladies he was working long and late hours organising a party for his brother. 'I'm having trouble getting a hall,' he said. The ladies never saw him again. At 1.00 p.m. on 3 July 1968, Detective Inspector John O'Driscoll and Detective Sergeant Edward (Ned) Ryan called. They went up to the room and opened up the newspaper parcels, to find 112 bottles of brandy, whiskey, vodka and liqueurs.

Tony Felloni was back in business, stealing cars and breaking into houses and shops. This was the Ireland of the late 1960s and 1970s. It was natural for Felloni to move into burglaries, robberies and car thefts; the wealth of the country had started to grow and people now had more things to steal. By the mid-seventies you were five times more likely to have your home or business broken into than you were in the mid-fifties. Your car was twenty-seven times more likely to be stolen, and overall the number of robberies was almost thirty times as high. Felloni wasn't three months out of prison in 1966 when he was found on Dollymount strand at 4.00 a.m. with housebreaking tools— a jemmy, a screwdriver and two pieces of cloth.

He hooked up with another local crook, Tony Duff, who was known as 'The Boss'. Born in Hardwicke Street flats, he had grown up with Felloni in the north inner city. Boss Duff was a tough, dangerous man who had a string of previous convictions for violence, larceny and robbery, but he was popular within his own community, where he was perceived as a so-called 'ordinary decent criminal'. In later life he was both friend and protector to Tony Felloni.

In the early hours of 16 January 1967, the two Tonys and another man broke into the Castle Golf Club in Rathfarnham. They looted the pavilion and the shop, making off with cases of Power's, Jameson and Crested 10 whiskeys and 30,000 cigarettes, along with two velvet curtains. The haul was worth nearly £500, over £5,000 today.[1] Two weeks later Felloni stole a car at Eccles Street in Dublin. The following week he was seen driving another stolen car, taken from Temple Street earlier that night. Felloni was followed by a patrol car after he drove out of Hardwicke Street flats and was arrested just past Trinity College.

Felloni now had a new mantra for the Gardaí when they charged him: 'I comprehend the charges but I refuse to accept them.' He was given plenty of time to comprehend them when he was put back in prison. He was refused bail and locked up pending his trial. Dissatisfied, Felloni decided to appeal the decision. On 18 March 1967 he wrote a letter from Mountjoy Jail to the county registrar asking for copies of the depositions in the case. He played the poor mouth and asked for the depositions for nothing, 'as I have no money or means of getting any'. 'I have no solicitor', he wrote, 'and I expect to be representing myself.'

Felloni already had a track record of sending flowery missives from the cells of the country's prisons. He became a bit of a jailhouse lawyer in Portlaoise while serving his three-year sentence. He had plenty of time on his hands and little else to occupy his mind but to think of ways to get out. On 17 July 1965, more than a year after his conviction, he thought he had grounds for an appeal. 'I wish to obtain a copy of the return for trial order in my case,' he wrote to the court registrar. 'I was not supplied with a copy at that time and now I am making an appeal.' Ironically, the time limit to apply for a certificate to appeal his conviction had expired five days earlier.

Now, two years later, he was again writing to the county court registrar as part of another attempt to get out of prison, even if he could do so only on bail. He sent a second letter on 28 March 1967. 'I am making an application for bail to the Supreme Court shortly,' he wrote, 'and I consider it a matter of cardinal importance that I have a copy of the depositions before the court.' His entreaties were of little use. Two weeks later he was convicted in the Circuit Court of stealing a car. Even his mother, who appeared as a witness in the case, couldn't keep him out of prison; he was jailed for three months.

Less than two months after his release he was picked up again in Terenure and charged in connection with the robbery at the Rathfarnham golf club. He pleaded guilty and on 6 July was convicted of receiving stolen goods. He was sent back to Mountjoy, this time for a year. The judge also took three other cases into account, two cases of possession of housebreaking implements and a third of stealing a £450 car. But the most notable aspect of the case was the fact that Felloni was arrested and prosecuted by Detective Inspector John O'Driscoll. Twenty-nine years later his son Sergeant John O'Driscoll was still chasing Felloni and his children.

Felloni was a habitual criminal who went back to stealing as soon as he got out of jail the following year. At around 10.30 p.m. on Sunday, 5 May 1968 Sergeant Tommy Boyle was passing Walker's on Upper Liffey Street in Dublin city centre. The sports and cycle shop was on the site where the new side entrance to Arnott's is today. 'I heard a sharp sound followed by a few heavy bangs,' he said. When he took a look at the front door he saw that the centre panel was out of place. Someone had pushed it out, climbed in and replaced it.

Boyle crossed the road and asked two passers-by to ring Store Street Gardaí. He waited and watched the door. Five minutes later Tony Felloni peeped out. Thinking it was all clear, he opened the door and walked out. He had timed his exit to coincide with Garda shift changes and didn't expect to be stopped.

'Felloni!'

Tony looked around, saw Boyle and ran.

'Anthony!' the Garda shouted as he went after him. He started gaining on him but Felloni wouldn't stop so he drew his baton and hit him on the back. Tony kept on running and got away.

Sergeant Boyle called to Ronaldo and Mary Felloni's house at one o'clock the following morning. No, they said, they hadn't seen their son Anthony and they didn't know where he was. At three o'clock that afternoon Felloni walked in to Store Street Garda Station and turned himself in. He was arrested and charged. 'I comprehend the charges but I refuse to accept them,' he said. The next day he appeared at the District Court, pleaded not guilty and elected for trial in the Circuit Court. He was released on bail and continued stealing.

Six weeks later Anthony Best and his wife, Josephine, moved into the house with the two women on Victoria Road. Josephine was from Harcourt Street flats, and she and Tony had carried this one off at least once before, when they moved into a house in Rathmines as Mr and Mrs Ward. Felloni now had a base from which to operate and somewhere safe to store stolen goods. A week after he moved into Rathgar he went on a three-day burglary binge.

In the early hours of 26 June the front door of Kelly's Hotel in Carrickhenry went in. The hotel was three miles outside Sligo town on the Dublin road. Felloni and two others broke into the cellar and loaded up their car with over 160 bottles of whiskeys, vodka, brandy and liqueurs, along with 10,000 cigarettes. In all they took over £350 worth of spirits and cigarettes with them back to Dublin. They didn't bother with any of the beer.[2]

The next day, some time between 9.00 a.m. and 1.00 p.m., Felloni broke into a house on Merrion Road. The house was in flats; there were three young girls living there. Felloni took all their jewellery, including gold watches, lockets, bangles and two engagement rings— in total worth over £175.[3] The next day he broke into another house at Orwell Park, where he stole six more pieces of expensive jewellery, worth over £370. One three-stone diamond engagement ring was valued at £225.[4]

In May and June 1968 Felloni was breaking into two houses a week on Dublin's south side. 'As a matter of fact,' he said, 'there are about fifteen or twenty in all.' The run came to an end after George Best's brother's flat was raided and some of the spirits from the Sligo burglary were found. The drink was traced back to Kelly's Hotel through a bottle of crème de menthe. There wasn't much demand for this liqueur in Carrickhenry and the odd time the barmen sold some they could never remember the price, so it had to be marked on the bottle. The price tag connected this bottle to Kelly's. The top on the bottle was also loose and the label was stained where the liqueur had leaked. By the time Felloni got it to Dublin it was empty.

'Hello, Mr Ryan, how are you?' Felloni said to Detective Sergeant Ned Ryan. They met in the Bridewell Garda Station at around 6.00 p.m. on 3 July. 'What is the value of the stuff you found in my flat?'

'About £300 to £350,' Ryan said, 'but we don't know the exact value yet.' He asked Felloni to tell him about it.

'What can I say, you found it in my gaff,' Felloni said. 'Did you find anything else?'

Ryan ignored the question and asked whether or not Felloni was going to make a written statement.

'What do you want a written statement for? I'm pleading guilty to receiving the stuff. I'll think it over tonight and let you know in the morning.' Tony decided not to make the statement.

Ned Ryan met him again the next day but Felloni still wouldn't tell him where the stolen goods came from.

'I don't know where the stuff is out of,' he said, 'It could be from heaven, but I got it from a man last Thursday evening and I knew it was stolen.' He was brought over to the District Court and charged in connection with the robberies. After that he tried to do a deal.

'There are a lot of things I have done that I would like to clear up at this stage,' Felloni told Ned Ryan.

'Such as what?'

'There are a few houses I broke into and I got jewellery and cash out of them. I don't know the exact addresses but if you tell me the houses that were broken into in the Rathmines and Donnybrook areas in the past three months, I will tell you the ones I did.'

Felloni offered to go with Ryan and John O'Driscoll in the squad car and show them the houses, but when they got as far as Christ Church Place, he changed his mind and asked to be brought back to his cell. He did, however, still agree to tell them which from a list were those houses he had burgled.

Ned Ryan named off four houses in Rathmines. The last one was in Orwell Park.

'I done that one,' Felloni said. 'Put me down for it. I think that was the house where I forced the front door.' He then offered to get the stolen jewellery back if he was released. 'There are two other blokes involved and they have the jewellery in a flat. If I tell you where it is they will know I have squealed.' Felloni still refused to make a written statement. 'I have told you enough', he said, 'to give myself three years.'

Two weeks later Felloni asked to speak to Ned Ryan again. He was anxious to get out of prison. 'I want to ask you some questions,' he said.

'By all means.'

'Mr Ryan, if I got bail I would be able to clear up all the crimes I have committed and get nearly all of the stolen stuff back for you.'

'Sorry,' the detective said, 'the position is I will be asking for custody at all times but you can look for bail in the District Court or apply to the High Court.'

Felloni tried to give Ryan a reason to trust him. He started offering crumbs. 'There's a house at Merrion Road which I broke into and got some jewellery out of. I'm almost certain it was the day before I broke into the house at Orwell Park.'

Ryan was unimpressed.

Felloni tried again. 'At the beginning of May 1968,' he said, 'I broke into a house at Leeson Street and I only got about £3 in cash in it.'

Ned Ryan still wouldn't budge.

Felloni looked at him, exasperated. 'Ah fuck it, Mr Ryan,' he cried, 'I'm telling you no more. I am really gone now for three years.'

In the end he got it nearly half right. On 17 October 1968 he was sentenced to fifteen months in prison for office-breaking. The other burglaries were taken into account.

Felloni was, however, learning to maximise his criminal activity while minimising the amount of time he spent in jail. He was already serving another sentence for housebreaking when he got the fifteen months; two weeks later he was back in the District Court, where he received another eight months for larceny and housebreaking. But each sentence he received over this period was for a number of offences. In August 1968, for example, he received two six-month sentences for housebreaking and larceny, but the sentences were concurrent. Similarly, in October and November, the sentences of fifteen and eight months were concurrent. So in spite of receiving sentences totalling almost three and a half years in three months, Tony Felloni was out again in less than a year.

Felloni's younger brother, Justin, was also a well-established criminal. He had fourteen convictions before he was twenty years old, including one for carrying a gun. The two brothers, along with another local criminal, operated a simple but effective pickpocketing scam in O'Connell Street in the 1960s. The system is still used by pickpockets all over the world today.

Three people were involved in the scam: the distracter, the hit man and the carrier. The distracter walked up to the target and accidentally on purpose bumped into him. Profuse apologies were followed by reassuring words and helpful offers; the target was detained long enough for the hit man to pick his pocket. Tony Felloni was the hit man. He was an excellent pickpocket. As soon as he got the wallet or purse, he passed it on to the carrier, who slid it into his pocket or slipped it into his newspaper. The system was simple, quick and effective, so much so that the Gardaí had to set up a surveillance operation in front of the GPO to stop it. On 4 November 1968 Tony Felloni was convicted in the District Court of larceny from the person.

Justin had his own scams. He ran a prostitution ring across from Heuston Station during 1967 and 1968, offering women to the country lorry-drivers who delivered to Dublin. They stopped off at a café on Benburb Street beside the quays. One night in September 1968 Justin offered a prostitute to a driver from Roscommon who was picking up from the cattle market. It was around quarter to twelve.

'Did you see a woman?' Justin asked the man as he came out of the café.

'No.'

'Would you take one if I got one?'

'I might,' the driver said.

'Go into the lorry with him, he's a man spending money,' Justin said to one of the prostitutes. He and another man also got in. Just then they saw two plain-clothes Gardaí. 'The law's around,' Justin shouted to the driver, 'Move!' The man drove the lorry around to Smithfield, where they started haggling about the price of the prostitute.

'She's worth more than thirty shillings,' Justin said.

'That's all I have,' the driver told him.

Justin insisted he must have more, and when the man continued to deny it decided to see for himself, searching his pockets and trying to take his watch. The driver got scared and blew the horn. Justin caught his arm and twisted it behind his back. 'Will I use the blade on him?' he asked the others. He took all the money the driver had, a five-pound note, a ten-shilling note, one shilling and a couple of pennies. All three of them hopped out of the cab, but Justin stopped and turned back. He saw the man was wearing a signet ring and pulled it off his finger before he ran off. 'Don't call the police,' he warned the driver, 'or else!'

The plain-clothes Gardaí were quickly upon them and all three were thrown into the back of a squad car. Justin had dumped the money and jewellery, but before he was taken away he got out of the squad car and showed the Gardaí where the stolen goods were. 'I plead guilty to robbing the money,' he said, 'but I didn't use any violence.' Justin was sent to prison for eighteen months on 3 December 1968. It was his second conviction for a prostitution-related offence. A year beforehand he was convicted of living on immoral earnings.

Tony and Justin worked together again in the 1970s but the partnership was never successful. Justin became a 'spunker', an alcoholic; he was totally unreliable. He smuggled bottles of whiskey on jobs, got drunk and was useless. He robbed supermarkets shouting 'Mise Éire!', mixing up his republican slogans. Once he fell asleep in the middle of a co-op robbery; another time he nearly electrocuted Tony by turning the electricity back on as his brother was dismantling an alarm. 'You nearly took the fucking hand off me!' Tony roared at him.

Tony Felloni carried on with his burglary career throughout the 1970s. He would steal anything. One night in October 1970 he broke into a house in Greenfield Park and stole two pairs of socks and eight Churchill coins from a boy who lived there. He stole a little girl's bracelet and a money box containing £1 10s. He was arrested for it, and over a year later was sentenced to six months in prison, on 8 February 1972 in the Dublin Circuit Court.

Felloni was not sent to prison immediately. He was released for a week when he agreed to be bound over to the peace and turn up at

Mountjoy Jail by 6.00 p.m. on 7 February. He never showed up to begin his sentence. A bench warrant was issued and he was arrested and imprisoned the next day. The state entered a *nolle prosequi* against him on another charge of stealing £600 and a briefcase from a house in Monkstown. Six days later he was given another nine months in the District Court for breaking and entering.

After that Tony had better luck as a criminal while Justin's circumstances got steadily worse. He had no fixed address throughout the late 1970s and 1980s and he became a wino. He got drunk, stole from parked cars and slept on the streets. He also began to molest children and in later life his older brother would have nothing to do with him. Tony would walk by when he saw him begging on the streets.

Justin Felloni went to London, where he died penniless and homeless on 4 April 1996 at a drop-in centre for alcoholics in Camden Town. The coroner certified the cause of death as 'sudden death in epilepsy'. His sister, Maria, brought his body back to Northern Ireland. Justin was forty-nine years old.

1.

30,000 cigarettes	£300
4 cases of Power's Gold Label	£96
2 velvet curtains	£25
1 case of Jameson 10	£24
1 case of Crested 10	£24
Cash	£8 16s
Total	£477 16s

2.

10,000 cigarettes	£121 17s 6d
48 bottles of Black & White Scotch	£100
48 bottles of Power's Gold Label	£93 12s
24 bottles of Jameson	£46 14s
18 bottles of Jameson Bresta	£4 2s 6d
5 bottles of Courvoisier	£3 5s
10 bottles of Baby Power's	£2 5s 10d
7 bottles of liqueurs (including crème de menthe)	£1 18s 6d
Half-bottle of vodka	£1 3s
5 baby vodkas	£1 2s 11d
2 bottles of Courvoisier brandy	13s
1 bottle of Redbreast whiskey	9s 4d
One-eighth bottle of Scotch	4s 8d
Total	£379 17s 9d

3.

Solitaire diamond ring	£30
Ladies' gold watch	£25
Gold ring with aquamarine stone	£25
Gold locket	£10
Engagement ring	£10
Gold cameo bracelet	£10
Gold pocket watch and chain	£7
Gold bangle	£6
Gold chain with charms	£6
Ladies' wristwatch	£5
Gold locket	£5
Gold pendant	£5
Gold eternity ring	£5
Silver bangle	£4
Signet ring	£3 10s
Pendant and chain	£2
Gold cross and chain	£1
Bracelet	£1
Total	£175 10s

4.

Three-stone diamond engagement ring	£225
Sapphire and diamond ring	£60
Gold brooch	£30
Gold heart-shaped pendant	£25
Gold square-shaped pendant	£25
Gold chain	£5
Total	£370

5 *The Felloni Gang 1973–78*

'He couldn't fart but there was a policeman beside him.' That's how one of Felloni's associates summed up his lot in the early 1970s as he tried to continue his career as a criminal in Dublin. He was having severe difficulties. Every detective in the city knew him. He could no longer move around freely without the risk of being stopped, questioned or searched by the Gardaí. Felloni decided to broaden his horizons and look for targets outside Dublin. He began to concentrate his activities in what was known as 'the sticks'.

Felloni was one of the first Dublin criminals to spot the potential for robbing down the country. Country people were far less security-conscious than their city cousins. They still left their homes open, their door on the latch or their key in the lock. Most people did not have phones and those that did had no direct dialling facility. Not only were their homes easier to break into, but it was harder for them to call for help. Above all, people in the country did not expect to be broken into.

Security was not as tight in the businesses either. Felloni knew that not only were isolated rural shops and factories easier to break into, there was less chance of him being disturbed. There were fewer Gardaí to worry about in the country. They had to travel longer distances and their response times therefore were not as fast as in the city. Felloni lived away from his wife and children in a mobile home at a caravan park in Tallaght. It wasn't a long drive to Blessington and beyond. As far as Felloni was concerned, the country was there for the taking.

He got together with a gang of eight other well-known criminals. They started breaking into factories, post offices, shops, creameries, garages, pubs and houses all over the country. They usually drove out of Dublin in the afternoon, broke into about four or five places and came back in the early hours of the morning. They had the use of at least twelve cars and vans, including two black Mercedes, a blue Anglia van and a White Humber Hunter. By the end of 1973 'The Felloni Gang' was the biggest of three such criminal gangs which were based in Dublin but robbed in the country. His friend Tony Duff ran one of the others.

Felloni's gang was prepared to travel anywhere and rob anything. They drove out of Dublin and parked their own car a few miles from whatever they intended to rob. They then stole another car locally and drove it to the post office, house or factory. The car was always taken from a house or somewhere it wouldn't be missed until morning, never from a pub or club where the owner would be looking for it at half eleven. They drove home in their own car when the job was done.

Everyone knew what they had to do, 'alarm, tools, van, in and gone'. The first thing, however, in a small country town was to ensure the Garda car was put out of action. The four tyres were slashed so the gang couldn't be chased. Telephone wires were also cut; alarms were disconnected. If the men thought the alarm might go off they broke in, hid, and watched the premises for about an hour. If the Gardaí didn't come they knew it was safe to go in.

Most of the tools they needed were stolen locally: a jemmy, a screwdriver, a tyre jack, an angle grinder and black paint. They broke in with the jemmy and screwdriver and they opened safes with the jacks and angle grinders. They painted the windows black on the inside so the light or the sparks from the safes couldn't be seen outside.

For heavy-duty jobs they wore overalls, wellingtons and masks over their mouths. Felloni still wore his smart clothes underneath. They didn't use gloves because in the eyes of the law these were housebreaking implements. Instead they wore two pairs of socks and used one pair as gloves so as not to leave fingerprints behind. They got rid of the overalls and ran magnets through their hair afterwards to make sure all the shards of metal were gone.

They usually carried sticks rather than guns and relied on surprise and violence. They covered their faces with balaclavas or makeshift masks made from the sleeves of jumpers. They put a knot in the bottom, burned two holes for the eyes and pulled the sleeve over their heads. When they came across householders or postmistresses, they attacked them and tied them up. Tony Felloni could be very vicious. 'He took terrible liberties, he had to be stopped,' one gang member said. 'If they didn't give him the keys quick enough he'd bleeding mill them.'

Felloni was arrested on 11 October 1974 and charged with a series of robberies on homes in Kildare and Westmeath. He was accused of breaking into one house and moving on to another when he got nothing there. In the second house the owner was beaten up and the gang got £1,500 in cash and £500 in traveller's cheques. Then they beat up his wife and took another £100 from her.

Tony was the only one of the four men charged who got bail (£200). The gang members opted for trial not in the midlands where the robberies took place but in the Central Criminal Court in Dublin, as they believed that the local district justice would give them harsher sentences. After a series of adjournments the case finally came to court in Dublin fourteen months later. The state entered a *nolle prosequi* on three of the men, including Felloni. On 4 December 1975 those three walked free. In 1983 the law was changed and the practice of transferring rural cases to the Central Criminal Court was done away with.

Felloni didn't like guns but he was on jobs where they were used, particularly if he worked with any of the other gangs. Tony Duff often carried one. The gang rarely brought a gun to the scene; it was there when the men arrived. A motorbike would deliver it and wait until the job was finished to take it away. Felloni would never be caught with a firearm although he was with another gang member when he was.

In July of 1975 John Bollard was charged with possession of tear-gas canisters and a RÖHM RG-3 pistol, a weapon derogatorily referred to by ballistics experts as a 'cheap Saturday night job'. Felloni was charged with assaulting Garda Patrick Lydon. The case took a year and a half to come to trial and on 28 January 1977 Felloni pleaded guilty to the assault charge. Bollard got a nine-month suspended sentence while Tony got six months suspended; he was also fined £50 and bound over to the peace for six years. However,

Tony couldn't keep his word for even six months—he was convicted on another assault charge on 9 June.

The gang usually didn't bring the goods back to Dublin the same night they took them. It was too dangerous. The Gardaí knew they were robbing down the country and set up checkpoints on the main roads back into the city. They were often caught trying to avoid these by taking the back roads. The car or cars would be stopped and searched but most of the time nothing was found. In October 1974 Felloni was stopped at a checkpoint in Church Street at 12.30 a.m. driving a green Cortina that he had reported stolen a month before.

Felloni buried bulky goods like jewellery and coinage in ditches and fields. He also hid stolen property in isolated farmhouses or left it with contacts and drove back down to collect it a few days later. If he robbed a post office, the postal service often ended up delivering its own stolen goods. Stamps, cash and postal orders were put into envelopes in the post office while it was being robbed. These were stamped or franked and dropped into postboxes in the area to be sent to safe houses.

The gang always took the stamper and the inkpad because these were among the most valuable items in the post office. They were taken to England with the stolen postal orders, which were then stamped and cashed in small denominations in the post offices of various English towns. The gang members posed as emigrants who had just received a postal order from home. By the time the orders were returned to Ireland the gang were long gone with the money. Stolen postal orders were worth their face value.

Felloni's gang also used the Well pub just outside Moate, Co. Westmeath for storing stolen goods. Noel Crowley and his wife, Madeline, bought the Well in June 1973. Crowley was born in Clare but spent a lot of his time in Dublin with Felloni and other criminals. He also had connections with the group Saor Éire, a collection of disaffected republicans and bank robbers. Crowley also owned a house on the Howth Road and a farm in Wicklow. He had a number of convictions for fraud, receiving stolen property and driving without insurance.

Noel Crowley provided a front which allowed the gang to hide and launder much of the stolen property. Gang members travelled out of Dublin in twos and threes and met in the pub. They often had a few pints and maybe a meal before heading off to rob. Stolen drink and cigarettes were stored in a room upstairs or in a shed at the back. The men could also lie low in the pub. Felloni was arrested there at six o'clock one morning in 1976 as he slept upstairs.

One bank holiday weekend the gang all met up in the Well, but too many arrived so they split up into two smaller groups. One group went north and west out towards Sligo and back via Galway. They robbed small shops, post offices, creameries and factories. The other group carried out a similar spree as they headed out as far as Limerick and back via Cork. The loot was all brought back and divided up in the pub.

On 4 July 1974 the Well was raided. Over 116,000 cigarettes were found in Crowley's bedroom, and a large quantity of spirits were found in the cellar. It had all been stolen from a wholesale grocer in Birr, Co. Offaly three weeks before. There was also a large quantity of tinned beans, peas, salad creams and baby food in the shed, where the door had been built up with concrete blocks and the windows sealed off with wooden shutters. The food had been stolen from a delivery van in Dublin.

Noel and Madeline Crowley were both charged with housebreaking and receiving stolen goods. Both were granted free legal aid after Noel Crowley said in court that he couldn't afford the cost of the trial. The Well, he said, was finished because the Gardaí raided it twice a week. His house on the Howth Road was heavily mortgaged and the farm in Wicklow could only feed a few horses. The charges against Madeline Crowley were later dropped and she was therefore acquitted. Gardaí believed she knew nothing about the crimes and had nothing to do with them. Her husband pleaded guilty and on 26 January 1977 Noel Crowley received a two-year suspended sentence.

In Felloni's gang criminals worked for their money. 'You'd go at ten o'clock, get a feed, have a pint, go on a spree, do a few at a time,' one former member recalled. 'You'd go into a field, have a sleep in the car, have a wash; bang, away you go again. You earned your few quid, I mean you really earned it.' They often worked on inside information from disgruntled or greedy employees who knew the layout of factories, the level of security and the amount of money on the premises. There was an accountant who worked for a number of pubs in the midlands. 'He told you how to get in and how not to get in,' a gang member said. 'There was always a job to do for him while you were there. Take the books out so he'd get more work out of the pub or something.'

It was specialised work with long hours and heavy lifting in hazardous conditions. 'You could pop the rivets out of Milner safes,' one gang member said. 'Chubb's were the hardest.' They spent one weekend, nearly three days, on one safe, to find there was nothing in it. They prised another safe out of concrete with a tyre jack, put it on cushions and car tyres and pulled it quietly away. They stole £600 in sixpenny bits from a safe in a Dublin shopping centre. The bag was buried down the country and later cashed for a fee by a local businessman in a supermarket in Ballina.

On another occasion Felloni and two others managed to get a safe out of a post office in the middle of the night without waking the people sleeping upstairs. They slid it out into the garden and guided it up the path to the eight-foot wall at the end, wondering how they were going to get it over. They popped it up against the wall to ponder their dilemma when, as if by magic, the door swung open. The safe was full of cash, postal orders and insurance stamps.

The gang specialised in stealing social insurance stamps. It was the main reason for breaking into factories, labour exchanges, creameries or places where people worked. Every employer had to stamp a card for every employee. It was the law. The employer deducted the employee's contribution from his or her salary, made up the difference and bought the stamps at the post office. Each employee's card was kept in the workplace and the employee could check the payments any time.

Different stamps covered different employees but most people paid around £3.42 while their employers paid £5.26, giving the stamp a face value of £8.68. Social insurance was therefore expensive for employers, with the majority paying one and a half times the amount their employees contributed. An employer with 500 workers paid out over £130,000 a year for stamps. The cost of the stamps increased throughout the 1970s until they were replaced by Pay-Related Social Insurance in 1979.

Social insurance stamps were almost as good as hard cash to thieves like Felloni. They were widely available and easily accessible.

They were stolen in sheets from post offices or steamed off cards stolen from workplaces. They were easy to carry, conceal and sell on. With no serial numbers or other identifiable mark, they were untraceable. Stolen stamps could not be distinguished from legitimate ones. There was a ready market of dishonest employers for the stamps; they not only saved on their own payments but kept the money they deducted from their employees. The employer with 500 workers could save £2,000 a week, over £100,000 a year.[1]

Some factories tried to prevent their stamps from being stolen by stamping the company name and address over them to render them useless to any other employer. The gang found a way around that. They put the stamps in a basin of light bleach and water, which dissolved the ink from the stamps as well as separating them from the cards.

The Department of Social Welfare then tried to introduce a dye into the stamps that would fade once they were put into water and bleach. The gang found a way around that too, using a lighter chemical—Milton, the baby bottle cleaner—to remove the stamps from the cards. A plate was then heated in the oven and the stamps were put on it to dry. The only drawback for the employers buying the stamps was that there was no glue on them. They had to stick them on their employees' cards themselves.

The return on stolen social insurance stamps was higher than on other stolen property. Under normal circumstances, the resale value on stolen goods is approximately a third. For insurance stamps it was a half. Felloni and the others carried them around in a matchbox. It was dropped on the street and picked up later if there was a danger of being caught. Tony Felloni had the contacts to sell his own stamps to and he operated as a fence for others. 'Tony had a market for anything,' a gang member said, 'from a needle to a submarine.'

One evening Felloni walked into Coolock Garda Station, an unusual event in itself. He asked to speak to a detective he knew. 'I owe you a favour,' he said to the man. He didn't owe him any favour. 'Do you want to recover some of the stamps that were taken in the post office raid last week?' he asked him. 'I happen to know where an amount of them were sold but you'll have to move fast.'

The detective got a warrant and went to the home of a well-known north city butcher. When asked, the man produced an envelope he had recently received in the post. There were six social insurance stamps in it. The butcher said the letter was unexpected and unsolicited. 'Felloni was such a cheapskate that he wasn't prepared to use enough stamps to set the man up,' the detective said later. If the butcher had been using stolen stamps, he'd have bought more than six.

Felloni had learned by now not to say anything to the Gardaí. He was smooth and self-assured, a man who talked a lot but said nothing. Superintendent Gerry Murray, who was based in the midlands for most of his career, remembers Tony Felloni as 'a remarkable man' in an interview situation.

'He would tell you about all the crime in the world but when it came to specifics he knew nothing. I asked him once if he had a dozen jobs planned for a night but got £20,000 in the first place he went in to, would he stop then or continue on robbing for the night. "Oh Jaysus, Mr Murray," he said to me, "that would be like getting a goal in the first minute of an All-Ireland final. Whereas if you went to three or four places and got nothing it would be hard after that to keep the team on their toes."'

Felloni knew a little about sports psychology. He claimed he never went robbing late on Saturday night because he was always watching *Match of the Day*. He practised his amateur psychology in the 1970s on the numerous occasions he was picked up for questioning by the Gardaí. 'Look, lads,' he once said to two detectives, 'I meet plenty of fellas like you. Some come the heavy, others produce the cigarettes. It's all the same to me because ye do all get the same result out of Tony Felloni so ye can have it any way ye want.' 'Felloni wouldn't admit he was alive,' Superintendent John Reynolds said.

An interview after one of his robberies in Wicklow turned into something of a cross between a pantomime and a game of verbal gymnastics. When the detective asked him if he had anything to say, he replied, 'You don't fucking think I'm going to admit just like that. I want a solicitor.' The solicitor arrived and spoke to him for about fifteen minutes. When the interview resumed, Tony was far less hostile. 'I want to help the guards in any way I can,' he declared. 'At the moment I can't recall with any accuracy the dates you mentioned.'

He appeared to slip up when he was asked what part of a car he was in. 'I was all over the car,' he said, 'but you won't find . . .' He stopped.

The detective pressed him. 'Find what?'

'I did not say.'

'I don't think your mind is too clear on events, is it accidental or intentional?' the detective asked.

'I won't say,' Felloni replied. He had recovered his composure and control.

'You might say in the morning,' the detective said.

'You know me, I'll talk all night without saying anything.' Felloni was true to his word. The morning session lasted less than a minute. Tony 'wasn't any clearer' about where he had been. And as one of the gang said about him, 'If he was caught he was caught on his own.' Felloni never named names.

Tony Felloni had decided from now on to admit nothing. If he was involved he had to be caught in the act, and even if he was caught red-handed, the case against him still had to be proved in court. Availing of the criminal legal aid scheme, Tony would take it all the way through the system if necessary, with the best lawyers fighting for him. If he wasn't happy, he would appeal. He appealed all three of his convictions for beating up his wife, Anne, but they were not overturned. However, one of his other convictions was.

Felloni had been convicted of loitering with intent to commit a felony. The offence took place at the Roundabout pub in Artane on 20 May 1975. A year and a half later he went to the High Court and applied for a conditional order directing the authorities to show why he should be put into Mountjoy Jail for three months.

On 26 November 1976 Felloni claimed in an affidavit that section 4 of the Vagrancy Act 1824 and section 13 of the Prevention of Crimes Act 1871 were unconstitutional and did not form any part of the law of the state. He cited the cases of three other men charged under the same Acts whose convictions were set aside when the DPP and the Attorney General consented to have them quashed. Mr Justice Murnaghan told Felloni he would give him an absolute order because the 1824 Act did not apply in the Republic. The Act, he said, had been superseded but the later Act had not been recited on the conviction. Felloni won the case and the conviction does not appear on his criminal record. The fact that the judge gave him an absolute order meant that Felloni won the case outright in the High Court; if the state had wanted to appeal, it would have had to go to the Supreme Court.

Felloni and his gang went all over the country. They robbed a pub in Wexford but got only a few hundred pounds instead of a few thousand. Losing their way, they asked directions from a farmer's wife, who later identified one of them. They tied up a woman in a post office in north county Dublin one evening, took the light bulb out of the hall and waited until the postmistress and her husband arrived back. They hit the man over the head and covered his face with a pillowcase, took the keys and tied the couple up. They made off with 'the labour money' from the safe but crashed the car on the way home. The gang also drove a car into a bog in Co. Offaly on the Ferbane–Ballycomber Road, having broken into the Robinson factory in Belmont.

They robbed the Fairyhouse racecourse twice. One of the nights they played a game of cards and had a few drinks there before taking spirits and cigarettes. On their return journey they robbed a butcher's shop: 'We drove back with the sausages hanging out the boot of the car.'

In Cavan they had to make a run for it when dogs chased them from the postmistress's house. The countryside was pitch-black and they jumped over a four-foot wall to find that 'It was like Beecher's Brook,' as one of them said—'there was a twelve-foot drop on the other side.'

One of the gang, a well-known criminal from Sheriff Street, broke his pelvis. Two of the others compounded his injuries by landing on top of him. They carried him off and left him at the Mater Hospital back in Dublin. It was the second time the same criminal had been hurt on a job. On the previous occasion he had been trying to break a plank with a kick and had put his boot through a nail. The others had laughed at him. Felloni also hurt his back when the car crashed on the way back from a job. He banged his head off the windscreen, but refused to be left behind. Another gang member carried him away screaming. His left middle finger is missing—a permanent reminder of his days on the road. He lost it after he tried to dive out of a window with wire mesh running through the glass.

The gang carried out a series of burglaries on the Ballyowen Road in Lucan. There were no motorways at the time, and Lucan and Leixlip were still country villages. Tony Duff and Justin Felloni were also on that job but Justin had too much to drink and got sick on his leather jacket. They stole about £500 in cash from one house along with a small amount of Dutch guilders—which later gave 'The Boss' away when they were found in his flat.

The Felloni gang were suspected of breaking into Chadwick's builders' supplies centre in Athlone in October of 1975 and stealing over £3,500 in stamps and £70 in cash. They were also thought to be behind the robbery at Claffey's drapery in Ballymahon, Co. Longford that September, when over £2,000 worth of clothes were stolen. In one night in January 1976 four premises within a half-mile radius were hit in Athboy, Co. Meath. Gang members were also spotted numerous times outside factories all over the country watching to see what time the wages were delivered.

Another post office robbery in Wicklow came to the Gardaí's attention only when they raided a gang member's flat and lifted the carpet. Right in the middle of the floor they found £500 in cash, the denominations and serial numbers coinciding exactly with the money stolen in Wicklow. One by one the members of the Felloni gang were getting caught and getting put away.

Felloni himself had managed to avoid getting caught for the robberies during the period the gang operated—from 1973 to mid-1977—yet he still spent around half that time in prison. Seven of the eight convictions he received were for assaults or driving offences. The closest the Gardaí got to catching him for the activities of the gang was when he was given a twelve-month suspended sentence for possession of housebreaking implements in October 1974.

The majority of Felloni's sentences were handed down in Dublin courts, although he was also caught with a stolen car in Tipperary and convicted of assault in Mullingar. The gang members varied over the years as they either dropped out or were locked up. Felloni was a constant factor who always came out of prison after relatively short spells only to resume his life of crime. But in the middle of 1977, after he had spent more than a year out of jail, Felloni's luck finally ran out. His problems began with his driver's licence.

Tony needed to be able to drive. It was a tool of his trade. The problem was not that he wasn't able to drive, but that legally he wasn't allowed to do so. The Gardaí in the country were sticklers when asking for a licence, tax and insurance. Even a polished, well-dressed, well-spoken bluffer like Felloni couldn't always talk his way out of a checkpoint.

He was caught a number of times driving stolen cars and driving without insurance, and at the end of January 1976 was convicted again in Dublin of driving without a licence or insurance. He was fined £2; he could afford that. He was sent to prison for six months; he could handle that. But the judge disqualified him from driving for a year and that was a problem. He'd be out in four months and he was a man who travelled the country. He needed his licence.

He appealed the decision to the Circuit Appeal Court but he was out of luck. The judge there not only reaffirmed the original decision but increased the period of disqualification from one to fifteen years. Felloni's licence was also endorsed in spite of the fact that he didn't have one. Four years later he was still sore about it and decided to appeal the decision again, this time from prison. He was partially successful.

In 1980 Tony Felloni was given permission to reapply for a driving licence. The court was told that he wanted his licence back to undergo a course so that he could get a job driving commercial vehicles. The judge decided he would not stand in the way of Felloni's rehabilitation but he stipulated that the prisoner could apply only for a licence for vehicles over two tons. Felloni could drive out to rob the post offices, creameries and factories of the country only in a lorry. He failed again four years later when he appealed the disqualification for a third time.

Leixlip marked the beginning of the end for the Felloni gang. It was in the early hours of Monday, 18 April 1977 when the front door of the gate lodge cottage at Killarkin Stud in Dunboyne, Co. Meath crashed in. The family were all in bed—the head groom, William Rochford, his wife, Mary Frances, sub-postmistress in Leixlip, and their two sons, James and Anthony. Three armed and masked men ran into their bedrooms. Billy Rochford was hit on the head with a stick and ordered to lie face down on the bed. 'I could hear them hitting my wife and asking her about the post office and where the keys were,' he said.

The gang had decided to do the job on the Sunday evening because it was the day of the National Football League final at Croke Park. Kerry beat Dublin by two points but the main topic of conversation for the supporters driving home was the demonstrations and disturbances on the pitch. The gang members timed their departure from Dublin to coincide with the thousands of Kerry supporters going home. They knew that three men in one car leaving Dublin on a match day would not raise Garda suspicions. But one Garda was suspicious.

A detective from Coolock, driving back to Dublin after the weekend, spotted three characters he knew very well. He pointed them out to his passenger. 'Mark my words,' he said. 'You read the papers tomorrow and you'll read all about what those three are doing tonight.' It did not make pleasant reading.

While their parents were being beaten, the Rochford children were being watched by another gang member, who ordered eleven-year-old James and his younger brother Anthony to cover their faces with the bedspread. In the other room, one of the men hit Mary Rochford across the face with a stick, and when they eventually got the keys from her, they slapped her until she told them which key was which.

One of the raiders headed for Leixlip and emptied the safe of all the cash, insurance stamps, postal orders, postage stamps, television licences and money orders. The two others watched the family. Mary Rochford was bleeding from a cut to the head and one of the men made her a cup of tea. James could hear her crying from his bed next door and looked out from under the bedclothes. His bedroom door opened out on to the living room and he could see a man standing there. He was about five foot eight inches, twenty-eight to thirty years of age, with reddish or dark brown hair and a moustache, and he wore a white jumper. Joe 'The Fly' Fagan had taken his mask off to get a drink. The boy watched him for about three minutes. Then Fagan put his mask back on, came in and carried the boys on his shoulders into their parents' room. 'We were thrown onto the bed and told to get into it,' James recalled.

The family's ordeal lasted about three hours. When the man returned from the post office, Billy and Anthony Rochford were tied together, James and his mother were taken out and tied up in the other bedroom. 'One of the raiders told me I wasn't to squeal to the cops or there would be guns waiting for me,' Billy said. He later freed himself and his family. The gang had ransacked the house and stole another £25 before leaving.

Joe Fagan was the only gang member ever convicted of the Leixlip post office robbery. There wasn't enough evidence to proceed against the others. Fagan claimed that he was at Croke Park on the day of the robbery, that he had a few drinks afterwards and went home to bed. Almost two years later, on 7 February 1979, he was sentenced to ten years in prison in the Central Criminal Court.

Two weeks after Leixlip Tony Felloni was caught.

There was a crossroads, a shop, a pub, a church, a school, a couple of houses and—most important of all—a post office in Ballacolla, Co. Laois. The phone rang in the Garda house at 4.00 a.m. It was the second time the silence in the sleepy little village had been broken in the early hours of Wednesday, 4 May 1977. The dog, which slept in the hall, had barked twenty minutes earlier and woken Sergeant Eddie Geraghty. He had just fallen back to sleep when the phone rang. The postmistress, Maureen Dillon, was on the other end of the line. The post office was being broken into. Two men had put a ladder up to the house and were climbing in the back window. She lived there and she was terrified. 'I suppose I should have copped it when the dog barked,' the sergeant thought as he jumped out of bed.

He pulled on his pants, jumper and shoes, and rang the nearby station in Abbeyleix for back-up. He grabbed a hurley and rushed out to the car to find all four tyres flat. As he ran the 100 or so yards towards the post office, two other men ran in the opposite direction. They split up. One man stole a bike. He cycled around until he got lost and was later picked up by Abbeyleix Gardaí.

The second man headed off across the fields. Geraghty went after him. In the darkness the thief became disorientated and as the sergeant caught up with him he threw himself on the ground, shouting, 'I'm an epileptic, I'm an epileptic!' Geraghty arrested him and took him to Abbeyleix station. Ballacolla was the last post office Tony Felloni robbed. One of the gang got away and back to Dublin.

At around 7.00 a.m. he told Anne Felloni her husband had been caught. 'She didn't give a fuck,' he said.

Felloni was charged in May 1977 and remanded to Abbeyleix District Court, but as in other cases he opted for trial in Dublin. He was prepared to plead guilty in the District Court, where the maximum sentence was a year in prison. But when the judge sent the case to a higher court, Tony pleaded not guilty, secured bail, and was able to stay out of prison for another year. In the Central Criminal Court he was found guilty of burglary and on 24 July 1978 was sent to prison for three years.

Tony Felloni can handle prison. Gardaí, prison officials and fellow criminals agree that he can do his time. 'Prison was no deterrent,' one of his gang said, 'Felloni had no fear of jail.' He was a model prisoner who served his time quietly and neither caused nor got involved in any trouble. He was usually able to get a good job inside, one that got him away from the general prison population and out of his cell for most of the day.

He made jeans in the workshop in Mountjoy Jail and became a 'trustee', a trusted prisoner. This allowed him more freedom. He was often out of his cell in the evenings working with a trades officer. He also read a lot in prison, often spending two or three days at a time alone in his cell, coming out only for his meals or another book. Felloni was sent to the training unit in Mountjoy in 1978 and as usual he earned full remission by being of good behaviour. He was given temporary release over Christmas in 1979 and returned to prison on St Stephen's Day. He was fully released on 24 September 1980.

Felloni's friend and fellow criminal Tony 'Boss' Duff also protected him in prison. The two met up again in jail in the late 1980s when both had moved away from burglary: Duff into armed bank robbery; Felloni into drugs. The Boss, however, did not survive long enough to look out for his friend in prison in the late 1990s. On Friday, 21 July 1995, Duff and three other men held up the Castletroy branch of Allied Irish Banks in Limerick. They managed to get away with £10,000 but the Gardaí were onto them. They chased Duff for five miles from Limerick city to the river Shannon at Clonlara. He was trapped but wouldn't give up. He jumped into the Shannon and tried to swim across but the current was too strong. The Boss's body was later recovered downriver.

Felloni's move into drugs was marked by what was expected to be a routine robbery in Co. Wicklow. There was no doubt that he took part in it but there was not enough evidence to make a case against him. It was a robbery he got away with; a robbery where there was no malicious intent, other than theft, on the part of any of those involved. But it was a robbery that led to a political storm, a public health crisis and the death of a young Dublin postman.

1. If a dishonest employer bought 500 stolen £8 stamps from Felloni at half price, it would cost him £2,000 (500 x £4). He could then keep his 500 employees' contributions of £3 each a week and steal £1,500. The total cost of the stolen insurance stamps to him was therefore only £500. If he were to buy his stamps legitimately from the post office they would cost him £2,500, along with his employees' £1,500. Buying stolen stamps saved him £2,000 a week, or £104,000 a year.

6 *Poison* *1980*

'I am completely innocent,' Tony Felloni told the judge in the Dublin District Court at 12.30 p.m. on 8 November 1980. He was charged with causing £288 worth of damage and stealing £597 worth of drugs and property from O'Byrne's chemist, in Aughrim in Co. Wicklow. The drugs included Diconal, pethidine, cocaine, Physeptone and strychnine. He was remanded in custody for a week.

Three weeks before, at 1.45 a.m. on Monday, 20 October, the desk sergeant at Clontarf Garda Station in Dublin received an urgent phone call. Five people in the area had been rushed to the Richmond Hospital. Gerard Cronin, Mona Maher, Samuel Kiely, Laurence Goulding and Christopher Herbert were together in a flat on St Laurence's Road when they all fell ill.

Half an hour later another call came in to Store Street Garda Station in the city centre. The inspector on duty was told that three seriously ill men had been brought in to Jervis Street Hospital. Two men in a red Cortina had dropped John Young, John Kelly and Gerard Cowzer at the hospital's casualty department, in strange and suspicious circumstances.

Doctors at the Richmond began examining the five from Clontarf. A powdery substance found in one of the men's pockets was sent for analysis to the twenty-four-hour laboratory at Jervis Street. A medical team over there was carrying out similar tests on the three other men. Doctors at both hospitals quickly came to the same conclusion. All eight patients were suffering from strychnine poisoning.

Emergency procedures were immediately put in place. The victims were transferred to intensive care and put on ventilators.

Their stomachs were pumped and efforts were made to resuscitate the most seriously ill. There was a gradual response in all cases but one. Gerard Cronin, who lived in the flat on St Laurence's Road, initially appeared to be responding to the treatment. However, later that morning his condition deteriorated and in spite of desperate efforts to revive him the 21-year-old postman never recovered. He died at one o'clock that Monday afternoon.

Gerard Cronin had snorted rat poison, thinking it was cocaine. The doctors and the Drug Squad detectives were now extremely worried. They had to find out whether any more of the poison was being sold as cocaine on the streets. They also had to establish how much of it was out there, who was selling it and why. But the first thing they had to do was ensure that no more people died.

'GET TO HOSPITAL QUICKLY!' That was the stark message splashed across the front pages of the newspapers and broadcast on radio and television news bulletins. The Gardaí sent out an urgent appeal to anyone who had bought illegal drugs the week before to see a doctor immediately. The director of the National Drugs Advisory Board issued a frighteningly frank public warning. 'People who take strychnine seldom recover,' Dr Allene Scott said. 'A teaspoon of strychnine would kill a farmyard full of rats.'

The registrar of the Drug Unit in Jervis Street Hospital explained to *The Irish Times* how the poison affects its victims. 'Strychnine is a fast-acting and painful poison,' Dr William Ryan said. 'Victims feel the first problems within minutes of taking it. Their backs become arched—they become almost S-shaped. Their arms and legs are hit by spasms, leaving their limbs stretched straight out.'

Dr Scott also pointed out that the only chance the young people in hospital had was the fact they had sniffed rather than swallowed the strychnine. The post-mortem on Gerard Cronin, however, showed that he could have swallowed some of the poison. The state pathologist, Dr John Harbison, found traces of it in his nose and mouth. People who snort cocaine sometimes put whatever remaining powder they can't sniff into their mouths, usually rubbing it around their teeth.

Cronin's death caused a public outcry over the availability of drugs and the extent of the drug problem in Ireland. He was the fourteenth victim of drug abuse that year. The mortality rate was double that of 1979 and more than three times that of the years before. The head of the Drug Squad, Detective Inspector Denis Mullins, warned that the availability of cocaine in Ireland was rising dramatically. He had no doubt that cocaine and heroin were being smuggled into Ireland in large quantities. 'The drug pusher', he said, 'does not guarantee his wares on the street.'

Doctors advised parents to keep a closer eye on their teenage children to make sure they were not dabbling in drugs. According to Dr William Ryan, there was a new group of young people experimenting with drugs. 'Here you have people who have not had much exposure to drugs and they will take something on somebody's word,' he said. 'This is horrifying and it's on the increase.'

He was also worried because none of the eight people poisoned was known to the staff at the Drug Unit in Jervis Street, the only state-funded treatment centre in the country, which dealt mainly with people in their late teens. This appeared to suggest that they were all comparatively new to the Dublin drugs scene.

The inevitable political uproar followed. 'STOP THIS MURDER FOR MONEY' screamed an *Irish Independent* headline. Fine Gael's spokesman on youth affairs, Enda Kenny, TD, left the country in no doubt as to his views. 'Pushers are hanged in other countries. They are responsible for giving out drugs to young people and eventually driving them crazy,' he was quoted as saying. 'There is no more pathetic sight, no more harrowing scene than that of a useful life ravaged by drug addiction. Pimps, pushers and those responsible must be under no illusion as to the extent of the law of punishment in this regard.'

Kenny wanted the Minister for Education, John Wilson, to launch a comprehensive education series which would fully enlighten parents, teachers and young people on the dangers of drug abuse. He called on Minister for Justice Gerry Collins to expand the Garda Drug Squad and provide the facilities necessary to combat 'this shocking indictment of society in 1980'.

All this bull and bluster died down within a week and as usual, politically, very little of any practical use happened. The remaining seven victims, six men and one woman, gradually recovered and were discharged from the hospitals one by one. The Gardaí had no doubt that both sets of victims got the poison from the same source. The investigation had to establish the connection between the two different groups and piece together the events that led to all eight being poisoned.

Initially there were fears that the rat poison was being deliberately sold to people who would not know the difference between it and cocaine. On Wednesday, 22 October 1980, *The Irish Times* reported a claim on its front page that one dealer was pushing the strychnine to another in revenge for a drug debt, the second dealer having failed to pay for around £2,000 worth of marijuana three months after getting it. But Drug Squad detectives quickly dismissed the story. They already had a firm indication where the poison came from. 'It's likely the strychnine was mistaken for cocaine during a raid on a chemist's shop down the country,' one said. 'It then went on to the market.'

Just after midnight on Sunday, 19 October, a young thief from the north side of Dublin met three men in Pearse Street in the city centre. The four had agreed to 'do a job' together. One of the men was from Tallaght and was out for the weekend on temporary release from the training unit at Mountjoy Jail; he knew he'd be back in prison by the time the robbery was discovered. The other two men were Gerry Cowzer and Tony Felloni.

The four had arranged to carry out the type of robbery which Felloni had plenty of experience of: a break-in at a creamery down the country. The thief had stolen a car earlier in the week and the gang drove down to the Aughrim branch of Premier Dairies. One of them took out a nail-puller and forced one of the office windows. He ripped away the venetian blinds and they all climbed in. They then tried to force open the locked main door inside but a curious passer-by interrupted them. 'Fuck off!' they told him but they knew they'd been rumbled. The job was off and the gang walked away, leaving behind a crowbar, a woollen cap and two full safes.

All was not lost, however. They walked up the main street of the village and when they saw Alice O'Byrne's chemist a new plan was hatched on the spot. One of them clambered up on the roof and pulled the wires out of the alarm box. All four then hopped over a brick wall at the back, smashed a pane of glass, opened the window and climbed into the shop.

They started in the dispensary at the back. There was only one floor to rob. They all wore gloves; there would be no fingerprints.

One of them found a cardboard box and he filled it with bottles of pills and medicines. He loaded up over 200 Diconal, Dalmane and pethidine tablets and phials of morphine injection, Omnopon and cocaine. He also put bottles of paraffin, arsenic, eye drops, Physeptone and two bottles of strychnine into the box and carried the lot back to the car at the creamery.

The other three followed with handfuls of jewellery—watches, lockets, brooches, earrings, charms, straps, pearls and a camera. They also took Mrs O'Byrne's chequebook with at least ten blank cheques still in it.

The gang left Aughrim at around 6.00 a.m. and headed back to Dublin. They stopped off at the Tallaght home of the man on temporary release. His wife knew only one of the other three men, Tony Felloni. The young thief was so tired that he sat down and fell fast asleep. He snored through the division of the spoils.

The others had a cup of tea as they sat in the sitting room 'divvying up' the haul. Ever the ladies' man, Tony picked some of the earrings up off the table and gave them to the woman of the house. She thought they looked cheap but took five pairs anyway and went into the kitchen to make her children their breakfast. The young man was roused with a kick and the three left without saying goodbye. The man on parole went up to bed.

They stopped off at one of the bridges over the Grand Canal on the way back to the city. The young thief got out of the car and threw the box into the water. There were only some bottles, mainly poison, and some powder in a bag left in it. Felloni and Cowzer had held on to the drugs they wanted. They then dropped him off in town and he took a bus home. It was the first time the young man had robbed with Tony Felloni and because the creamery job had failed, he never got a penny for his night's work. He had no interest in the drugs or jewellery. He wasn't offered a cut from them.

It wasn't until 4.15 p.m. that day that Alice O'Byrne discovered her chemist shop had been broken into. She went down in the afternoon to check the premises but as she opened the front door, she knew immediately something was wrong. There was silence, when the alarm should have been ringing. She went in through the shop to the dispensary at the back and found the window open and broken.

The drawers had been pulled out, the contents scattered all over the floor. The jewellery display cabinet had been ransacked. The filing cabinet in which the dangerous drugs were kept had been forced, and the three drugs drawers were all prised open. The alarm bell had been ripped off the wall and around £300 worth of damage had been done to the shop. The value of the stolen drugs and jewellery was more than double that.

At the same time fifty miles away in Dublin Christopher Herbert was thinking of going for a pint. Herbert was a builder's foreman who lived in Clontarf, down the road from Gerry Cronin. He worked on the IDA site in Pearse Street and he also had a part-time job as a barman in the Dockers pub on the quays. It was there that he went that Sunday for a few autumn evening pints. Later on he headed up to the Countess Bar on Townsend Street, where he bumped into his cousin Gerry Cowzer. The two of them had a pint together.

'Have ya any smoke, Christy?' Cowzer asked him; by smoke he meant hash. Herbert told him he had only a little bit for himself, but Cowzer offered to do a deal with him. He said he had a bit of cocaine and he would swap it for some hash. Herbert agreed and they exchanged drugs in the car park. Cowzer had the 'cocaine' in a bottle in his car. Slowly and carefully he poured a small amount of the white powder into some cigarette paper and handed the package to his cousin.

Cowzer raved about his 'cocaine'. 'It's old,' he told Herbert, 'so it's supposed to be good.' He also said he had more drugs, heroin and opium tablets, in the boot of the car. Herbert gave him some of his hash and the two went their separate ways. Christy Herbert went back to the Dockers. Gerry Cowzer walked back into the Countess Bar.

Herbert got the bus home to Clontarf after closing time. He stopped for chips and decided to call in on his friend Gerry Cronin. Cronin lived with his girlfriend, Mona Maher, in the top-storey flat of a house on St Laurence's Road. She worked as a nurses' aid. The couple had been living together for about six months. It was just before midnight when Cronin opened the door to his drunken friend.

Laurence Goulding and Samuel Kiely were also there when Herbert arrived. Kiely had lived abroad for a few years and had only recently arrived back in Ireland from Denmark. He was stuck for a place to stay and Gerry and Mona were putting him up for a while.

He didn't really know Laurence Goulding, but they had made friends earlier that evening and had smoked a bit of hash together.

Christopher Herbert didn't know Goulding either; he met him for the first time that night. But feeling generous, he took out his white powder and told everyone it was cocaine. 'Would you like to try a "snort"?' he asked the people in the flat. They all said they would and the sugary crystal powder was poured out onto a big mirror. It was then divided into ten white lines. A pound note was rolled up into a thin cylinder and the 'cocaine' was snorted and passed from one to the other.

One of the men took the first good snort. When he tried for a second one his nose started to bleed. Another man took at least four snorts but then felt ill and left to go to bed. He had difficulty breathing and didn't make it to the bedroom, collapsing in the hallway. His joints started to lock and he began to take fits.

Two of the others went out to help him. They struggled with him and managed to get him as far as the bedroom. They put him lying on the bed, but then he became violently ill. He started retching and suffering convulsions. Another of the men found that his own legs had started to get heavy. He was having difficulty moving them. Two more people began to get spasms, while the fifth collapsed and began to lapse in and out of consciousness.

All five were feeling the effects, with some clearly worse than others. Christopher Herbert told one of the men who wasn't as badly affected to go to his flat and get some sleeping tablets. 'Get some Mondrex,' he said, 'it'll ease the pain.' But when the man came back twenty minutes later he saw the situation had deteriorated even further. At least two of the other four were seriously ill. One of them complained he wasn't able to move because his joints were locking. Another had crawled down three flights of stairs and out onto the street. It was almost 1.30 a.m. It was time to get help. An ambulance was called.

Three of the victims were out on the street when the ambulance came. They were whining and crying and very distressed. All three complained of collapse in their legs. They were put into the back of the van. One of them told the ambulance men what condition the other two were in and where to find them. The paramedics rushed upstairs, where they found the other victims lying on the floor.

One man's eyes and mouth were open but he was unable to speak. He stared blankly ahead. He suffered spasms continuously. The ambulance men decided to take him first and one of them ran back downstairs to get a stretcher. The other remained in the bedroom with the victims, talking to them, comforting them and encouraging them to try to move their limbs. He radioed in for a second ambulance.

In the meantime the condition of two of the other three victims in the ambulance began to deteriorate even further. The psychological as well as the physical effects of the poison were beginning to take hold. Both became paranoid and frightened. They begged the ambulance man who came down for the stretcher not to go back upstairs.

'Don't leave, don't leave us here,' they pleaded with him. 'We don't want to die.' He looked at them and realised he couldn't go, so he waited with them until the second ambulance arrived. The stretchers were then rushed upstairs and the three most seriously ill were the first to be brought to hospital. Neighbours and tenants woken by the banging and screaming stood around helpless, watching in tears as all five victims were taken away.

At 1.45 a.m., after he had been given the barest details about the incident, the sergeant in Clontarf drove to St Laurence's Road. The house was in darkness. He knocked on the door and woke some of the other tenants. He spoke to them before heading for the Richmond Hospital. One of the victims there told him they all took what they thought was cocaine. He didn't think it was cocaine now!

Meanwhile, Gerry Cowzer had stayed on drinking in the Countess Bar that night. He rolled and smoked a joint from the hash. Two other local men, John Kelly and John Young, joined him later. Young lived in Markievicz House, a block of Corporation flats down the road from the pub. He was twenty-seven years old and out of work. His neighbour John Kelly was thirty-nine. He still lived at home in the nearby Pearse House flats with his mother and two younger brothers. They all made leather goods and sold them at the weekend in Dublin's Dandelion Market.

There was a party in Raheny that night and all three decided to go. Cowzer drove them out there, along with the brother of the woman who was hosting it. When they walked in the door one of the guests said to them, 'You're ahead of the drink, lads.' They had got there early, it was just past closing time. When they were offered a drink, Cowzer whispered he had something better. 'I scored some coke on Stephen's Green earlier today,' he told the others excitedly. The woman's brother exploded: 'None of that in this house', he roared. 'Outside! If you want to do anything go out to the car and do it.'

Thinking that was the end of the matter, he went off to get the three lads a drink. When he came back and found they had actually gone out to the car, he stormed out after them and a row erupted in the front garden. 'Would you do this at your own fucking sister's house?' he shouted. 'Don't worry,' one of the young men replied, 'It's only coke, it will only speed you up.' But he wasn't prepared to listen to any explanations or excuses. 'Fuck off, all three of you, and don't bother coming back in to this party.'

The three shrugged and carried on regardless. Sitting in the car, Cowzer poured some of the white powder onto the top of a cigarette packet and drew three lines in it with his finger. He pulled out a pound note and rolled it up. Each man then put a line of the 'cocaine' on the back of his hand. Each sniffed his in turn. The effects became apparent almost immediately.

The first man began to feel sick after only the second snort. He got out of the car, took three steps, felt his legs getting stiff and fell forward onto the grass. He then began to suffer spasms. The second man also got out of the car. At first he thought his friend was messing, but that was until his own jaw tightened up and his legs became stiff at the knees. He decided to walk around for a bit and then he went back into the house. He had a bottle of stout because he thought it would make him feel better. Instead, he went back outside because he knew he was getting worse.

Word spread through the party that something was seriously wrong. A woman approached the host's brother and told him a man had fallen outside. When he went out he could see one of the three men on his knees. He asked to be put lying down in the back of a van, but as soon as he was touched he began to scream. He kept begging to be taken to hospital. The other two were also suffering. One was sitting on a wall nearby and when the other was lifted up and put sitting beside him he immediately got sick. The other man was lockjawed but kept deluding himself that he'd be all right if he could get into a van, lie down and sleep.

Cowzer, Kelly and Young were seriously ill. Two of them were feeling paranoid and frightened. They screamed if anyone touched them. The third had already passed out. Two men came out from the party, put all three into a car and drove them to hospital. Two of the victims managed to stagger in to Jervis Street. The third had to be carried to a trolley. 'Ah, we just saw them on the road and picked them up,' one of the drivers told a nurse. 'Where exactly did you pick them up?' she asked. 'Ah, somewhere on the road,' he said before the two men disappeared. They didn't leave their names.

Cowzer, Kelly and Young told the medical staff they were at a party in Raheny. They said they'd been drinking and smoking pot, but their stories diverged and became increasingly vague. At first they said their drinks had been spiked. Then Cowzer admitted that all three had sniffed what they thought was cocaine. He said he had also taken some Diconal tablets.[1]

The men kept changing their stories in the hospital. One said the party was somewhere in Coolock, not Raheny, and again another said someone had put something in his drink. He said he had taken some of the 'cocaine' in a drink of orange. He remained relatively calm while the other two were very distressed and frightened. All three were in pain, and exhibited signs of 'Carpopedal Spasm', i.e. they lapsed into spasms when their hands or feet were touched. Cowzer was at this stage beginning to turn blue, a symptom of a condition known as cyanosis.

A team of nurses and doctors began treating all three, taking off some of their clothes, cutting off the others. The men's chances of survival were put at fifty-fifty. The stories of spiked drinks, smoking hash, snorting cocaine and parties on the north side didn't add up; the stories didn't match the symptoms. The medical staff were becoming increasingly worried because the men wouldn't tell them exactly what happened. The breakthrough finally came when one of them could no longer hide his fear.

'What would happen to me if I had taken strychnine?' he asked a student nurse as she was taking his clothes off him. She immediately reported this to the consultant in charge and at last the hospital knew what it was dealing with. The men were transferred to the Intensive

Care Unit, and toxicology reports later confirmed that they had indeed sniffed rat poison. All three were seriously ill when first admitted but they all made a full recovery. Over in the Richmond Gerard Cronin wasn't so lucky.

Two days later Tony Felloni went to see Gerry Cowzer in hospital. Tony was telling everyone he now worked as a salad chef in a restaurant in town. Few if any believed he had moved into legitimate employment. He hadn't. He had, however, split up with Anne again and could be seen around the city with his latest girlfriend, 'a newer, younger model'. Cowzer had met her with him the week before in a city centre bar.

Tony walked into the Intensive Care Unit and sat down beside his friend. Cowzer's condition was gradually improving but he remained seriously ill. He was allowed visitors for only short periods of time. Felloni didn't bring any oranges or Lucozade. 'He came to see me', Cowzer said, 'because he was worried about me.' But Tony was more worried about what Cowzer intended to say to his other prospective visitors, the Gardaí.

Cowzer decided his story would be that he broke into a car parked in a shopping centre and found a number of bottles in the boot. There would be arsenic in a blue bottle, and gear in a bag. The bottles were all the same, all marked poison, but Cowzer would say he tasted powder in one of them and thought it was cocaine. He had, he would admit, tasted 'coke' before.

He remembered he also had to introduce Diconal into the story because on the night he was admitted to hospital he told the medical staff he had taken some Diconal tablets. He would therefore say he kept the Diconal from the car for himself, but gave his cousin Christopher Herbert some of the strychnine, thinking it was coke. He did this, he would say, even though 'poison' was marked on the bottle. The story was agreed and Tony left the hospital satisfied his friend was sick, but not in the head. Tony's name wouldn't even be mentioned.

As he lay there recovering in the hospital bed Gerard Cowzer was truly baffled. He just couldn't figure it out. 'I never made a mistake before, I would know the difference between coke and strychnine,' he mused. 'I would know by the taste. Coke is like sugar, coke is more crystallised.' He remembered swapping the strychnine for hash with his cousin but he genuinely believed he was giving him cocaine. Cowzer had been poisoned once before but he thought that was just because of bad LSD.

It didn't take detectives long to discover that the Aughrim pharmacy was the most likely source of the poison. They settled on it after cross-referencing the strychnine with a list of all chemists recently burgled. Forensic tests and medical reference numbers later confirmed it did actually come from O'Byrne's chemist. They also drew up a list of criminals known for breaking into chemists. Cowzer's name appeared on that list and the suspects were narrowed down to him and his associates. Confidential information, prison records and good police work enabled them to fill in the rest of the picture.

At eight the following morning the Gardaí arrived at the house in Tallaght. The place was searched but only the earrings were recovered. The woman who had got them from Felloni claimed that it had never dawned on her that they were stolen. She insisted her husband was not involved in the robbery. 'Sure he was in bed with me,' she said, 'all Saturday night.' She told the Gardaí he had been with her all weekend while he was out on temporary release. Wife and prison: the perfect alibi.

Detectives went to see her husband in Mountjoy Jail and told him the stolen jewellery was found at his wife's home. He was handed a copy of what his wife said to the Gardaí. The man, however, was a seasoned criminal. He had robbed with Tony Felloni throughout the 1970s and had been through interrogations like this before. He remained unmoved; he had nothing to lose. He was back in prison when the others were sniffing the 'cocaine'. He confirmed he was out on parole that weekend but refused to say anything else until he had spoken to his wife and solicitor.

The young thief was arrested and he was scared. He'd read in the papers that eight people had been poisoned and one of them had died. It dawned on him now where the drugs they had stolen had ended up. Even though he had taken none of the drugs or jewellery, he knew he was an accessory because he was on the job. He claimed that on the night of the robbery he was out cider-drinking with his friends. No, he couldn't name any of the friends he was with. He said he went home afterwards and went to bed, but he was unsure of the places, dates and times.

The young thief's father arrived at the Garda station where his son was being held. He too knew that one person was already dead and he was afraid others could die. He pleaded with his son to tell the Gardaí what happened to the drugs. The young man finally relented. He admitted his part in the robbery and he also admitted dumping some of the stolen poisons in the Grand Canal. The Garda Sub-Aqua Unit later recovered bottles labelled 'Aughrim Pharmacy'. They found Dalmane, arsenic, strychnine and a white powder in a plastic bag submerged among the weeds.

The young thief was charged with trespass, stealing and malicious damage to the pharmacy. He admitted his own involvement but that was as far as he would go. At seventeen years of age he was not as brazen or as hardened as the others were, but he still refused to name them as accomplices. The man in prison didn't talk either and when Cowzer and Felloni were arrested neither did they.

Cowzer was first pulled in four days after the poisoning. He was arrested on the steps of the hospital as soon as he was discharged. His story now was that he had paid £120 for cocaine to a man he didn't know. He said he'd bought it in Nassau Street with money he got from a friend the previous Friday. He remembered, he told the guards, because after he made the deal he walked his mother down to Bingo.

The story, however, contradicted one he told in the hospital a few days before, when he said he had traded some 'dike' tablets for cocaine with a man he met near the Shelbourne Hotel. He had, he said, been out looking for hash. It also contradicted the story he had arranged with Felloni in the hospital. Cowzer had in fact told six different Gardaí three different stories about where he got the drug. But Gerard Cowzer was of course a very sick man then; he may not have known exactly what he was saying.

'I don't know anything about it, I was not there,' he said when he was asked about the Aughrim break-in. 'I done loads of chemists' down the country, I was peddling drugs but I gave it up.' He told detectives anxious to account for all the strychnine that he had got rid of all the bottles of poison, including the one they had all snorted from. The Gardaí found this difficult to believe because Cowzer had spent the entire time since he poisoned himself either in hospital or in custody. But Cowzer was adamant. 'You can take it', he insisted, 'that all that gear is now in the river.'

Tony Felloni was picked up two weeks later as he was walking down Talbot Street at ten past midnight. He admitted nothing in custody, and along with Cowzer he was charged with theft and causing damage at the Wicklow chemist's. Tony declared his innocence. Cowzer replied, 'Nothing to say.' After his court appearance Cowzer had to be taken from the Garda station back into hospital. He still hadn't fully recovered from the effects of the strychnine.

Forty detectives interviewed almost 100 people in the investigation into the break-in which indirectly led to the poisoning of eight people and the subsequent death of Gerry Cronin. There was, however, no evidence of malicious intent on anybody's part. Tony Felloni and Gerry Cowzer, along with the young thief and the Tallaght prisoner, set out that night to rob the creamery in Aughrim. They broke into the chemist only when forced to abort that job.

No one set out to kill Gerry Cronin either. It was never intended that anyone should die, and all those poisoned really believed they were snorting cocaine. The source of the poison, Gerry Cowzer, was common to all eight victims, but Cowzer himself also believed the strychnine was cocaine. Even though the bottle was clearly marked poison, he snorted it himself and gave some of it to his cousin and friends.

The charges against the three men did not stand up and the case never went to trial. The Garda file was sent to the Director of Public Prosecutions, who directed that no prosecution should take place. There wasn't enough evidence to proceed against the men. Tony Felloni had got away again. The case, however, marked the beginning of a determined effort by the detective sergeant who arrested Felloni to put him behind bars. It was an ambition that took him another sixteen years and John Long was a detective superintendent before he achieved it.

The case was also significant because it marked a turning point in Tony Felloni's career. He graduated from crime ordinary, robberies and tie-ups, to the developing and ultimately more lucrative world of drugs. By 1980 'King Scum' had thirty convictions for offences ranging from burglary to assault, larceny to blackmail. But up to that time he never had a conviction for drugs. After 1980, however, he never had a conviction for anything else.

1. Diconal is a tablet, a strong painkiller sometimes used in the treatment of cancer, but because it is an opiate it was particularly popular with drug users in the late 1970s and early 1980s. It was crushed into a powder and injected in solution form when heroin wasn't available. Doctors today can still recognise the signs of Diconal abuse among the city's older drug addicts. They tend to have enlarged 'Diconal' hands from injecting the crushed tablets into their veins. Drug addicts today tend to use the sleeping tablet Rohypnol instead. It has not been detected in urine samples so addicts can abuse it and continue on treatment programmes. It is also better known as the 'date rape' drug. A number of people have had their drinks spiked, fallen asleep drugged, and woken up later to find they have been robbed and/or raped. The company which manufactures it has, however, changed the constituents so that it now turns blue in drinks. Both Diconal and Rohypnol are controlled drugs and it is a criminal offence to possess or supply them.

7 'King Scum' 1980–85

'If you think we're bad, wait till you see what's coming after us.' That was the prophetic statement made by Larry Dunne, Dublin's biggest heroin dealer in the early 1980s, as he was being taken away to begin a ten-year jail sentence. The Dunnes effectively introduced heroin to Dublin and controlled its supply throughout the city for a number of years.

Many politicians and senior Gardaí naively believed that the imprisonment of Larry and the rest of the Dunnes, and the smashing of their drugs operation, marked the beginning of the end of the heroin epidemic in Dublin. But Larry knew better and he was proved right. When he went to jail the market he had established still needed to be supplied. The thousands of hooked and desperate junkies still had to have their heroin daily and they didn't care who supplied it.

Organised criminals had begun pushing heroin in the capital in the late seventies and their success was reflected in the corresponding misery on the streets. There was a dramatic increase in the number of addicts seeking treatment in Dublin. The country's main treatment centre at Jervis Street Hospital dealt with just over 550 patients in 1980. Within three years that figure had trebled.

An American priest, Monsignor William O'Brien, who ran one of the world's biggest rehabilitation centres for addicts in New York, visited Dublin in April 1982. He was shocked by what he saw. Dublin, he said, had the worst pre-adolescent heroin problem he had ever seen. The devastation the Dunnes had caused was clearly illustrated in a report the following year prepared by the Medico-Social Research Board. It showed that 10 per cent of the people in

Dublin's north inner city between the ages of fifteen and twenty-four were heroin addicts. Drug addiction was worse here than it was in the black ghettos of New York in 1970 during the Vietnam War, when the epidemic there was at its height.

But all this became public knowledge only when the report was leaked to *The Irish Times*. The vast majority of the country's politicians didn't know, didn't care or didn't accept that there was a serious heroin problem in Dublin. In 1982 the government transferred 20 per cent of the Drug Squad officers to the Serious Crime Squad, showing just how far out of touch it was. The Minister for Justice, Seán Doherty, responded to criticism of the decision in the Dáil by saying that the expertise of individual Drug Squad officers would be a useful addition to the Serious Crime Squad.

Two years later, when the extent of the epidemic was clear and unavoidable, the government launched a well-publicised attack on crime. The strength of the Drug Squad, however, was increased to just thirty-five and only thirteen of those officers were on duty at any one time. In the Dáil, the Independent TD for Dublin Central, Tony Gregory, slated the policy: 'The government', he said, 'is clearly not serious about tackling the drugs problem.'

Larry Dunne abandoned his heroin business and went on the run in June of 1983. It was the last day of his second drugs trial and he knew he was about to go to jail. Gardaí had found seventy grams of heroin—enough to make over 5,000 street deals—hidden in a pillowcase at his Corporation house in Carrickmount Drive in Rathfarnham in Dublin. With Larry out of the way, there was nothing to stop Tony Felloni moving in on his business. By the time Larry was recaptured and sent to jail two years later, Felloni was the biggest heroin supplier in the north inner city, the biggest market in Dublin.

Tony first became interested in drugs after his release from Mountjoy Jail in September 1980. One of the men who robbed with him in the 1970s, a criminal from Kilbarrack in Dublin, had started selling heroin and advised Tony to do the same. Tony could see it was a lucrative business. He knew the Dunnes and envied them for the money they were making. At first he tried to buy heroin from them at wholesale rates but he refused to pay the price they were asking. He decided to look elsewhere and went to England.

Felloni got a new look and a new friend. He had his hair permed and teamed up with 29-year-old Paul Kirwin from Rathfarnham in Dublin. Neither of them knew it but they were under Garda surveillance when they flew to London to buy heroin in the summer of 1981. Felloni had over £2,000 in cash on him. They never made it past the airport. The Gardaí alerted the police in Britain and Felloni and Kirwin were arrested as they tried to cut a deal with a group of Greeks.

Felloni apparently admitted that he was there to buy heroin. Conspiracy is not an offence in Ireland and he didn't think he could be convicted for it. He soon realised, however, that it is an offence in Britain because he was charged and on 8 July was remanded in custody. Four months later he was convicted at Kingston Crown Court in Surrey of conspiracy to supply drugs. On 30 November 1981 Felloni was sentenced to four years in prison, Kirwin to three.

Two weeks later his wife and children moved out of Bridgefoot Street flats and into their first house at Palmerston Place, a quiet little street just off Dorset Street in the north inner city. Anne says she paid over £30,000 cash for the house. She also redecorated it and put in new furniture from Lanigan's in Capel Street and new carpets from Navan. Wherever she got the money, she didn't get it selling drugs. Anne Felloni has no drugs convictions at all. Two months later the house was raided and a furious Anne attacked the Gardaí. On 11 March 1982 she was given six months in the District Court for obstructing and assaulting a Garda. It was the second time in five weeks she was convicted of the offence.

During the two years and eight months Tony Felloni spent in jail he made a number of contacts in the British drug trade. On 5 March 1984 he was released and he was deported from England at noon the same day. His arrival back in Dublin coincided with an unprecedented demand for heroin among the city's underprivileged, unemployed and poorly educated addicts. Felloni quickly realised that in the aftermath of the collapse of the Dunnes' operation, not only was there a ready market for the drug, but there were few other criminals prepared to supply it. Most who were, were already in jail.

In the late 1970s and early 1980s, heroin was sold in £10 packs, rising to £20 over the years. Felloni changed that in 1984/5. He took over the market in the north inner city, the biggest in Dublin, controlled it and put up the price to £40. One of his legacies to the city's addicts is the £40 deal.

Heroin in Dublin today is half the price it was in the mid-1980s, and the market now is far more diverse. Hundreds of addicts, couriers and mules smuggle heroin and other drugs into Ireland every day from London, Liverpool and Amsterdam. But fourteen years ago the situation was very different. Tony Felloni was one of a handful of criminals who controlled the sale and supply of heroin in Dublin by arranging the importation and organising the distribution.

He brought heroin in from England, buying both from his English contacts and from a Dublin dealer who was living in London. Tony had known this man for years. He was from the north inner city and had previous drug convictions. Not one for trusting others, Felloni personally cut and packaged his own deals. He cut the heroin with glucose, citric acid or milk powder, diluting only as much as he needed for two or three days. He brought it out in small quantities for sale on the streets. Felloni was paying between £1,500 and £2,000 for an ounce of heroin. When diluted, distributed and sold as street deals it could make him around £25,000.[1]

At the height of his operation, Tony's mules and couriers were bringing in as much as nine ounces some weeks, with a street value of around £250,000. However, he never made that much. After selling some wholesale, some himself and the rest through pushers, he made around £115,000 profit.[2] His couriers carried the drugs externally, hiding them in clothes or on their bodies as they went through the airports and ports. The mules were more desperate and took a far greater risk. They concealed the heroin internally in what customs officers call 'swallowing or stuffing'.

Unlike his predecessor, Larry 'Doesn't Carry' Dunne, Tony moved some of his own heroin around the city. He also sold to addicts at street level. He carried deals around either in his hand or in his mouth so he could conceal them and dispose of them quickly if necessary. He took out his false teeth and put them in his pocket before he popped the heroin in his mouth. If Tony's false teeth were out he was probably carrying. If his teeth were in he was probably supervising.

Tony Felloni quickly became the main operator in the north inner city. In late 1984 he operated a schedule selling from selected pubs throughout the day. As well as heroin, his pushers sold small amounts of marijuana and cannabis resin to the more affluent middle-class teenagers and university students. They bought it in O'Connell Street or upstairs at a nearby pub in Dorset Street.

Tony's pushers sold along a patch of O'Connell Street that ran from Abbey Street to Bachelor's Walk on the quays. They also operated out of a snooker hall located in a long dark basement in the city centre. The addicts had to go downstairs into the crowded smoky snooker room. There was an exit door leading to a lane at the back. It was very difficult for the Gardaí to get in without first being spotted, and there was plenty of time to get rid of the drugs or to get out fast in the event of a raid. It was an ideal trading post for Felloni's pushers and customers. The addicts who didn't go down to the snooker hall hung around on the street outside. They could be seen lining up for heroin amid the unsuspecting shoppers.

Tony started off selling to the inner-city addicts. His business took off, however, and more junkies came in from the suburbs to buy from him, from Ballyfermot and Finglas, from Tallaght and Ballymun. 'Felloni', one said, 'had a reputation for supplying the best "gear" and unlike other dealers he rarely ran out.'[3] When Gardaí stopped and searched drug addicts they found Tony Felloni's telephone number over and over again.

He recruited an army of young addicts to sell on the streets for him. Dependent and dispensable, they were easily replaced if they were arrested. He would meet his pushers, one at a time, in the side streets and lanes beside his home in Palmerston Place, or on the Western Way, the road at the back, but he was cautious and constantly changed his routine.

He collected the money from his dealer addicts before he handed over a batch of heroin, twelve to fifteen street deals, or 'Q's. A Q is supposed to be enough for one fix, although chronic addicts will often inject or 'bang up' two or three at one time. The severity of the addiction determines how many Qs a junkie will need for a hit or a 'turn-on', and how many turn-ons he or she will need in a day.

Each individual Q is about a tenth of a gram. Half the size of a thumbnail, it comes wrapped in plastic. All the Qs to make up a batch are held together in the corner of a small plastic bag. Tony dealt in hundreds of thousands of pounds worth of heroin but he only ever carried fifties or hundreds at a time. This reduced the risk of him being robbed of or arrested with a substantial quantity. He wouldn't lose much in the case of the former; he would face a less serious sentence in the event of the latter.

Pushers buy heroin in batches from suppliers and sell it on in Qs. Tony usually allowed each of his pushers a cut of three Qs from every batch; that was how he paid them. But since most were addicts themselves they just shot their three Qs into their own veins. Tony often reduced their cuts if he felt they were becoming careless or more heavily addicted. The reasons why were not always clear but there was nothing they could do about it.

Tony Felloni gained a reputation among drug addicts for cruelty and meanness. 'You could be dealing with him for a year,' one said, 'come up to him dying sick and he'd give you nothing.' Anne remembered Tony throwing one junkie's money out on the road because he was short £2. 'He said, "No! If you went into a shop to buy something and you were £2 short you wouldn't get it." Any time I ever asked him for money he would tell me to "Go and fuck off! You're getting nothing, you can go out and earn it yourself."'

Tony sold much of his heroin from home but he also sold from his parents' flat in Dominick Street and along the balconies of the nearby flat complexes. Neighbours met a steady stream of sick young junkies on their way in there. The elderly residents, three times as old but twice as healthy, found themselves being 'hit on'. The junkies threatened, cajoled and begged for everything, from cigarettes to money for their heroin. 'I'll pray for you, son,' was the most they got from the poor pensioners.

Felloni did not care who he sold to. Friends, family or neighbours—all were given heroin as long as they had money. If he decided to sell to someone who was short he would reduce the cut, no matter how desperate the addict was. Tony sold drugs purely for money. He didn't touch the stuff himself.

His ability to identify susceptible young women led him to recruit teenage girls to sell for him. Much as he had done with the country girls over twenty years before, he chatted up and charmed disadvantaged Dublin girls. He slept with many and coerced some into selling heroin in the flats and on the streets. At forty-one years of age he was as vain and as fashion-conscious as ever. He dyed his hair auburn and got himself a girlfriend twenty years younger. She too sold heroin for him.

In one well-known incident Felloni set three young girls up in an abandoned Corporation flat in Mountain View Court in Summerhill. The heroin was delivered to and sold from there throughout the afternoon. Every time there was a knock at the door, one of the girls would take the heroin into the bathroom, hold it over the toilet and prepare to flush. If the caller was an addict, he or she was sold a fix. If the knock signalled a raid, the heroin was gone.

Business was interrupted for a time by a group of residents, an ad hoc anti-drugs group, who got together and threw the three out of the flat. But Tony was not prepared to give up that easily and he ordered the girls to go back in. The residents threw them out again, and Tony put them back. The game of tit-for-tat ended when the residents took the front door off the flat. Tony didn't come to put it back on and the flat was abandoned; it was too open for heroin dealing. A week later Dublin Corporation boarded it up.

One of Tony's most addicted customers was his own brother-in-law, Patrick Flynn. 'Padser' was Anne's younger brother, twenty-two years of age. He also sold for Felloni but when it came to buying heroin he didn't receive any favours from his relation. Padser bought his heroin like everyone else, sometimes in the nearby flats, sometimes at his sister's house; there was no discount and no special treatment. Tony Felloni could never be accused of nepotism. Neighbours would hear him knocking frantically at the front, calling at the back or shouting through the letter box of 11 Palmerston Place, 'It's Padser, it's Padser, for fuck's sake lemme in!'

Padser could arrive at any time of the day or night. A serious drug addict, he needed at least five fixes a day. His habit was costing him over £700 a week. In desperation one day he came and went from the house five times in the space of half an hour right in the middle of Tony's lunch. When he finally did get to buy his Q, he popped it in his mouth, and meandered off, checking he was not being followed. He walked in the middle of the road, looking back over both his shoulders, and moved onto the footpath only to let cars pass.

There were a number of factors during 1984 and 1985 that made it relatively easy for Felloni to run his heroin business with impunity. The demise of the Dunnes, the jailing of other major dealers, the increasing number of chronic addicts and the lack of treatment places all helped to make him one of the biggest suppliers in Dublin. But Tony had the added advantage of having spent the previous three years in prison in Britain. He was not known as a heroin dealer in Dublin. He still had no convictions for drugs here, in spite of having served time in England for conspiracy to supply. He had been out of the country during the previous clampdown on heroin dealers and was therefore not well known to the majority of the Gardaí stationed in the north city. Most of them didn't find out about his British conviction until 1986.

Felloni was also a beneficiary of official complacency as regards the heroin problem in the area. After the recent successes of the Garda undercover squad, the 'Mockeys', and the Concerned Parents movement, there was a tendency for both sides to rest on their laurels. But the problem hadn't gone away, and it was in this climate that Felloni's operation grew and prospered.

The Concerned Parents movement began in early 1983 in Hardwicke Street flats in the north inner city, when a Catholic priest called a meeting of the residents and set up a local committee to tackle the drugs problem in the area. They held mass meetings which often became heated as angry residents vented their fears for their children and their frustration at watching heroin dealers operate openly in the flats. They organised patrols, approached drug dealers and asked them to stop dealing or get out. They moved in and cleaned up the flats when the dealers left. This idea of people power spread to the other flat complexes on both sides of the city, and similar committees were set up in Dolphin House, St Teresa's Gardens, Seán MacDermott Street, Ballybough and Dún Laoghaire. By September, the individual committees had started liaising with each other and calling themselves the Concerned Parents against Drugs.

For a year and a half they took direct action against people they believed were dealing drugs in the communities, without either the support or approval of the statutory authorities. Throughout 1983 and into the middle of 1984, mass meetings were held, suspected dealers' homes were marched on and many either left voluntarily or were forcibly evicted. In Crumlin, roadblocks were set up and some people were searched. Allegations of intimidation, violence and IRA infiltration followed and the Concerned Parents found themselves at loggerheads not only with the Gardaí but with the criminal fraternity.

The activities of the Concerned Parents peaked with the O'Connell Street march on Wednesday, 29 February 1984, when 2,000 residents, community leaders and inner-city children marched to the Taoiseach's office. They carried banners, placards and a coffin, and handed in letters condemning Garret FitzGerald and the Minister for Justice, Michael Noonan, for their failure to tackle the worsening drug problem. There was a lull in the movement's activities in the north inner city in the late summer of that year, and that vacuum allowed Felloni to set up and run his heroin business.

Business was booming in and around Palmerston Place. From 8.00 a.m. to 2.00 a.m. the following morning there was a steady stream of addicts coming to buy heroin. They arrived in taxis and cars, on bikes and on foot. 'You could score at Felloni's day and night,' they said.

Tony operated a system with them to make sure he wasn't being set up. The addict phoned first, let the number ring three times and then hung up. He phoned back immediately and Tony picked up the phone and told him where to go. 'You made no mention of the gear, he'd just say to you to meet him at a spot near the house or the flats and you'd wait there for a few minutes.'

The financial rewards from selling heroin are obvious if one is prepared to ignore the consequences. Tony Felloni was. His attitude was in marked contrast to many of his fellow criminals and former associates who would have nothing to do with drug dealing. They realised that most dealers don't last long in the business—they either get caught by the authorities or get killed by their adversaries.

They also realised that there were serious social as well as occupational implications for a burglar or thief who set himself up as a drug dealer. Communities once tolerant, even supportive of the so-called ordinary decent criminal turned against the man who they felt had turned against them by selling heroin in their area. In many cases they co-operated with the Gardaí to put such dealers out of business. Co-operation on the drug issue was not perceived as betrayal.

Professional criminals such as the Monk and the General resolutely refused to get involved in drug dealing. They not only recognised the inherent dangers but witnessed at first hand the devastation heroin caused within their own communities and realised that dealing could lose them the tacit support of friends and neighbours. The Monk made headlines in 1996 when he attended an anti-drugs rally in the north city. Four years after his death the General is still respected, in a warped kind of way, for his anti-drugs stance.

Tony Felloni was a hardened, experienced and popular criminal, but he lost the respect of much of the criminal fraternity when he moved into heroin. But Tony didn't care about the other criminals or the community. They in turn could not understand his callousness. Here was a man who had grown up in north Dublin. Now he was prepared to destroy it. He showed no regard for the lives, health and welfare of his neighbours and their children. He was more than happy to ply them with heroin and profit from their pathetic addictions. Many in the area cannot forgive him even today for destroying the lives of people he knew and grew up with and devastating the community from which he himself came.

Local residents could not understand how Felloni could get away with dealing so openly. One man whose mother ran a business near the house in Palmerston Place came home on holidays and couldn't believe his eyes. He himself had grown up in the neighbourhood before he emigrated but he was stunned at the complete transformation that drugs and drug dealing had brought. Working as an engineer in South Africa, he had never seen anything like this before.

His mother's house provided a front row seat for the drug dealing spectacle. The engineer wanted others to realise what was going on so he videoed the addicts coming and going from in and around Tony's house. He gave it to the residents' group, and it was handed in to the Gardaí as proof of the extent of the problem. By this time the anger of the local community had turned to outright hostility, which was played out in a very public and tragicomic fashion.

A group of anti-drug activists from the north inner city, led by Paddy Malone and Mick Rafferty, began following Tony Felloni around. They harassed, ridiculed and abused him in public in an attempt to upset him and destabilise his business. 'You're now in the presence of a scumbag,' they bellowed through a megaphone. They chased him off his O'Connell Street patch, down Henry Street, through shops and out of the city centre. When Tony ran, they ran after him through the crowds of bemused and bewildered Dublin shoppers. 'That's the drug dealer Tony Felloni,' they announced, 'he's selling heroin to our children.'

On one such occasion a small group including Malone, local TD Tony Gregory and an elderly local woman known as Sister Corbally waited for Felloni outside the GPO. They watched as he walked down O'Connell Street, flanked by two young women who carried the heroin in case he was stopped. Tony never spotted the group waiting for him. As he came closer, this small, frail but furious sixty-year-old woman made her way through the passing shoppers and stopped directly in front of him. Sister Corbally was about three feet shorter than Felloni was but she was not afraid of him. She drew back her hand and slapped him right across the face. 'Murderer!' she screamed. 'Murdering drug dealer!' Her son was a heroin addict who bought from Felloni.

Community anger spilled out into protests and vigils as thousands of people marched on the house in Palmerston Place. The Gardaí feared trouble and the marches were heavily policed. One night it looked as if the Riot Squad and the Dog Unit had been brought in because men with dogs, batons and helmets eyed the marchers suspiciously.

The show of force served only to increase mistrust and resentment of Garda motives and priorities. The local community saw the machinery of the state being mobilised to guard a drug dealer. The people were made to feel they were the criminals, harassing a man and his young family in his own home. The irony of the situation as far as the community was concerned was that a man who consistently flouted the law was being fully and unjustly protected by it. The community was being alienated, the wrong message was being sent out.

Tony didn't care about the residents or their protests. He laughed when the Concerned Parents hung a wreath on his door, a symbol of the number of local people who had died from heroin. He certainly wasn't worried they might pose a threat. Felloni may not have had a reputation for violence, but he was prepared to fight if he had to. He had worked with serious, violent criminals in the past and he had the money to pay for the muscle he needed. Many local people were too scared to take him on.

Tony Gregory put down a number of questions in the Dáil asking what the government and the Gardaí were doing about Tony Felloni, though he could not actually name him. He outlined the damage Felloni was causing in the north inner city and called for the re-establishment of the Mockeys. As early as November 1984 he tried to identify Felloni publicly as one of the biggest heroin dealers in the city by naming him in a Dáil question to the Minister for Justice.

TDs have the right of absolute privilege in the Dáil. They cannot be sued for anything they say in the House, no matter how scandalous, libellous or inaccurate it turns out to be. Gregory was extremely frustrated by the apparent indifference of the government to Felloni's operation. He pointed out that even though the Garda Drug Squad knew all about his activities, they had neither the manpower nor the resources to put him out of business. He asked Michael Noonan whether or not he was aware of Tony Felloni's activities and if he was confident that he would be apprehended 'before there are [any] further deaths'. The question never got a public airing. The Ceann Comhairle ruled it out of order and Tony Felloni's identity as a drug trafficker was protected.

It was some consolation to Gregory that twelve years later when he tried the same tactic in a Dáil committee, it worked. He succeeded in naming for the first time in public another north city heroin dealer, Tommy Mullen. In January 1998 Mullen was convicted in England of conspiracy to supply heroin and sent to prison for eighteen years. The fact that two years earlier Gregory identified in the Dáil the man who until then had been known only as 'The Boxer' enabled the media to follow suit.

The public at large really became aware of the extent of Tony Felloni's drug dealing activities only in December of 1984, when the *Sunday World* published a series of articles about 'the vile and kinky lifestyle of Dublin's top death dealer King Scum'. 'He's nasty, he has unpleasant habits, he likes kinky sex,' the newspaper claimed. It estimated his fortune at the time at 'anywhere between £100,000 and a quarter of a million pounds'. The *Sunday Tribune* also photographed Tony standing on O'Connell Street talking to two of his pushers.

Public and political criticism of the Gardaí began to mount. There was a growing perception, particularly among north city community activists, that the force was either unable or unwilling to tackle the worsening drugs crisis. A man known only to the general public as 'King Scum' personified the problem. Everybody in the area knew who he was.

The time had come for the Gardaí to act. It wasn't enough that they had already begun a number of covert surveillance operations in and around the capital's main street. They had succeeded only in arresting and charging a few of the city's addicts and small-time pushers. Felloni was still able to operate at will. The Drug Squad knew all about his heroin network in late 1984, but it was to be another year before a concerted and determined Garda operation was set up to close him down.

General Note

The examples at the end of this and other chapters are calculated to give the reader an idea of how heroin is valued. However, they should not be seen as a definitive guide—because there is no definitive guide. Drug prices are influenced by many factors, such as

—the purity of the drug, in this case heroin
—the amount bought
—the price negotiated
—who Felloni was buying from
—his relationship with his supplier
—the availability of the drug on the market
—whether Tony was selling alone or with others
—whether he was selling wholesale to other dealers (as was the case when he brought in large quantities) or retail to pushers and pusher addicts
—whether it was a combination of both
—his expenses, such as travel, accommodation, partners, criminal payments and expenses for himself to arrange the deal or for his couriers and mules to travel out and bring the drugs back
—costs incurred when one of his shipments or couriers/mules was intercepted by Gardaí, customs or foreign police

1. Tony was paying between £1,500 and £2,000 for an ounce of heroin. Most weeks he brought in two or three ounces, but some weeks, perhaps on average once every six weeks, he brought in as much as nine ounces in one week.

1 ounce = 28 grams
1 gram = 10 fixes
28 grams = 280 fixes
280 fixes = 1 ounce

But Felloni would cut 50–60 per cent pure heroin twice or even three times, so one ounce cut say the average figure of two and a half times would give him 700 fixes.

Seven hundred fixes at £40 each would make £28,000 on the street. Subtract say £2,000 cost and another £1,000 expenses per ounce, and Felloni made £25,000 on the individual ounce when he sold it himself. If he sold an ounce through his pushers, he would have to give them around three fixes in every ten, so he would lose between £7,500 and £8,000, thereby making around £17,000 on that ounce, give or take a few hundred pounds.

2. In the week he brought in nine ounces he would not, however, make nine times that figure, because at least half of that would be sold on the wholesale market to other dealers who were cutting up and selling on to pushers. Say five of the nine ounces were sold wholesale for around three times the cost. Five ounces sold at £6,000 (three times £2,000 cost per ounce) each made £30,000. The other four were diluted as above to make £112,000 worth (4 x £28,000). Total on nine ounces is £112,000 + £30,000 = £142,000. Subtract £18,000 cost (nine £2,000 ounces) plus another £9,000 expenses etc. (£1,000 per ounce average) and this leaves Felloni with £115,000 profit.

3. Tony's reputation for selling 'good gear' came from the junkies who bought from him. Drug dealers do not have access to forensic laboratories to determine the purity of the heroin they are buying. The way they ensure it is good is to test it on a junkie first of all. The junkie will be given a free fix and he will tell the buyer whether it is good or bad gear, i.e. if the purity level is high or low.

Gardaí often watched known drug dealers head to England and bring with them a known drug addict to test the heroin and then courier it back in to Ireland. In later years, Tony was able to use his drug-addicted son Luigi to test the quality of his heroin for him. Luigi would travel to London and test the quality of the heroin personally before buying it, then give it to a 'mule' to bring back.

8 George
1985–86

'Tony Felloni was a difficult man to keep an eye on. It was a difficult job to keep him under surveillance.' A young Garda who spent a lot of time hiding around corners and standing in shadows, doorways and sheds remembers the Christmas and New Year period of 1985–6. 'He walked quickly in short rapid steps. He didn't say much and he didn't hang around for long in any one spot. He dressed well, but didn't drink much. He didn't seem to spend much of his money and I never knew him to take a foreign holiday. He never told anyone where he was going and he never kept to the same routine.'

By the end of 1985 the new Store Street Drug Unit, successors to the 'Mockeys', had Tony Felloni under surveillance. Their predecessors had put his predecessors, the Dunnes, out of business, and they intended that history should repeat itself. The Mockeys were a group of unknown, undercover Gardaí who adopted the antics, the demeanour and the hours of the drug addicts. In the two years they operated, 1982 and 1983, they were responsible for over half of the drug busts in the north inner city. They didn't look, talk or dress like Gardaí. They operated as mock addicts, hence the name.

The tactics of the Mockeys were once again adopted when it came to targeting Tony Felloni. There was, however, one notable difference the second time round: the approach was approved, formalised and supervised. The new Drug Unit was set up in Store Street under Detective Sergeant John Long. He picked a team of eight Gardaí, six from Store Street, the remaining two from Crumlin and the city centre.

The unit was set up with one primary objective—to smash Tony Felloni's heroin business. But before the team even began to target him, John Long was promoted to detective inspector and transferred to Tallaght. The timing was unfortunate for the man who remembered Felloni from the poisoning episode five years earlier. He played no further part in the move to convict him. From then on an experienced detective Garda, Mickey Finn, led the operation on the ground. He knew Felloni and Felloni knew him; but Felloni didn't know any of the other members of the squad.

In December of 1985 the Drug Unit set up Operation George. George was the code name given to Felloni when the team members were in radio contact with one another. '11.43 a.m. George has just come out of the house.' 'Female walking with George towards Mountjoy Square.' Everybody knew that 'George' was the main supplier of heroin in the area; the aim was to get enough evidence to prove that in court.

The team had to identify exactly how he sold his heroin and then catch him in the act to secure a conviction. Finn set up a surveillance operation to identify Felloni's contacts, habits and modus operandi. A number of houses and flats were borrowed or rented in and around his home at 11 Palmerston Place. The surveillance team had sight of both the front and the back doors at all times.

They also had to follow Tony around. They did so in a variety of disguises on foot, on bikes, on buses and in cars. They dressed as busmen, binmen, office workers and nuns. They posed as mechanics and maintenance men, pretended they worked for the post office and the ESB. Ironically one of the most effective surveillance uniforms was often that of a Garda. Tony knew he was being watched and he expected to see a policeman around. He became suspicious if there was none to be seen. A uniformed Garda not only reassured him, but distracted him from the actual surveillance operation in progress.

Thirteen years later, the same tactic worked perfectly for the north-central Drug Unit, when as plain-clothes officers they went back into uniform to catch the notorious heroin supplier 'Country Mick'. The unsuspecting Michael Heeney was driving in from his home in Duleek, Co. Meath to deliver heroin to his pushers in Dublin city. He stopped his car at a checkpoint manned by members of the Drug Unit in uniform and he was caught with heroin hidden in his sock and in the boot of the car. On 20 July 1998 he was jailed for twelve years.

But Tony Felloni took precautions. He had his own counter-surveillance measures. He could leave his house on foot, but catch a bus further down the road. He would then get off the bus before his intended destination and walk or take a taxi the rest of the way. He would often go in to a shop and browse for a while. He might walk in one door of a pub and walk out the other; or he might sit down inside and have an orange juice just to check if anyone was following him. He was extremely careful and he kept changing his movements. He was therefore exceedingly difficult to stay with and the manpower needed was often unavailable. The logistics of hiding, moving around and changing personnel along the route meant Felloni regularly gave the Gardaí the slip.

Ever vigilant and always prepared for the inevitable raid, Tony stored his heroin outside the house. He brought it in, in small amounts, only when he needed to dilute, sell or package it. He kept a fire blazing in the house day and night, even in summer, and sat beside it when he handled his heroin, so that if the Gardaí burst in he could throw the drugs on it. He was becoming so confident that on one occasion he left the window open in advance of a raid so that the Drug Squad wouldn't have to smash their way in. The raid was abandoned as pointless. The element of surprise was gone and nothing would be found.

Surveillance on Tony Felloni's home in the middle of the winter was not a pleasant way to spend Christmas and the New Year. The Gardaí stood and stared at the house all day. They blew on their hands and stamped their feet in an attempt to stay warm. They worked in twos and threes in six- or eight-hour shifts at different vantage points around number 11. They also watched his parents' flat in nearby Dominick Street and a flat in Ballymun that he had recently started to visit, sometimes staying for five or six hours until 1.00 a.m. Every incident was noted, no matter how trivial or insignificant.

Drug addicts are unpredictable and drug dealers paranoid about maintaining the same routine. Yet a pattern developed around Tony's home because certain things happened every day, even if they happened at different times. The same faces began to appear. Known heroin pushers and addicts knocked on his front door one day, but waited around at the back gate the next. Some hung around alone or in small groups near the house waiting for Felloni to come out. Others bought in the yards or along the balconies of the nearby flats, or in the pub down the road.

The surveillance team watched as Tony moved in and out of the house, back and forth between the pub, the flats and his parents' flat. His nephew Billy McHugh also began arriving at the house. Billy would walk up to the door or arrive in a taxi but he always brought a bag with him. It appeared he was expected. The door would open quickly, and Billy would be in and gone in less than three minutes.

One day Luigi ran to the local pub and came back to the house with a bag in his hand. Five minutes later he ran back down to the pub, went in for a minute and came back home. He was out again almost immediately and straight down to the pub for a third time. Ten minutes later he walked back home with his father, but two minutes after that they both came out again and went back to the pub. After spending a few minutes there they finally came home together for the evening. Luigi made four round trips to the pub within the space of half an hour, ferrying what the Gardaí watching believed was cash and drugs between the two.

The breakthrough in Operation George finally came early in the afternoon of 15 January 1986. Tony came out of his kitchen into his back garden and climbed onto the wall dividing his house from his neighbour's. He walked along the wall to the roof of the shed next door, put his hand under the slates and took out a black sock. He brought the sock back into his house.

Five minutes later he came back out again and put the sock back in the same spot. This time, however, he had a packet of heroin in his other hand. He took that back into the kitchen with him and closed the door. The detectives had been waiting for something like this to happen. Now they had discovered one of Tony's hiding places. They moved in as soon as they were sure Tony had left the house to sell the heroin. There was nobody else at home. Two of them sneaked into his neighbour's garden, snatched the sock and brought it back to the van. Mickey Finn took a look inside and saw two quarter-ounce bags of heroin, with an estimated street value of £6,500.[1]

Finn switched the drugs for two tea bags of approximately the same size and weight and held on to the heroin. He gave the sock to one of the detectives, who put it back under the slates. The trap was set and the team were ready. Ten minutes later their luck ran out. First of all, just as he was climbing into the garden next door to wait, Finn got an urgent message that 'George' had returned. Then his walkie-talkie slipped and crashed onto the footpath on Western Way. A passer-by picked it up and walked off down the street with it. Mickey Finn had to get out of the garden to get it back. It was broken. Now he was out of position and he couldn't risk going back into the garden in case Tony saw him. A tense, confusing and frustrating situation had developed.

Just then Felloni came out into his own garden. He hopped up on the wall again, walked over to his neighbour's shed and rooted the sock out from under the slates. He took it back into the house and didn't come out again for the rest of the day. The Gardaí were left wondering whether or not the entire operation was blown. They decided to stay with it for at least a few more days.

Inside Tony went berserk when he realised that he had tea instead of heroin to sell. He knew he was under surveillance but he didn't think the Gardaí had taken his drugs. He immediately suspected his brother-in-law of robbing him. Padser had been in the house at lunchtime. He was a junkie and he knew Tony's set-up. Tony came to the conclusion that Anne's brother was the only one who could have stolen his heroin. Tony intended to deal with Padser later, but he never got the chance.

The following night the Drug Unit waited on Western Way beside the little green gate at the back of his house. Western Way is a quiet road with no houses. Dimly lit, it is seldom used by pedestrians after dark. One of Tony's busiest times was between seven and nine in the evening, when he would come out the back door to meet pushers and addicts. The detectives had already searched and detained some of them earlier that evening. They knew most of them but that night, 16 January, there was only one man they were waiting for. They stopped the addicts and waited for Tony in their place.

At nine o'clock Tony opened the back gate and two detectives grabbed him. He started to struggle. He tried to close the gate but the detectives held on to him. He had a mouthful of heroin deals; his false teeth were out. When the guards stopped him and told him they wanted to search him, he fought and kicked and succeeded in swallowing the lot. Once he was sure the heroin was gone, he calmed down and claimed he didn't realise they were Gardaí. 'I didn't believe you when you told me you were the police, I thought you were someone else,' he said. 'I was never so happy to see the police in all my life.'

It is doubtful that Tony was happy to see the police, but it does seem he was genuinely relieved that it was the Gardaí and not the IRA who had him. He had been worried for some time that 'the Provos' might take him out. They had already publicly warned drug dealers, and people in the north city were sick and tired of Felloni's drug dealing. They threatened to go to the IRA and ask the paramilitaries to shoot him. Although the idea was talked about among sections of the community, it did not receive serious consideration. But Tony wasn't told that and he still believed his life could be in danger.

One night when both he and Anne had gone out, two men knocked on the door at Palmerston Place. It was just before midnight. Ann, then fourteen, was babysitting. 'Where's your mother and father?' the men asked as they walked in past her. 'Out!' she told them. They took a quick look around, and before leaving warned her, 'Keep this door bolted and locked. When your father comes back, tell him we were looking for him.' The two men were from the Garda Special Branch. They too had heard about the threats of an IRA attack.

Tony became so concerned about his safety that he approached the local Sinn Féin representative on Dublin Corporation, Christy Burke.

'Felloni walked into my office on Blessington Street one day and began to say he knew all about me, that he knew where I lived and what my movements were. "Are you threatening me?" I asked him. "Because if anything happens to me your days are over!"'

Christy Burke claims that Felloni then offered him half a million pounds to get 'the movement' to protect him and his heroin trade. No deal was ever done.

Back at Palmerston Place, Tony was held and handcuffed. He was brought into his own kitchen and put sitting on a chair. His wife looked on as the Gardaí began to search the house. They found over

£964 in three separate bundles of cash, and a further £20 in sterling. There was also a jar of glucose used for diluting the heroin and a bundle of cellophane bags for packaging it into deals.

'I know nothing about that,' Tony said when he was shown the money.

'It's not mine, my money's in my bag,' said Anne.

'It's Anne's house,' Tony protested. 'She owns it. I think you know that.' He also tried to blame her for the rest of the paraphernalia. He admitted only to owning the £100 found in his pocket. Gardaí believed that Tony was making large amounts of cash which was held in different accounts in the city. But in the 1980s that money was never pursued.

The addicts remained oblivious to the raid. The phone kept ringing and the orders kept coming in. There were sick, emaciated, desperate young men and women hanging around outside the house. Mickey Finn took a call from an addict known as 'Ringo'.

'Tony,' he said.

'Yeah,' said Finn.

'I need two Qs.'

'OK, where?'

'The pub,' Ringo said. 'In ten minutes.'

Although Felloni was renowned for not handing over the heroin if the addicts didn't have all the money, he complained that they still kept 'trying it on'. So it was with poor old Ringo. Tony charged £40 a Q but when Mickey Finn and another detective met and searched him Ringo had only £79 in his pocket for two Qs. Finn teased Felloni when he got back to the house. 'Ringo was leaving you a pound short, Tony.'

This was not the first time Gardaí had posed as drug dealers in the dealer's own home. The Mockeys first did it to Mickey Dunne in 1982. Mickey sold heroin from his flat in Fatima Mansions, doing so much business that the flat was nicknamed 'Dunnes Stores'. When the Mockeys raided it in August of that year nine addicts called for heroin in two hours. They demanded to see Mickey and the detectives let them. They demanded their fixes and some refused to leave without one, even after Mickey told them they had walked into a raid. The Mockeys were forced to call a halt to the whole thing when they ran out of handcuffs.

At Palmerston Place, five addicts were arrested in the first half-hour. As the search of his house continued, Tony relaxed. He made a cup of coffee for Mickey Finn and talked about how long he knew him. Finn had known Felloni since the 1960s. He knew he was a hardened, experienced professional criminal who now controlled one of the largest heroin distribution operations in Dublin. He also knew he beat up his wife and that his eldest son was serving a two-year sentence in a juvenile detention centre. He neither liked nor respected the man and he had no interest in having a cosy little chat with him.

'Would you mind coming out to the yard outside, there's something I want to ask you?' Finn said to him.

The detective pointed to the shed next door and asked Tony about hiding his heroin there.

'Nothing to say,' Tony replied.

An impromptu reconstruction was set up to refresh his memory. As Tony looked on, another detective walked along the wall and put his hand into the hole under the slates. When asked to explain what the Garda was doing, Tony again replied, 'Nothing to say.' He wasn't biting; the conversation was on the record. He was arrested and brought to Store Street station, where he was put into a cell. Mickey Finn and three other detectives then headed for Ballymun and the final part of Operation George.

They arrived just after midnight at 28 Silloge Road, a seventh-floor flat in one of the blocks beside Ballymun's seven towers. Billy McHugh lived there with his girlfriend and their two-year-old daughter. Billy opened the door, saw the Gardaí and immediately tried to close it again. The detectives held it, produced the search warrant, pushed the door open and walked straight in.

Billy McHugh is Maria 'Deenie' Felloni's elder child. Convicted with Tony in 1964 for her part in the blackmail conspiracy, Deenie left Dublin after her release from prison and went to England. There she married a man from Sligo, William McHugh. They had two sons, Billy and Justin.

Billy had very little contact with his mother in the early 1980s. She was living in Belfast, while he was staying with his grandparents, Ronaldo and Mary, in the Dominick Street flat. He moved into the flat in Ballymun with his girlfriend in 1984. He had never been in trouble before and he was not a drug addict; yet he ended up working in his uncle's heroin business.

'Any heroin in the flat, Billy?'

'No,' he replied.

Twenty minutes later the Gardaí found two weighing scales and a bag of brown powder. The heroin was hidden in a sock in the bedroom. Billy insisted he hadn't known what was in the sock.

'I was minding it for Tony Felloni,' he told them. 'I got a few bob off him for looking after it.' Billy's girlfriend was not supposed to know what he was doing. 'I didn't want her to find it,' he said. She didn't receive any money as a result of Billy's involvement with heroin and now the father of her child was going to jail.

It was a friendly conversation with his enterprising Uncle Tony that had landed Billy McHugh in this mess. They were chatting at his grandparents. It was 11 December. 'Would you like to make a few bob for the Christmas?' his uncle asked him. Two days later he gave him a weighing scales and a bag of heroin, and told him to put them in a safe place in his flat. Billy put the scales in a wardrobe and the heroin into a sock drawer and waited for Tony to get in touch.

Tony arrived at the flat at around 9.00 p.m. the next evening. 'Yes,' he said, 'I'd love a cup of tea.' He then asked for his things and Billy brought him into the bedroom. Tony set up the scales on a piece of hardboard to make it level and took out the white plastic bag with the brown powder. He turned to his nephew: 'Close the door on your way out.' Tony spent three-quarters of an hour diluting his heroin in Billy's bedroom.

When he came out into the kitchen he acted like a consultant after a major operation telling a nurse to finish stitching the patient. He washed his hands and started giving the orders. 'This is what I want you to do,' he said. He had a big bag of heroin and three smaller bags and he told Billy to put the 'stuff' in the drawer. The three smaller bags had two packets of heroin each and the big one had three packets and was marked with an X. Then he told Billy to ring him in the morning to find out which bag to bring in. He was too mean to make the phone call himself. The next day Billy was instructed to bring him one of the smaller bags.

Over the next four weeks Billy delivered bags of heroin from his flat in Ballymun to Tony's home in Palmerston Place. Tony's business was doing so well that Billy had to bring him his heroin every day and sometimes twice a day. But Tony always knew how much was left in the flat and he always knew when to come out to Ballymun to mix some more. He would go out to the flat every week and dilute his heroin in the bedroom. The young couple kept glucose in the kitchen to put in their baby's milk. Tony used it to cut his heroin.

The last time Billy delivered heroin was on the morning of the raid on his flat. When he rang Tony he discovered he was annoyed and suspicious about the tea bags. He told Billy not to come directly to the house but to meet him beside a guest house in Glasnevin, the Addison Lodge. Tony arrived there after going through his elaborate personal anti-surveillance routine. This included a final stop-off in front of the Tolka House pub 500 yards away to shake off anyone following him. He walked to the guest house, met his nephew and walked back with him to the Tolka House. The heroin was discreetly handed over outside.

Tony was not a reputable businessman and consequently, as his nephew found out to his cost, he was not an honourable employer. 'I'll look after you, I'll give you a few bob,' he told Billy before he hired him. He did not tell him how much or how often. His promises were vague. The first time Tony paid Billy he gave him £200. The next two payments were of £100 each, and the last time he was paid, Billy got £200. For £600, Tony had the full use of Billy's flat; his nephew became his employee and he was the one taking the bigger risk, storing and delivering heroin and on call twenty-four hours a day.

Five ounces of heroin worth over £100,000 were found in Billy's flat. Tony Felloni was still in the Garda station when he heard it had been discovered. He bent his head, put one hand to his face and took a deep breath. 'Oh God,' he sighed. As the seriousness of the situation dawned on him, he became flustered and flushed. For a time it even appeared he might admit to the crime. 'I could get life for this, couldn't I,' he said, 'or at least fourteen years.' He was quiet in himself, soft-spoken and uncharacteristically circumspect. When asked about the drugs he replied, 'I can't say anything about it for the moment but you know what I will have to do when the time comes.'

He asked for a smoke and pondered his predicament aloud, speaking to everybody and yet nobody in particular.

'What could I get for this?' he asked one of the detectives. 'I'm forty-three years of age.' The detectives watched him and wondered whether he would talk about the drugs. 'I know I should tell you,' he said. 'I want to but I just can't.' He asked to be allowed some time alone to think.

It will never be known whether Tony's behaviour was real or rehearsed, whether he was genuinely thinking of confessing or simply playing for time. What is known, however, is that thirty minutes later he was back to his normal, formal, uncooperative self. When he was asked to tell the truth, he replied, 'It's against my principles to do that.' He was advised to 'Forget principles and think of the future,' but by then it was too late. Tony Felloni had reverted to type. 'I want to make it quite clear from the outset that I am completely innocent,' he declared. 'I now request to see a doctor about my back, I injured it a few days ago.'

At 4.30 a.m. he was transferred to the Bridewell Garda Station beside the Dublin District Courts. His nephew was locked up in a cell in Ballymun Garda Station that night. The two of them were charged with possession and supply of heroin later that day. They were brought before the District Court on 17 January and remanded in custody. Gardaí noticed a dramatic decrease in the sale of heroin in the city once Tony Felloni was taken off the street.

Nineteen-year-old Billy McHugh now found himself locked up in the juvenile prison, St Patrick's Institution, and facing a long stretch inside. It was the first time he had ever been in jail; he had no previous convictions. For £600 he could now see he had been used. Billy began to think about all this and began to feel betrayed. Tony had already refused to accept responsibility for the heroin and Billy now feared he was being left to take the rap. He felt that the whole family, including his grandparents, were conspiring against him, and his suspicions were confirmed when he couldn't get bail the following week.

The District Court fixed Billy's bail at £10,000, an amount of money he couldn't raise on his own. He asked his grandmother, with whom he had lived for a number of years, to go bail for him. Mary Felloni held the purse strings for her son. But Tony was determined to keep Billy in jail and Granny Mary wouldn't help him. 'Make sure the little bastard doesn't get bail,' Tony was overheard saying to his wife

Eighteen-year-old Tony Felloni walking along O'Connell Street in June 1961

Tony with his mother, Mary (Courtesy Sunday World)

Seventeen-year-old Anne Flynn,
Tony's wife, at the Tramps' Ball in
the Mansion House in 1967

A letter written by Tony Felloni from Mountjoy
in connection with a bail application, 1967

Wanted!
Leader of 'The Felloni Gang',
1973

Justin Felloni, Tony's brother

Justin McHugh, Tony's nephew

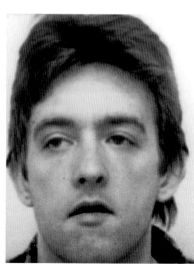

Mario Felloni, Tony's son

Ann Felloni junior, Tony's daughter

*Luigi Felloni, Tony's son, as a child
at a Christmas party in the house*

Regina (top) and Lena Felloni, Tony's daughters

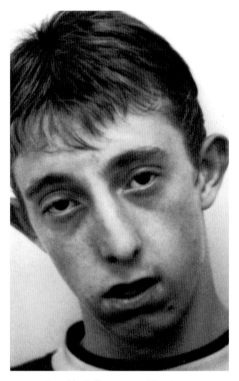

Ronaldo Felloni junior, Tony's son

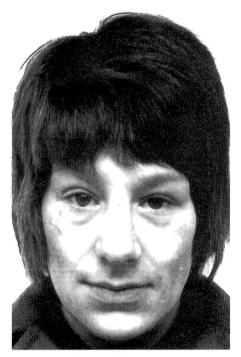

Maria 'Deenie' Felloni, Tony's sister

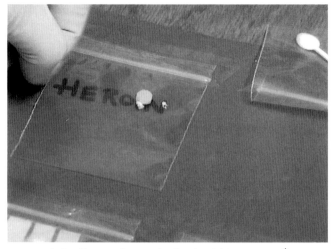

A Q of heroin, the size of a thumbnail (Courtesy RTÉ)

The shaving brushes Felloni used to conceal heroin (Courtesy RTÉ)

Qs—individual fixes—and cash (Courtesy RTÉ)

*Heroin and one of the plastic spoons which Felloni used for measuring it
(Courtesy RTÉ)*

No Stamp Duty.

To the Registrar for Registering Deeds and soforth in IRELAND

102

I, ANTHONY FELLONI of 11 PALMERSTON PLACE, DUBLIN 7 married woman aged 21 years and upwards do solemnly and sincerely declare as follows:-

1. I am the lawful ~~wife~~ HUSBAND of Anne Felloni of 11 PALMERSTON PLACE, DUBLIN 7.

2. I married the said Anne Felloni on 1st day of Sept 1969 at ST MICHAEL'S Church PALMERS ~~—~~

3. The said ANNE FELLONI. has an interest in the premises known as 11 PALMERSTON PLACE DUBLIN 7 ~~Dublin~~

4. The said premises ANNE FELLONI and I ANTHONY FELLONI comprises the family home of the said ANNE FELLONI

5. I make this Declaration for the purpose of registering in the Registry of Deeds pursuant to the Registration of Deeds Act 1707 a Notice under Section 12 of the Family Home Protection Act 1976.

6. I make this Declaration conscientiously believing the same to be true and by virtue of the Statutory Declarations Act 1938.

DECLARED before me by the said
Anthony Felloni this 26 st
day of Aug 1989 at
399 North Circular Road Dublin   Sign Here.

and I know the Declarant   Anthony Felloni

_____
COMMISSIONER FOR OATHS.

Felloni's oath of 26 July 1989 confirming his marriage to Anne on 1 September 1969

Ann Felloni and Santa Claus, Mountjoy, Christmas 1997

Ann and Regina, the Felloni sisters, in prison,
Christmas 1997

at the court hearing. Billy heard about it and hated him for it. Believing he was being set up, he sent word from the prison four days later that he wanted to talk.

Billy told the detectives everything. How Tony first brought him into the kitchen in Palmerston Place, showed him the scales and the bag of heroin he took out of a sock, and told him to hide them in the flat. Billy told them about Felloni's visits to weigh and cut the heroin in the bedroom. He also detailed four weeks of daily deliveries. 'There was no change in this routine,' he said.

Gardaí now accepted that Billy McHugh was only a 'pawn' who had been used by his uncle. Two weeks later on 7 February his bail was reduced in the High Court, but he still hadn't the money to get out of prison. Felloni continued to order people not to go bail for him. Billy spent two more months on remand in prison before finally being released on bail until his trial.

The Gardaí vigorously opposed Felloni's own bail applications both at the District Court and the subsequent High Court hearing. They said he would interfere with witnesses and would not stand trial. Mickey Finn admitted that Felloni had a good record of turning up for various trials but stressed that this was by far the most serious charge he had ever faced.

Finn also pointed out that Felloni had expressed concerns about his sentence if convicted. Mr Justice Rory O'Hanlon refused bail because of the seriousness of the charge. Tony Felloni considered taking the case to the Supreme Court but never did. He remained in custody until he was sentenced four months later. It turned out that his concerns were fully justified.

On 2 July 1986 the Dublin Circuit Criminal Court adjourned in uproar. The president of the court, Mr Justice Frank Roe, was outraged. A number of women at the back of the courtroom started to clap and shout and cheer. Tony Felloni had finally been sent to prison for drug dealing in Dublin. He had pleaded guilty to possession of almost £110,000 worth of heroin with intent to supply. He admitted having the heroin both at his home and at the Ballymun flat in January. The group of mothers from Dorset Street, Frederick Street and Hardwicke Street flats were ecstatic.

The judge immediately adjourned the hearing. 'The women's behaviour', he said, 'is in gross contempt of court.' If he had known who they were, he said, he would have had them removed. 'This is particularly unfair to the defendant, who has pleaded guilty and received a severe sentence. I suggest that if the Gardaí know who these people are they can consider taking steps against them.' The suggestion didn't receive too much consideration. No action was ever taken against the women.

The hostile scenes continued outside. Felloni was handcuffed to prison officers and taken from the court before the judge returned to the bench. But he had to be brought in again quickly because the crowd of local residents and community activists had resumed their protest in front of the court. They carried banners and shouted abuse. Calm was finally restored inside and Mr Justice Roe came back and made an order for the destruction of the drugs.

Felloni's barrister, Greg Murphy, had argued in his defence that Tony was a petty criminal in Dublin and that other people were involved in this offence. He also pointed out that Tony's wife, Anne, was a drug abuser and he asked for leniency because Tony had pleaded guilty. In sentencing, judges always take a guilty plea into consideration. It saves time and expense for the prosecution and it spares witnesses and victims the trauma of having to give evidence in open court.

But Mr Justice Roe wanted a second opinion on Felloni and Mickey Finn was recalled to the stand. Finn said he had known Felloni for twenty years, during which time he was associated with people involved in serious crime. He would not, he insisted, accept that Tony Felloni was a petty criminal. He agreed that there were other people involved in this offence but pointed out that Felloni sold heroin in quarter-ounces, the level at which dealers supply to pushers. 'He was the man', Finn said, 'with the controlling interest.'

Mickey Finn left the judge in no doubt as to the damage caused by Tony Felloni's operation over the previous two years. He pointed out that the lucrative heroin business that Tony had taken over from Larry Dunne had now been taken over and carried on by someone else. 'Heroin', he said, 'is still a major problem in Dublin and there is a constant supply available.' Tony's criminal record was also given in evidence. The court heard he had twenty-five previous convictions; he actually had thirty-one.

The judge looked at his last conviction, conspiracy to supply heroin five years earlier in England. He took a particularly dim view of that. 'You have deliberately decided to come back into the business of supplying heroin, and you have done it with your eyes open,' he said. Dressed in a grey leather jacket, grey trousers, blue shirt and striped tie, Tony Felloni stared straight ahead. 'The court must make it clear to those who distribute drugs in a major way that they can expect severe sentences. The lowest I can impose in this case is ten years.' Felloni showed no emotion whatever.

The lowest, however, was too low for many of the residents of Dublin's north inner city. Tony Gregory bitterly criticised the sentence, especially in light of the fact that the law had changed in the last three weeks. The government had increased the maximum sentence for drug trafficking from fourteen years to life. 'The Dáil has reflected its abhorrence of drug trafficking by introducing a life sentence for serious drug traffickers,' he said afterwards, 'but this has been ignored by the courts. If ever there was a candidate for this sentence, that candidate is Tony Felloni.'

Handcuffed to a prison officer with a coat covering his head, 'King Scum' was led from the court into a prison van through a cacophony of cheers, jeers and sneers. He was driven away to Mountjoy to begin his longest stretch in prison so far. His wife watched from the side of the Chancery Street court building. Two days later in the same court before the same judge, Billy McHugh was given a chance. Judge Frank Roe adjourned the case for a year and Billy walked free.

The *Sunday Tribune* that weekend ran a story about Tony's drug dealing under the headline 'The end of Felloni's dealing days'. The article turned out to be somewhat premature. Felloni served his time in Limerick, Portlaoise and Mountjoy Jails. He was a top-security prisoner and always considered high-risk on transfers. But once again Felloni was a model prisoner. He earned his remission and served only seven years of his ten-year sentence. He was released in the summer of 1993, fit, healthy and ready to take up where he had left off. Felloni's 'dealing days' were far from over. He had contributed so much to Dublin's first heroin epidemic in the 1980s. He came out of prison in time to contribute to the second one in the 1990s.

1. The two packets of heroin weighed between five grams and a quarter of an ounce, around seven grams. The purity level was high so the Gardaí estimated that when it was cut to the street level of between 15 and 20 per cent, there would be four fixes for every quarter-gram, sixteen per gram and eighty for every five-gram packet, each fix selling on the street for £40. The packet with five grams of heroin was therefore worth £3,200; the second packet contained a little bit more so the Gardaí allowed another £100, rounding the value of the whole lot up to £6,500.

9 Sister Anne
1969–98

Anne Felloni spends much of her time wandering around the streets of Dublin. Four-year-old Ellavita is often with her holding her mother's hand. 'Salve Regina Mater Misericordia Vita'. Ella-vita, her life. Anne took the name of her youngest child from the Latin version of the 'Hail Holy Queen', the Catholic prayer to the Virgin Mary.

Ellavita was conceived after Tony Felloni came out of prison in 1993, in spite of her mother's well-publicised dislike of her husband. Anne was forty-three when the child was born. She says she spent only one night with Felloni and just happened to conceive then: 'It doesn't mean to say because you have a child with a man you lie with him every night.' She was in prison when she realised she was pregnant with her ninth child.

All Tony and Anne's children have Italian names. Anne says this is because 'Felloni is of Italian descent'. Mario, the eldest boy, was called after Tony's mother, Mary. Antoinette, or Ann, is called after her mother. Luigi is named rather bizarrely after the Italian footballer Luigi Riva, and that's as much of an explanation as his mother will give. Lena is named after a friend of Anne's, an old neighbour Lena Smith, Regina is named after her grandmother, who was known as 'Queenie', and Ronaldo is called after his grandfather.

Four years after the birth of her youngest child, Anne is still looking for places to steal from. 'I walked out of Clery's with a television set,' she says. 'I walked out of a shop in Camden Street with a Superser.' Her job is becoming increasingly difficult, however. She is still well known in the shops and to the Gardaí. She appeared in

115

the Dublin District Court in February 1998 charged with stealing a £50 jacket from Marks & Spencer's in July 1997 and £112 worth of clothes from Dunnes Stores in Crumlin. She spent the following week on remand in a cell in Mountjoy Jail. 'It's the small things you get done for,' she says. For her forty-fifth and most recent conviction, on 15 July 1998, Anne Felloni was given a nine-month suspended sentence and bound to the peace for two years.

With Tony in prison and his mother dead, Anne moved in to the flat in Dominick Street with Ellavita. Ronaldo was still living there and Anne looked after him until he went into the nursing home in Bray. However, Dublin Corporation evicted her in July of 1997, and said it would not be recommending that she be rehoused. She remains bitter about that decision because she herself has no convictions for drugs. She is, she claims, being victimised for the drug dealing that went on there, in which she says she was not involved. The flat was later burned out in mysterious circumstances.

Nineteen ninety-seven was a tough year for Anne. She was homeless and she and her child slept on friends' sofas, stayed at her sister's flat or lived in Eastern Health Board bed and breakfast rooms. She went back on the drug she claims she had managed to get off. Anne Felloni was a heroin addict for five years in the 1980s. Towards the end of 1997, she could be seen on the streets carrying a large bottle of Physeptone around in her handbag. The litre of the methadone maintenance drug was supposed to last her a fortnight.

Anne admits that Tony Felloni did not put her on drugs. She was dabbling in heroin before he started selling it. 'I was messing around with it, but I never sold,' she says, 'and I was never convicted of drugs.' She claims, however, that the frequency and the severity of the beatings she received from him contributed to her subsequent heroin addiction.

There is little doubt that Tony Felloni was extremely violent towards his wife. She went through a particularly bad patch in the late 1970s: 'They were the most terrible years I spent with him.' In spite of the fact that she secured barring orders against him, he managed to beat her up on several occasions and get away with it.

She still remembers the first time he hit her. It was in 1967 before they were married. She had decided to leave him: 'It was either a good run or a bad stand. I had to get away from him because he was doing my head in.' Tony was in Mountjoy so Anne wrote him a letter telling him she intended to marry someone else. She then went to London, but he followed her over as soon as he got out.

Anne was robbing with a gang of tough young Irish criminals in England. The men drove and kept a lookout while the women stole. She was finished with Felloni and seeing other people. Tony also had his own girlfriend but Anne says that when he saw her with other men he became very jealous. One night he waited for her outside her flat in Earls Court. Anne arrived home at 2.00 a.m. Tony asked her to stop seeing other men but she refused and a row broke out. Tony ended the row abruptly. 'He hit me with a bottle over the head and put me in hospital,' she says.

Anne's friends in London went looking for him, but Tony had disappeared. He went back to Ireland and spent most of that year in prison. Before he left London, however, he 'borrowed' money from his Irish girlfriend in England. Her father later visited Tony in Mountjoy to try to get the money back.

Tony and Anne married two years later. She says that is when the beatings began in earnest. They had a violent, volatile relationship, despite spending much of their married life apart in jail. During their first ten years together Anne notched up ten convictions, while he was sent to prison sixteen times. 'He was totally obnoxious towards me, there was nothing civil about him and over the years I spent with him, it was so bad I was sometimes suicidal.'

She says he would beat her up whether she was pregnant or not. Tony hit her across the head with a hatchet while she was expecting their second child, Ann. 'I remember when I was expecting Lena,' she says. 'He jumped on me on the floor, put his knees on my two hands and he gave me a walloping. I had to go down to the Rotunda and stay in. I remember after I had Luigi he nearly left me for dead.'

On the morning that their eldest child was making his first Communion, Anne says she had to have her head stitched in Mercer's Hospital before she went to the church. 'He was after beating the head off me prior to that. I was washing Mario and he came in mouldy drunk and battered me.'

She missed the start of the mass. As she arrived at the church with a scarf covering her bandaged head and matted hair, her mother, Christina, met her at the door. She asked Anne why she was late and why she hadn't got her hair done. Anne removed the scarf and showed her. The wound reopened and blood began to seep through the bandage down onto her good white jacket. 'I think he got away with that one,' she says. Tony never made it to his son's Communion.

Tony's attacks on his wife were explosive and unpredictable. 'Nothing would actually happen, nothing had to happen,' she says. 'It was just whatever humour he came home in, we all fell the victim for it.' Some of the time they were drink or drugs related, other times they arose out of something trivial. A job might have gone wrong, Anne might have refused to get him something or his shirts might not have been properly pressed—in the end Anne refused to do his ironing so he sent his shirts down to his mother.

'He was a complete schizo, the man was totally possessed by the devil. He was two people in one day, two people in one hour,' she says. 'He'd be very nice, and all of a sudden he'd turn it on and you'd get a bang of a hammer or a hatchet or something; for nothing, for nothing at all.' A passionate Fulham supporter, Tony would throw the plates, pots, pans and the dinner at her if she didn't wake him up in time for a match. He'd be catching up on sleep after being out robbing the night before. Anne's friends used to say she had a head like the map of Ireland because of all the stitches. 'All in all I have about 300 stitches all over my body from him.'

'He also nearly lost his mind', she recalls, 'when at one stage both his dole and medical cards were withdrawn.' He couldn't see a doctor for nothing and he had to pay for any medical treatment he needed. He suffered from tennis elbow, and the pain of that along with the loss of his benefits made him more irritable and violent. 'It was worth it,' she says, 'just to see him upset.'

According to Anne, his mother never intervened. She says Mary Felloni sat throughout one beating and afterwards slipped quietly upstairs to knit a cardigan for Lena. 'He'd bring fellas home all hours of the night and you had to get out of bed and do them steaks and make them food,' Anne says. 'If you didn't, when they would be gone—you might as well get up and do them cos your life wouldn't be worth . . . and my children was looking at this.'

Ann Felloni still remembers as a child lying awake upstairs with some of her brothers and sisters, crying, listening to their father and mother fighting. She hurled abuse; he punched and kicked; she fought back whatever way she could.

Ann recalls one particular beating when her mother came home after having been missing for a fortnight, leaving the children—aged six to thirteen—in the hands of their father. Tony was apoplectic with rage. He waited up nights for her. The night she staggered in drunk, Ann was minding the other children. Tony was out. It was eleven o'clock.

'Where is he?' Anne asked her daughter.

'Ma, leggit, quick. He's gonna kill you. He's been sitting in for two weeks waiting on you,' Ann pleaded.

'I don't give a bollox,' her mother said, and with that she fell asleep on the sofa.

Ann started to panic. She put the kids on red alert, warning them not to move out of the bedroom. A silence settled on the house but then in the distance she heard the clink of bottles.

'Oh no,' she whispered to herself. 'He has drink on him, that's enough.'

In came Tony with a crate of drink and two women.

'Oho,' he announced, 'she's home.' He stood over Anne as she slept, inspecting her. 'Same clothes, same nose,' he said. 'Yes, it's her. She hasn't changed.'

'Now, Tony,' one of the women said, 'please leave her out.'

'Don't start,' he snapped at her. 'Wait till she wakes up.'

Ann sat watching all this, nervously smoking a cigarette. Tony continued drinking and the more he drank the angrier he became. He began to insult the women. His daughter thought this was a ploy to get rid of them, but the women realised what he was trying to do and wouldn't move.

Anne woke up at 3.00 a.m. 'Oh my darling husband, in my home having a party. Has it been like this for the past two weeks?'

A row began. It soon turned nasty as stories of blackmail were aired and allegations of infidelity were made. Tony remained chillingly calm for a while. 'That's right, that's right,' he said.

Suddenly he exploded. He hit her a few times with the bottles and his fists before the others stepped in and pulled him away. He sat back down and drank some more. Then he got up and started again. Every time he stopped, she cursed and shouted at him. Provoked, he got up and hit her again. The others kept telling her to shut up but she wouldn't. Ann says the beatings continued on and off for about two hours.

The next morning Anne lay in bed bloodied and bruised. Tony got up as the children pottered around before school.

'Right, babyers,' he said. 'What do youse want for breakfast?'

'Mars bars and crisps,' one of them shouted back.

'Where's my Ma, Da?' one of the younger children asked after a while.

'Ah she's up in bed,' he replied casually.

Tony Felloni has six convictions for assault, three of which are for assaulting his wife. 'They were really bad assaults, they'd have to be bad before I got the police,' she says, 'and I can assure you they were bad assaults.' One day she went into the Bridewell Garda Station and showed the Gardaí what he had done to her. They went back to the flat with her to arrest him.

'What about it?' he said to the Gardaí. 'All right, I'll come with you but you'll have to wait until I get dressed.' He went into the back room and came out ten minutes later dressed for arrest in a shirt and tie and a navy suit. The Gardaí escorted him out of the flat, with Tony leading the way. When he got to the first floor balcony he took two steps forward, put his hand on the railing, vaulted twelve feet down to the ground and disappeared. Three days later he was picked up in Swords.

On 9 June 1977 he was sent to prison for six months for beating Anne up. He lodged an appeal and was out on bail within three weeks. Two weeks later he was sent back to jail, but the sentence was later reduced to five months on appeal. With time off for good behaviour Tony Felloni was out by October. Four months later he was before the District Court again on another charge of unlawfully assaulting his wife. He was found guilty on 17 February 1978 and again sentenced to six months in prison. Once more he lodged an appeal and four days later he was out on bail.

He was back again in the District Court four months later after he went for Anne with a carving knife. Again he was found guilty and again he was sentenced to six months. He appealed the decision and was released on bail while the appeal was heard. He remained free all summer as it took over two months for the case to come back to court. But this time the Circuit Appeal Court reaffirmed Judge Donal Carney's original sentence. Tony Felloni was jailed for six months. He had been convicted of assaulting his wife three times in just over a year.

Prison, barring orders or threats to call the Gardaí did little to discourage Tony's violence towards his wife. Anne says that he ignored barring orders, and that when she warned him she would call the guards, he threatened to kill her: 'If I'm going to Mountjoy, I'll kill you altogether first.' If the Gardaí did come, she says, he'd lie low until things quietened down.

'One time I left him and left the children with his mother and the next thing I heard he had my children in a home in Goldenbridge,' says Anne. 'Mario, Ann, Luigi, twice he put them away.' She says she came back home when she heard, but Tony had told the nuns she was a wayward mother and the head nun at the orphanage refused to hand over the children. 'So I just told her to go and fuck herself and to get the police,' Anne says, 'cos the police would have backed me up as regards the reason why I left my children.' The children still remember the orphanage today.

But Anne was also capable of being extremely violent, and she often attacked Felloni. He has a six-inch scar on the left of his chest from when his wife got out of bed at 5.00 a.m. and stabbed him while he slept. 'He dragged me out of bed and gave me a hammering at two o'clock in the morning. When I looked in the mirror and saw the state of myself I went mad.' When Tony had his left middle finger sewn back on after it was sheared off during a robbery, Anne later bit it during a row. It became infected, developed gangrene and eventually had to be amputated.

More than a third of Anne's forty-five criminal convictions are for assault or causing actual bodily harm. She has a number of convictions for attacking Gardaí. 'Anne could be quite a vicious thing when she wanted to be,' one senior officer said. During some of her earlier court appearances she cursed and abused the judge. In June of 1980 she smashed a plate over a security guard's head in Brown Thomas in Grafton Street. He had approached her in the sandwich bar on suspicion of shoplifting. The man was treated for a severe gash on his head. Anne was given a suspended sentence. Six years later she was jailed for six months after she was caught stealing three suits from the same shop.

On Saturday afternoon, 18 July 1981 she got into a row with a group of women outside a shop in Meath Street in the south inner city. Anne attacked one of them, Marie O'Kelly, and stabbed her with a knife in the face. Nine months later, on Mario's twelfth birthday, she was convicted by a jury in the Circuit Criminal Court of unlawful wounding and assault occasioning actual bodily harm. She was sent to prison for two years. She appealed the decision to the Court of Criminal Appeal. Eight months later it upheld the original two-year sentence, but suspended the remainder of her prison term and bound her to the peace.

Anne was quite lucky in the courts. She was convicted ten times in nine years between 1973 and early 1982 for shoplifting, burglary, obstruction and assault, but during that time she was never sent to prison. The majority of her appearances were in the District Court; the majority of her offences were considered petty. She was usually treated leniently and she appealed if she was unhappy with a court's decision. She didn't have to pay either as she was entitled to legal aid. Anne avoided prison for more than half of her crimes. She was fined, bound to the peace, given probation or given a suspended sentence.

In 1981, for example, Mr Justice Thomas Finlay gave her six months for assault. Her barrister, Adrian Hardiman, pointed out that she was bringing up her seven children on her own because Tony was on remand on a drug charge in England. The judge looked down at Anne from the bench. 'I am suspending the sentence because without you your children would have to be taken into care,' he said. 'But I warn you, Mrs Felloni, not to appear before me again on a similar charge or I will give you six months' imprisonment in addition to any sentence you might receive for any further offence.' Four months later Anne was back in the District Court on a charge of resisting arrest and obstructing a Garda.

Anne Felloni is still, however, best known for her shoplifting ability. She was renowned for her variety of disguises—as a schoolgirl, as a society woman but most notably as a nun. On one occasion she went into a jewellery shop in Grafton Street disguised as one of the Sisters of Charity. She told the young man behind the counter that the order wanted to buy a present for the Mother Superior. It was

Mother's golden jubilee, she said, and the sisters wanted to mark it with one of the most expensive pieces of gold jewellery in the shop. The assistant took out around ten of the best bracelets, crosses and pendants and laid them out in a line across the top of the counter. 'Sister Anne' began to examine them.

Suddenly three men burst in, shouting, roaring and threatening staff. In less than thirty seconds they had grabbed all the jewellery and headed out the door. Poor Sister Anne was so shocked and overcome by all this criminal commotion that she fainted and fell right across the doorway. Funnily enough, she fainted after the robbers had made their escape but before the staff could get out after them. With Sister Anne slumped across the floor they couldn't pull the door open fast enough.

Another time Sister Anne was 'shopping' in Dublin city centre when her behaviour brought her to the attention of a store detective. He was puzzled as he watched her push skirts and blouses into her habit. After a while he went over to ask her what she was doing. He was stunned when she turned around and pulled a knife on him.

The store detective disarmed Anne, took her into the back and called the Gardaí. Anne knew she was caught red-handed and stoically awaited her fate. She sat quietly in the back room and after a while asked the store detective for a cigarette. He gave her one and she lit it up. She took one long pull from it, looked the man in the eye and said with a straight face, 'You young people, you've no fucking respect for the cloth any more.'

Anne became so familiar to both Gardaí and store detectives in Dublin that they would pull the wigs off her and publicly order her out of shops. She was such a persistent shoplifter that she was often at the centre of a bizarre game of human tennis. The players were Gardaí from both sides of the river Liffey, O'Connell Bridge was the net dividing the two city centre stations, and Anne Felloni was the ball, batted back and forth between them.

Pearse Street Gardaí, who are responsible for the Grafton Street area, would deposit Anne over on the north side of the Liffey, where she became the responsibility of Store Street Gardaí. 'Any shoplifting you have to do now, Anne,' they told her, 'you can try it on over there.' Their colleagues in Store Street policed the Henry Street shops. If they saw Anne they would quite literally return the compliment.

She was often followed by a Garda as she made her way out of a shop with stolen goods, only to stumble into another one outside. 'Here, take them,' she said to the baffled Garda. 'Take the fucking things after all you've done for me and all the times you've saved me from my murdering husband.' She knew this particular Garda well over the years and called in to the Bridewell with stolen brand new first edition books for him. He laughed but wouldn't, couldn't take them. But for all her shoplifting she never had much to show for it. 'I earn it like a horse,' she'd say, 'and spend it like an ass.'

But Anne Felloni was nobody's fool. She turned adversity to advantage and used her notoriety to great effect. Once she walked into a shop every security man and store detective zoned in on her immediately. They tried to throw her out but Anne wouldn't leave. She shouted about her rights, she told them all to 'Fuck off!' She said they could all follow her shopping if they liked. She would keep up the floor show for as long as was necessary for the rest of the team to clean out the shop. When Anne got the 'billy', the nod that they had enough stolen, she would calm down instantly and walk quietly out the door. Anne Felloni was the perfect decoy.

Anne and her children suffered greatly because of their association with heroin. Once she started smoking it she developed a serious habit. She was not an intravenous user: 'I never used a needle in my life.' She says the first time Tony gave her heroin was in 1984 when she was seriously ill. 'He was giving me drugs—heroin—in the bedroom.' She became disorientated. Her daughter Ann remembers her cleaning a window with a toothbrush and afterwards nearly drowning in the bath. Her brother Padser, also a drug addict, came in, saw her condition and got her to hospital.

Anne was in hospital for weeks. She was first brought to Jervis Street, and then transferred to the Rotunda because she was pregnant. She was so ill that there was a doubt over whether or not she would survive. She kept drifting in and out of consciousness. She remembers the doctors telling Tony that either his wife or his baby was going to die. 'Does anyone care about this woman?' one doctor asked.

Anne lapsed into a semi-coma, her legs swelled up and she was jaundiced. She says the doctor told her that at one point she was clinically dead. Anne survived, her baby didn't. 'I went into labour and the baby was born,' she says. 'He died and he's buried in Glasnevin. I wasn't at the funeral. I was in hospital.' Benito Felloni was born prematurely on 9 September 1984, weighing two pounds. He died two days later.

The Fellonis lived in six different houses and flats during their turbulent marriage. All but one were paid for by the state. They started off in the 1970s renting a room in a Corporation flat in Summerhill in the north inner city. Then they moved up the road to a two-bedroom home in Dorset Street. They were there for seven years until the Corporation evicted them.

Anne claims that when she had gone to see Tony in prison one day, Mario got into a row with a young girl over a skipping rope when he went to buy ice cream. She says the girl's father intervened and smashed Mario's head off the ice cream van. The boy needed four stitches and Anne went looking for her neighbour. When she couldn't find him, she says she set his cars on fire.

From there it was on to a flat in Bridgefoot Street across the road from the Guinness Brewery. After that the family moved into the house in Palmerston Place, the base for Tony's heroin operation in the mid-1980s. Anne says she bought it with her own money but won't say where an unemployed, heroin-addicted mother of six got more than £30,000. 'Where's the snow that fell last year?' she says. 'It's nobody's business where I got that money.' She denies she got it selling drugs.

The house was sold in March of 1990 after Anne came out of prison and found, among others, her two eldest heroin-addicted children living there. She says Ann and Mario had sold all the furniture to buy drugs. From then on she lived away from Tony. She moved into a flat in St Michael's Estate in Inchicore and for a short time he lived there with her after he came out of prison in 1993. It didn't work out and Tony moved in with his parents in Dominick Street.

While he sold drugs in the 1990s, Anne lived a chaotic life, first as a pregnant woman, then as the mother of a baby girl. She was given twelve months in October 1993 for larceny, six months in November 1995 for larceny and assault, and nine months in November of 1996 for larceny. The last sentence was suspended and she was bound to the peace for three years. She was also granted temporary release from prison on a number of occasions, and failed to return at least four times in 1995 and 1996.

By the end of 1997 Anne Felloni had secured a year's lease on a private house in the south inner city. She said she was paying £80 a week for herself and her daughter, half of which was covered by rent allowance. When asked why she didn't leave Tony Felloni years ago, she replied, 'I had nowhere else to go.'

Lena Felloni still wonders why her mother didn't act once Tony was put away. 'Why didn't she take the opportunity to bring us all together when he got the ten years in prison?' she asks.

'I used listen to her give out about him when she had a few large bottles in her,' 27-year-old Ann says about her mother. '"I was a decent woman until I met your father," she would say.'

'Ah yeah, go way outa that, you were shoplifting all your life,' her eldest daughter would reply.

'Your father had to buy his name to marry me.'

'That's a fucking joke, Ma.'

In June 1996 Anne Felloni talked to a Sunday newspaper about her life with Tony Felloni. She showed the reporter the stitches in her skull where she said she was hit by a hatchet. She pointed to a scar near her eye where she claimed she was hit by a bottle. She said she had stitches to her ear after her husband tried to bite it off; and she showed the reporter scars on both her legs, which she said she sustained after she was thrown through a window. The interview appeared in the *Sunday Independent* of 23 June 1996. It was Veronica Guerin's last published article.

10 *Teddy Bear* *1993–95*

It all began as a joke. One bored Garda started humming a nursery rhyme over the radio: 'If you go down to the woods today you're sure of a big surprise.' The Drug Squad had been dug in for the best part of two months. So far they hadn't had much success. Some were cramped into unmarked cars; others were hiding in the woods behind trees. 'If you go down to the woods today you'd better go in disguise.'

Five miles out from the city centre on the old Dublin Airport road, Santry Woods was one of a number of places Tony Felloni was now hiding his heroin. Two hundred and fifty acres of dense wood and thick undergrowth were proving hard to keep under surveillance. There was no single point from where most of the woods could be watched. The terrain was difficult, the view was poor and the vantage points were clearly visible. Unmarked cars parked nearby would give the game away. As unpredictable as ever, Tony came and left the woods at different times each day. The manpower required made it impossible to cover him all the time.

He would usually drive up the old airport road, park in the housing estate opposite the woods, cross the road and jump over the four-foot wall. He sometimes carried a spade. There were numerous hiding places for heroin in the woods. It was wrapped in sealed plastic and kept in ordinary watertight household containers such as biscuit tins or coffee jars. It was hidden in tree hollows or buried in holes in the ground, but it was never kept in the same spot for long. Tony changed his hiding place as often as three times a day.

'The Teddy Bear's Picnic' whistled down the radio began as an amusing distraction to alleviate the boredom. It developed into a signal marking the arrival of the teddy bear. Felloni had changed his modus operandi from 1986. He didn't want to repeat the mistakes of eight years ago and attract hundreds of junkies and unwanted attention by having heroin in his home. Now he stored it miles from Dominick Street flats. Less than a year out of prison after serving his longest sentence to date, Tony Felloni was back in the drug business.

The city that Felloni came out of prison to in 1993 was in the grip of another heroin epidemic. There were over 3,000 drug addicts in Dublin, some as young as thirteen years of age. The numbers seeking treatment at the National Drug Treatment Centre in Pearse Street were up more than 25 per cent on the previous year, and continued to rise over the next three years. They are still growing, but the centre has been told it can not treat any more than the current number of addicts at its city clinic after a group of local business people took it to court.

The increase in drug addiction in Dublin was also reflected in the crime figures as addicts robbed, mugged, burgled and attacked people to get the money they needed. Syringe robberies became the hallmark horror crime of the mid-1990s. The number of attacks plummeted almost overnight, however, when the government introduced sentences of anything from seven years to life for the offence.

The director of the country's longest-established drug treatment centre at Coolmine in Dublin did not mince his words. 'Heroin is flooding onto the city's streets again, abuse of it is rapidly increasing,' Jim Comberton warned as early as October of 1993. 'It's causing untold misery.' Dublin's drug addicts were estimated to be spending one million pounds a week on heroin. There was money to be made out of the misery business.

Tony kept telling his doting mother during his seven years in jail that he was out of the drug business for good. Mary Felloni would relay this news to her sceptical neighbours, and ask them to pray that her son would get out of jail 'sooner than he should'. She visited him in Mountjoy every week. She delivered messages for him, looked after his finances and even made sure he had the newspapers to read. Tony promised her he would not go back to selling heroin when he was released. It was a promise he didn't keep.

The prison authorities began preparing Tony for his release around six months before it was due. He was granted temporary release for the Christmas of 1992, but he stayed in a hotel because there was no room for him at his parents' flat. He was subsequently allowed out of prison for other short spells up until his full release in July 1993. At first he moved back in with Anne and for a while they appeared to get on well. Tony made an attempt to do up the flat in Inchicore and Anne became pregnant. But the reunion didn't last long. They separated again and Tony moved in with his parents.

Tony found it difficult on the outside. After spending so much of his life in jail, he had become somewhat institutionalised and couldn't adjust to all the changes. 'Jesus,' he said, 'I can't even cope with crossing the road now, never mind the new motorways and telephones.' The cars were all different, the buses too fast, the roads too big, the money had changed and the phonecards made the telephones too complicated.

For a while he lived the quiet life, going for the odd pint in the Granby or the All Stars pubs in Dorset Street. He watched the 1994 World Cup in the pubs. Fanatical about football, he would tape the matches and watch them again at home. But Tony was a loner. He was never much of a drinker and he had few real friends. He did not know how to hold down a regular job, nor was he prepared to do so. 'I was getting lonely going into pubs at night,' he said, 'you just drift back into the scene.' Tony drifted back into crime, the only occupation he ever really knew. And he knew drug dealing was where the real money was.

By the middle of 1994, Tony Felloni was once again running a wholesale heroin distribution operation for the north city. His approach was different to that of the capital's other main suppliers because he handled the drugs personally and therefore exposed himself to a greater risk of getting caught. He was too mean to let others handle his drugs or money and he didn't trust anyone.

Felloni was now operating in the wholesale heroin market, and while there is little relationship between wholesale and retail heroin prices, clearly the more he bought the cheaper he got it. A kilo of heroin in London cost him about £25,000; that would make him at least £40,000 profit on the Dublin wholesale market.[1] But a kilo of heroin was a lot to try to smuggle in one go, so Tony usually brought in his heroin in ounces. He was paying around £1,250 an ounce and bringing substantial quantities in from England. At one point he was bringing in as much as ten ounces a week, sometimes with a purity level as high as 60–70 per cent. This would be cut once by Tony and sold on to pushers who would cut it again to bring it to the street level of between 15 and 20 per cent. One fix weighed around one-tenth of a gram and cost between £20 and £30. An initial investment of £25,000 could yield profits for Tony of over £45,000.[2]

Tony disputed these figures and blamed the media for blowing his earnings out of proportion. 'If you read the papers, they'd make you a fortune. If I was making that kind of money, I'd be a rich man,' he complained. 'Sure youse see how the papers put up the value of heroin. If there was that kind of money in it you'd only have to do it once.' Like a regular businessman he too was concerned about his overheads. 'I have to pay people, Aer Lingus aren't sponsoring me,' he said.

Tony was the brains behind the operation; he organised and financed it. It was he alone who had the foreign contacts to negotiate for and import the heroin and it was he who set up the distribution network in Ireland to sell it on. He employed others to work for him. He had good contacts in England and the heroin his people brought in for him was 'high-quality gear'. In many ways it had to be; Dublin was and still is a highly competitive market.

With over 3,000 addicts in the city at the time, Tony had no trouble selling his heroin, in spite of the fact that there was a lot of it coming in. But he still complained that he wasn't making that much money. He was cagey when dealing with prospective buyers. He claimed he didn't know just how good his heroin was. 'I don't know exactly,' he replied when asked about its purity, 'but it's good, otherwise it just wouldn't sell. There's a lot of gear out there, you know.'

Tony kept changing his hiding place in Santry and Teddy Bear was not having much success. He would dig up the heroin and bury it again in another part of the woods. Tony was now the Garda national Drug Squad's number one target. But they could never be sure whether he was carrying and were reluctant to move in on him for fear of blowing their cover. Tony had to be caught red-handed. They searched the woods for the heroin so as to lay a trap for him, but they only ever came across the holes in the ground where the drug had been. And as the weeks went by it became clear Tony was on to them.

As an experienced criminal he had developed a sixth sense of paranoia, an uncanny knack for sensing danger. His movements became even more unpredictable. He used the woods less and the Drug Squad realised that the operation had been compromised. They discovered he had transferred his hideout four miles away from Santry Woods to a patch of open ground behind the Royal Oak pub in Finglas. They transferred Teddy Bear with him.

Twenty-three-year-old Justin McHugh was Tony's nephew, Deenie's younger son. He was from Rathglen, Co. Antrim, but was now in Dublin, single, broke and unemployed. He dabbled in ecstasy but didn't use heroin. Eight years earlier, his older brother had been caught storing and carrying heroin for Tony. Justin had not learned from Billy's mistake.

Like his brother before him, Justin lived in Dominick Street with Tony's parents, sharing the small back bedroom with his uncle. Tony sent Justin to do the pick-ups and deliveries for him. He paid him £300 to drive out to Finglas on his motorbike and pick up the heroin.

The heroin was in a coffee jar hidden in a hole at the bottom of a tree, covered by a sod of grass. The tree served as a marker. Justin always approached the drugs carefully, nervously. He looked around and checked whether it was safe to move in. When he decided it was, he walked straight to the jar, unscrewed the top and took out a plastic bag. He replaced the jar and got out of there fast. The retrieval usually took about twenty minutes. Justin spent most of that time making sure it was safe.

The land at the back of the Royal Oak posed the same problems for the Drug Squad as Santry Woods had. Again there was too much ground to cover and too many ways in and out. Justin was regularly seen coming and going and the Drug Squad knew he was being used as the courier. Tony didn't go into the woods although he was seen hanging around the pub nearby.

The Drug Squad dug in and prepared for a long wait. They watched in all weathers for the next three weeks. It was damp in the mornings, cold in the evenings, and the ants bit the detectives who forgot to tuck their trousers into their socks. They were so well camouflaged that children played beside them during the day. Cider-drinkers oblivious to their presence shouted and fought there at night. At times they almost walked on top of them.

On Saturday afternoon, 6 August 1994, Justin came and left the woods again. The Drug Squad watched him from a distance. They couldn't pinpoint the precise location where Tony's heroin was hidden but started looking in the general area. For four days they searched without success. Then on Wednesday as they were dug in, one of the detectives heard a rustling. By the time he got to the spot where the noise came from, the courier had gone, but at least the Drug Squad now knew where to look. They moved in and started digging. Twenty minutes later they found fifteen packets of heroin wrapped in plastic and buried in a sealed coffee jar. Each packet weighed over 13 grams. In all there was over 208 grams of 56 per cent pure heroin with a street value of over £100,000.[3]

The officer leading the investigation, Detective Inspector Malachy Mulligan, decided to put the heroin under twenty-four-hour surveillance. He hoped Tony would come and collect it, but knew it was more likely to be his nephew. Justin's description was given to the Gardaí, who settled in and waited. Two days later, on Friday morning at around ten fifteen, Justin came back. He made his usual checks before he took one of the packages of heroin from the jar. Two Drug Squad officers stopped him as he walked off with it. Justin threw the package away and tried to run, but didn't get far before he was caught. He struggled, but was told to calm down because he couldn't get away. One of the Gardaí walked back and picked the package of heroin out of the grass.

'I only came in here to have a piss,' Justin protested. He denied all knowledge of the drugs and refused to give his name. When he was searched he was found to have several false driving licences on him. He was asked his name again. 'It's on the driving licence,' he said, but he wouldn't say which one. He also had a packet of condoms on him but he knew it would be a while before he'd get a chance to use them. 'They're no good to me now,' he said. 'I'll be thirty-one when I get out of prison, but I'll still be young enough to have sex.'

Justin McHugh was taken to Finglas Garda Station but he had already announced he wasn't talking. 'I'm saying fuck all about that gear,' he declared. He wouldn't answer any questions in the station either. He started singing and at one stage put his head down and pretended to be asleep. Then he sat up and ordered smoked cod, chips and fresh orange juice. He knew he was caught and he expected to go to prison for about ten years. But he remained defiant. 'I'll do my time,' he told the guards.

Later that day the Drug Squad raided the Fellonis' flat where Justin was staying. They knocked on the door of number 73; when they got no reply the door went in. They found Tony's elderly parents, Ronaldo and Mary, sitting together in a corner of the living room. In the back bedroom, they found £1,300 Irish and £56 sterling in a Bank of Ireland money bag. In a second money bag there was another £700 sterling and £90 Irish. There was also a pair of surgical gloves, white plastic bags and a receipt for a weighing scales. The receipt was made out to Justin McHugh.

There was now enough evidence to charge Justin. He was brought before a special sitting of the Dublin District Court at half eight that evening, 12 August, charged with possession and supply of heroin, and remanded in custody. The Gardaí successfully opposed bail. Malachy Mulligan told the court he knew that Tony's address was not Justin's permanent home. He believed Justin would not stand trial and was more likely to leave the jurisdiction and head back to Antrim.

Six months later Justin pleaded guilty and was sentenced to four and a half years in prison. The final eighteen months were suspended and the judge allowed the balance of the sentence to be reviewed in November 1996. By that time Justin McHugh was a changed man. He was no longer the cocky, defiant, tough youngster of two years before. After a spell in Mountjoy, where heroin, cocaine and hash are easily available, he was stunned by what he had seen drugs do to people. His probation reports were good and he had done so well in the educational unit that he had been made part of the staff.

'My client passed very close to the flame,' his counsel, Mill Arden, said, 'and he got burned.' The judge suspended the balance of McHugh's sentence 'on condition that he stays out of Dublin for the next five years, and lives in the North'. He was, however, to remain in contact with the probation service there and abide by its supervision. The judge also ordered him to enter into a bond to honour these conditions. 'That will keep his cough quiet,' he mused. The court had accepted that Justin was not 'the main man', his uncle was.

Justin McHugh was the first person in Tony's new distribution network to be caught and convicted. As pleased as the Drug Squad were with his arrest, their main aim was to smash the operation by putting the main man back in jail. Two weeks after Justin's arrest, a phone call to a Garda retirement party heralded the beginning of Tony Felloni's retirement. There was still a long way to go.

On 24 August 1994 John Long, now a detective superintendent, was at the send-off party for his boss, Chief Superintendent John Murphy. Long was the only member of his team who was able to go that night. Fifteen other Drug Squad detectives had booked and paid for tables, but they all had to pull out because of a last-minute sting. In the early hours of the morning towards the end of the function, John Long got the phone call he'd been hoping for. 'We were just in time for the Teddy Bear's picnic!'

It was around this time that Tony Felloni first dabbled in heroin. 'Would you believe it, I never touched the stuff myself until I came out after the ten-year stretch?' he said. 'I just couldn't handle it.' Tony started chasing the dragon—smoking heroin. Like his wife, he never liked needles, even at the doctor or the dentist. His own drug use corresponded with a move away from intravenous drug abuse. There was an increasing awareness that sharing needles could lead to Aids. The numbers being treated for heroin addiction continued to increase and the demand for 'gear' was stronger than ever. But many addicts now smoked rather than injected.

Tony had also teamed up with an unemployed drug addict during the summer of 1994. Jason Doyle had five convictions, including one for drugs, by the time he was twenty-one. He lived in Ballymun, and he and Felloni found a 'safe house' there in the home of a man they both knew well. Doyle knew Eddie 'Ego' McLoughlin all his life; Felloni knew him a lot longer.

Eddie, alias Nicholas alias Michael McLoughlin or Edward Ryan, was a friend of Tony Felloni's back in the 1960s. 'Ego' notched up eleven convictions between 1962 and 1980. Most were for criminal damage but one was for an indecent assault, for which he was sentenced to fifteen months. He hadn't been in trouble since. His wife had never been in trouble in her life, and neither of them had ever used drugs. But Eddie was out of work and needed money.

Felloni became a regular visitor to Ballymun. He and Jason drove there in his new car, a white Nissan Micra. Tony was never one for the trappings of wealth. Regina Felloni sometimes accompanied them. This was the first indication that the eighteen-year-old was involved in her father's drug business. All three were seen going into Ego McLoughlin's home at Belclare Park.

The McLoughlins had lived there for the past eighteen years. Felloni had started using their home as a clearing house only in the past month. He called around once or twice a week and paid Eddie 'a few pounds' for the use of his kitchen. Felloni and Doyle arrived late at night or in the early hours. They cut and packaged the heroin there but they always took it with them when they left.

On Wednesday evening, 24 August, the Drug Squad got a tip-off. One of Felloni's carriers had got through with a large amount of heroin. It was due to be sorted out in McLoughlin's home that night. The heroin was to be repackaged and stored elsewhere. Plans to attend John Murphy's retirement party went out the window and were replaced by plans to move on Felloni. Detective Garda P.J. Carey went straight to the District Court and had a search warrant for Belclare Park by 9.00 p.m.

The stake-out began an hour and a half later. Two detectives waited across the road from the house; they watched the front door. Another hid 200 yards down the road and watched for Felloni and Doyle to arrive. Seven other Drug Squad officers sat and waited in unmarked cars nearby. Two men called in to the house at around 1.30 a.m. They were later found to have nothing to do with the drugs. Half an hour later, the main players arrived. The white Micra cruised slowly up the road and parked a small distance away from the house. Tony and Jason Doyle walked back up the road, knocked on the front door and went inside. It was 2.05 a.m. The order was given: 'Move into position.'

The Gardaí quietly surrounded the house. Two of them who were at the back of the house could see Felloni and Doyle through a downstairs window. They were sitting at the dining room table. Eddie McLoughlin was standing beside them. Tony was wearing surgical gloves. He took a small packet of heroin from a larger parcel on the table, he carefully unwrapped it and put it on a weighing scales. His movements were slow, deliberate and very precise. At the same time Doyle was examining a number of plastic packets on the table in front of him. The Gardaí watched them for nearly an hour. At 3.00 a.m. the order was radioed through to the teams at the front and the back of the house: 'GO!'

135

'Gardaí, open up! Gardaí, open up!' P.J. Carey shouted. No one answered, but then there wasn't time. The front door crashed in and ten Drug Squad officers barrelled in behind it. Tony didn't even get time to stand up before one of them was on top of him. The officers made straight for his hands. A plastic bag containing over thirty-five grams of heroin was taken from him; his surgical gloves were swiftly removed. 'Jesus, it's a wonder I didn't die of a heart attack with the fright I got when you lot came through the door,' he spluttered. 'I got some fright, I'm not as young as I was.'

He certainly wasn't as young, or as sharp, or as fast, as Jason Doyle. He sprang to his feet immediately, dropped four packages of heroin on the floor and headed for the kitchen before he too was caught. Eddie McLoughlin and the other two men were also held as the search began. Two female Gardaí charged upstairs two steps at a time. Eddie's wife was in bed; in another bedroom the couple's fourteen-year-old son was fast asleep.

Tony was asked about the heroin. He put his hands in the air. 'What can I say?'

Eddie McLoughlin refused point-blank to answer any questions. 'No way, I'm not a grass, I'm signing fuck all,' he said. 'Ask Tony and Jayo. I just let them use the gaff.' He wouldn't say why he allowed them to 'use the gaff', whether he got paid for letting them use it, how often they used it or what they used it for.

'Whose idea was it, Eddie?' one of the detectives asked him.

'Well, it wasn't fucking mine,' he said. 'I told you to go and ask Tony and Jayo, they'll explain everything.'

The seizure was significant. When it was all picked up off the floor and laid out on the table in plastic bags and parcels of cling film, there was a total of ten and a half ounces in eleven separate packages. The individual quantities ranged from half an ounce to an ounce and a quarter. The purity of the heroin was high, between 50 and 60 per cent. There was no question of it being for personal use, it had to be cut for sale on the street. Tony claimed he didn't know how much the haul was worth. 'I forget,' he said. Initial estimates put its street value at nearly a quarter of a million pounds.[4]

The paraphernalia included wrapping paper, a calculator, a scissors, a roll of cling film, plastic bags, pieces of knotted plastic, two phonecards and a pair of plastic gloves. There was also a portable electronic weighing scales in a pouch on the table. It still showed the reading of the last package of heroin weighed—G28.25. And there was a selection of condoms with the tops cut off. Clearly the heroin had just been imported.

Drugs like heroin or cocaine are packed into condoms and either swallowed or stuffed by a person referred to as a 'mule'. He or she greases the rubber on the outside and swallows the package like a capsule or stuffs it up the backside like a suppository. Women also insert them in their vaginas. The drugs are then carried through ports and airports. Felloni and Doyle were caught emptying the heroin out of the condoms, checking the quantity and the quality, and repackaging it for storage or sale on the wholesale market. There were no dilutants such as glucose found in the house.

Everyone was searched but only Jason Doyle had anything of significance, £735 in cash. At around 4.00 a.m. all five men were arrested. Tony Felloni, Jason Doyle and Eddie McLoughlin were taken to Santry Garda Station; the other two men spent the night in Whitehall. The Gardaí were later satisfied they were only visiting the house when the Drug Squad raided. The next morning they were given their breakfast of choice before being released without charge—chips, Coke, tea, sandwiches and a bottle of milk.

The size of the haul confirmed what the Drug Squad had long suspected. Tony Felloni was a wholesale drug supplier. He and Jason Doyle were selling heroin in ounces to dealers who would cut it down to the street deals or Qs. The dealers would then sell it on to Dublin's junkies. Some weeks Tony would sell as much as nine or ten ounces, in addition to what he and Doyle used themselves. Tony had by this time developed a significant habit. He and Doyle were both prescribed Physeptone, the heroin substitute, while they were in custody.

Doyle and McLoughlin had already made it clear that neither of them would be talking to the Gardaí.

'I'm not saying anything, I'm finished talking to you,' Doyle said. 'I'm caught so charge me and bring me to the Joy.'

McLoughlin's big worry was that people would think he was a rat. He would not say anything unless Tony cleared it first. 'If I make a statement and he doesn't like it,' he told them, 'then people will think I'm a grass. If Tony says make a statement then I will.' He wouldn't even say what his own role was without first deferring to the man who ran the business. 'No Tony, no statement,' he said. 'Tony's a friend of mine.'

But Tony didn't demonstrate the same level of loyalty to his friend. 'I have done my time,' he said, 'I owe fuck all to anyone.' He believed in particular that he owed 'fuck all' to Ego McLoughlin. 'He was well looked after,' he told the guards, 'he can look after himself.' Tony knew he was looking at the real possibility of a life sentence on this charge. 'When I heard that door go in last night,' he said, 'all I could see was the calendar pages flicking away in front of me.'

But in spite of his apparent concern and anxiety, he held on to his old 'con' values in custody. Tony Felloni had 'Nothing to say.' To the innocuous questions he chose to answer, he gave vague, evasive and unhelpful replies. To the other questions he just sang dumb. When asked about the four other people in the house he said they would all have to speak for themselves. When asked about the circumstances of his arrest the previous night, he just shrugged his shoulders and sighed, 'What more can I say?'

He cheered up when his favourite daughter came to see him. Regina and Tony are extremely close and loyal to each other. She was seen with Tony and Jason Doyle on a number of occasions in Ballymun, but wasn't there the night the house was raided. She stayed with her father for about half an hour.

At five thirty that evening Tony Felloni was charged with possession of nearly a quarter of a million pounds worth of heroin and possession with intent to supply. Jason Doyle had been charged with the same offences two hours earlier. Both were brought before a special sitting of the Dublin District Court and remanded in custody at nine that night. 'Things couldn't be much worse now,' Felloni moaned. 'I don't know if I can do time again.' His melancholia didn't last too long. Both men were later released on bail.

On 22 September, nearly a month after he was charged, Tony was granted bail in the High Court. He signed a bond of £10,000 and his 'bagman', his mother, came forward and lodged £20,000 in court. He agreed to sign on daily at Store Street Garda Station between 9.00 a.m. and 9.00 p.m. and he abided by the conditions of his bail. But that did not mean he had to stop selling heroin. Tony was back in business as soon as he was released from jail.

The Drug Squad kept an eye on him once he was out and soon realised they had to set another trap for him. After Ballymun, he trusted fewer people than ever. He wasn't using any of his previous safe houses or flats but he was still hiding his drugs in the open. He couldn't go back to Santry Woods or the land at the back of the Royal Oak pub so he found a new hiding place in a field off Kinsealy Lane in north Dublin. It was less than a mile away from the home of the former Taoiseach Charles Haughey. This time he would do the pick-ups and deliveries himself.

Tony had changed his car since coming out of prison, but that didn't protect him from the surveillance. In January 1995 it was spotted at a garage in Malahide in north Dublin and later parked around Kinsealy Lane. The entrepreneur Tony Felloni had chosen to hide his heroin on open ground in front of Kinsealy Business Park.

As soon as he drove away, the Drug Squad began a search of the area, which lasted two days. On Sunday evening, 15 January, they found a coffee jar buried near the gable end of a disused house. The hiding place was covered with a brick. Inside the jar there were five plastic-wrapped packages of heroin. The jar was replaced and the area was put under surveillance. The detectives blackened up and took up vantage points around the house. It was Royal Oak all over again except this time they wouldn't have as long to wait.

At around 10.00 p.m., Tony drove up the lane with Regina. He parked by the roadside, left his daughter in the car and walked over towards his hiding place. He looked over his shoulder a few times before sliding back the brick and picking up the coffee jar. He was wearing a pair of dark gloves. Once he was holding the heroin the Drug Squad moved in and literally caught him red-handed again. Tony was disgusted, complaining, 'You lot can turn up anywhere.'

The five packages each weighed around an ounce; there was a total of 142 grams of heroin in the coffee jar. The purity at over 45 per cent indicated that Tony was still in the wholesale side of the heroin business. The estimated street value of the seizure was over £55,000.[5] Tony and Regina were both arrested and taken to Malahide Garda Station. They were questioned until midnight and again from eight the following morning. As usual Tony would talk only to his solicitor. 'I can't make a fucking statement,' he said, 'you know I can't.'

Tony Felloni believed the Gardaí were the one group of people you didn't speak to. He once said to a sergeant who asked him about other heroin dealers in Dublin, 'It would be unethical for me to talk to you about things like that.' Tony was an articulate man who could say a lot without saying anything. He often verbally agreed with Garda allegations as they were put to him, but he wouldn't sign a memo of any such conversation. He wouldn't admit anything for the record either and consistently refused to sign statements. In Irish law no inference as to a person's innocence or guilt can ever be drawn from such behaviour. It is a law which frustrates and often infuriates Gardaí and one which was changed after the Omagh bombing in August 1998. This amendment, which allows courts to draw an inference from a suspect's refusal to answer questions, applies to subversives rather than criminals.

Regina was released without charge the following day. Tony, however, was again charged with possession of heroin with intent to supply and brought to the District Court. 'What do you reckon, lads?' he joked. 'I suppose bail is out of the question.' But Tony had the last laugh. He spent only a week in custody before he applied for and was granted bail. Bail was fixed in his own bond of £10,000 and a further independent surety of £30,000 (or two of £15,000).

Eddie McLoughlin was given a five-year suspended sentence after he admitted allowing his house to be used as a distribution centre for heroin. Jason Doyle was jailed for four years for the possession and supply of £150,000 worth of the drug. The street price of heroin had plummeted by the time Doyle was convicted because there was so much of it available. As a consequence the value of the seizure had dropped by £70,000 between the time it was captured and the time Doyle was sentenced.

Doyle was later sentenced to a further eighteen months in prison after he was convicted of assaulting a security guard. John Byrne was on duty at the Northside Shopping Centre in Coolock in Dublin just before Christmas, 1994. He stopped Doyle and told him he could not bring his bicycle into the shopping centre. Doyle attacked him, and bit him on the face. The eighteen months were added on to his four-year sentence.

Meanwhile Tony Felloni was down twice, but was still out on the streets and still selling heroin. He reorganised and rationalised his operation, and moved it away from the suburbs of Santry, Ballymun and Kinsealy, back to his home base in the north inner city. The national Drug Squad had charged him twice; he now became the responsibility of the Divisional Drug Unit in Store Street.

But if Tony Felloni thought they would leave him alone until he was sentenced he was badly mistaken. In fact the Divisional Drug Unit took a special interest in him and his family. They set up a Garda operation to target the Fellonis that was unique in the history of the state. They not only zoned in on a major criminal's illegal activity, but for the first time ever they went after his money.

1. Kilo

Tony was paying £25,000 for a kilo of heroin worth £200,000 on the street.

    1 kilo = 1,000 grams

    1 gram = 10 fixes

    1 fix = £20 to £30, say £20

    10 fixes per gram = £200

    10,000 fixes = £200,000 minimum street value (value increases depending on
    purity and how many times it is cut)

However, no supplier ever gets that much money and Tony was selling wholesale. Wholesale value in Dublin was about three times the initial cost. Tony would have made around £40,000 on his kilo after cost and expenses (£25,000 x 3 = £75,000, minus £25,000 cost and say £10,000 expenses for mules, couriers, travel, criminal partners, etc.).

2. Ounces

Tony was paying around £1,250 an ounce

    1 ounce = 28 grams

    10 ounces = 280 grams

    10 fixes per gram = 2,800 fixes

    1 fix = £20 to £30, say £20

    2,800 fixes = £56,000 minimum street value (value increases depending on
    purity and how many times it is cut)

Ten ounces a week cost Tony £12,500 (£1,250 an ounce). He would then cut his ten ounces of 60 per cent pure to make at least twenty ounces. He would sell each one wholesale at around three times the cost, between £3,500 and £4,000 each, say £70,000 (£3,500 x 20), leaving him with a profit of around £47,500 on ten ounces after cost and expenses (£70,000 minus £12,500 cost and say £10,000 for mules, couriers, travel, accommodation and criminal payments, etc. = £47,500).

3. At 56 per cent pure, the heroin would have to be cut down at least twice if not three times to bring it down to street levels of 15 to 20 per cent. Cut the 208 grams say two and a half times to make 520 grams. With ten to fifteen 'Q's or street deals to a gram, there were at least 5,200 fixes to be sold at a minimum of £20 each, making the haul worth around £104,000.

4. At between 50 and 60 per cent pure, this was another high-quality seizure of heroin that again would have to be cut down twice or three times. Ten and a half ounces is around 294 grams. After cutting it down two and a half times to bring it to street purity levels, there would be around 735 grams. With ten to fifteen 'Q's or street deals in each gram, there were at least 7,350 Qs. The original £1/4 million estimate was based on an individual Q or fix costing the maximum £30 (£7,350 x 30 = £220,500). When the case came to the sentence hearing almost two years later, the price of heroin had dropped significantly. The revised estimate was based on 7,350 street deals at £20 each, thereby valuing the haul at around £150,000 (£7,350 x 20 = £147,000).

5. At 45 per cent pure, this seizure would be cut once, doubling the 142 grams to 284 grams. A minimum of ten Qs from each gram meant there were 2,840 street deals at £20, giving the haul a total street value of £56,800.

11 Operation Pizza 1995–96

'Ireckon I'm looking at life on this one,' Tony Felloni said when he was caught again selling heroin. 'I am fucked. I will die in prison this time.' Felloni knew he was in serious trouble and had little chance of leniency. 'Sure I've got previous as long as a roll of wallpaper. This is my third time caught dealing in heroin,' he said. 'I got four years in England and ten years here the last time.' But Felloni was not prepared to climb into a coffin yet. He decided to maximise his earnings before he was sent to jail again, reasoning that he might as well be hung for a sheep as a lamb.

Tony Felloni decided to consolidate and scale down his operation. He transferred his base back to the north inner city and centred it in the Dominick Street flat complex where his parents lived. He still bought heroin on the wholesale market but he was back retailing it himself in street-level quantities. He only trusted and worked with his own family now, particularly Luigi and Regina, and he dealt in smaller quantities of heroin. 'If we all stick together in this,' he said to them, 'we'll be unbeatable.'

It quickly became apparent that Felloni was out of jail and back in business. The residents of Dominick Street flats watched the steady stream of emaciated drug addicts coming and going from number 73. On busy days there was someone at the door looking to buy heroin on average every five minutes. The addicts hung around the balconies and playgrounds, waiting to 'score'. They would shoot up on the landings and stairwells, and some were found lying stoned on the concrete steps with bloodstained needles still hanging from their arms.

The complaints flooded in to the office of the Divisional Drug Unit at Store Street Garda Station. The phones were hopping with angry callers; downstairs at reception the residents were furious, berating whatever Garda was dealing with the public. People stopped uniformed Gardaí on the beat, pointing out what was happening and demanding to know why something wasn't being done. 'King Scum' had begun dealing heroin again.

The residents also made representations to Dublin Corporation and the offices of their TDs and councillors. The immediate area around their homes was being turned into one big shooting gallery. They were afraid to let their children out to play. When they themselves tried to go out they were lucky if the addicts simply harassed them and begged them for money. The more addicted and aggressive junkies pulled a syringe and robbed them anyway.

Tony didn't give a damn about his neighbours and continued to sell heroin from the flat. He remained cautious and still stored most of the drugs nearby outside his home. The dark pram and bicycle sheds downstairs were ideal. They were protected from surveillance and his hiding places there were impossible to find. He still kept all the equipment to make up street deals in the flat: surgical gloves, weighing scales, cling film and plastic bags.

Tony's parents were well aware of what was going on. At best they were ambivalent, at worst they aided and abetted him. His mother, Mary, always stood by him. She often posted his bail to get him out of jail while he awaited trial and she presented herself as a character witness in court to try to secure for him more lenient sentences. She looked after his money when he was in jail, she knew about his heroin operation and she promised the neighbours he would stop dealing. An hour after he was arrested on 16 January 1986 as part of Operation George, her home at 73 Lower Dominick Street was raided. Detectives took away a bag of cash which she told them belonged to her. It was forensically examined and found to contain traces of heroin. A file was prepared for the Director of Public Prosecutions but no charges were laid against her.

Tony's father, Ronaldo, was not only in the flat many of the times the Gardaí searched it, he actually tried to obstruct them so they wouldn't find any drugs. Even though he was by then an old man, he had, on at least one occasion, to be physically removed from the room being searched. He often abused the Gardaí and insisted there were no drugs in the flat. When the heroin was found and shown to him, he just shrugged his shoulders and grunted at them. Regina says he owns the house on Mellowes Road in Finglas with her, which they bought on or about 14 December 1995, one week before her twentieth birthday.

The North Central Drug Unit were well aware of Tony's activities and determined to put a stop to them. The unit had and still have a policy of targeting heroin dealers because they do the most damage. Heroin accounts for around 17 per cent of all drug seizures in Ireland. In Dublin it accounts for 38 per cent. But in the north inner city, heroin accounts for over 75 per cent of all drugs seized, evidence not only of the extent of the problem in the area but of the priority accorded to it by the Gardaí there.

Another operation was set up to target Felloni—the third in less than a year. Eight members of the Divisional Drug Unit sat in a cramped and dusty second-floor office in the late Victorian building that was Store Street Garda Station. They tossed around suggestions for a name. They tried Operation Co-operation! Operation Family Tree! The Italian Connection! They settled on Operation Pizza.

It was not the first time the name had been used in a drug busting operation. In the late 1970s and early 1980s the Mafia operated a heroin and cocaine distribution network between Sicily and New York. The drug route, code-named the Pizza Connection, made millions of dollars for the world's largest criminal organisation. But the US attorney for the Southern District of New York smashed the drug importation ring in 1983. Rudolph Giuliani secured the imprisonment of eight members of New York's Cosa Nostra ruling 'commission' and went on to become the mayor of New York. Even though Tony's father originally came from Sicily, any parallels between New York and Dublin, the Mafia and the Fellonis, ended with the name Pizza.

The Felloni family were not at all happy about Operation Pizza. They were obviously hostile to a Garda operation designed to destroy the family's drug business, but were also highly insulted by the name Pizza. They complained to the Gardaí that it was derogatory and racist. Regina felt particularly aggrieved, and seemed to miss the point that the title had its origins in the family's Italian descent. 'It's very unfair of the cops to call it Operation Pizza,' she moaned, 'just because I've got a few spots on my face.'

Operation Pizza was a very different Garda operation from any of the previous ones that had caught Felloni because it targeted his heroin dealing network in its entirety: his clearing houses, his customers, his couriers, his hiding places, his assets and his children. The fact that Tony had already been caught twice was irrelevant as far as the detectives in Store Street were concerned and it was certainly no guarantee of immunity. It served only to strengthen the resolve of the unit to put Felloni out of business again. They refused to allow him to abuse the law and embarrass the Gardaí. Tony Felloni would not be ignored.

Pizza centred on Tony's parents' flat at 73 Lower Dominick Street, where he lived and operated from. For most of 1995 the flat was one of the main selling points for heroin in the north inner city. The Divisional Drug Unit had it under surveillance and Tony had been arrested and pulled in a number of times. His response was always the same. 'Nothing to say,' was repeated like a mantra. He also used a polite form as an alternative: 'I've absolutely nothing to say until my solicitor arrives.' Tony Felloni always had to be caught in the act.

It wasn't until the late summer that the Drug Unit finally got their first shot at him. Garda Angela Willis received information from a reliable source about how the heroin was being sold from the flat and what safeguards were in operation in case of a raid. The detail corresponded with the information the unit had gathered from their surveillance on the flat.

Willis had already been granted a warrant to search the flat by the District Court almost three weeks before, but until now there had been no opportunity to use it. The unit couldn't risk blowing the surveillance operation by raiding the flat and finding nothing. They had to sit tight and be sure the heroin was there before they made their move. It was a bright summer's evening on 29 July when they decided to go in.

At around seven thirty a team of eight Gardaí ran up the stairs and clattered along the first floor balcony. The sergeant in charge, Willie Johnson, knocked on the front door but they all knew he couldn't wait long for an answer. When there was no reply the door went in and the Drug Unit went straight in after it. Johnson, first through the door, charged through the living room and headed for the back of the flat. As he ran into the kitchen he came face to face with Tony running out. Johnson grabbed him and there was a struggle between them. Tony threw a small white bag over the sergeant's shoulder towards the fire. The bag missed the flames, hit the tiles at the side of the fireplace and landed on the ground beside the TV.

Tony knew he was caught again. He was brought back into the kitchen and put sitting on a chair. Luigi was also in the flat. When Tony was shown the search warrant, he read it briefly, and wearily told the Gardaí to go ahead. There was tinfoil, cling film, a bag of white powder, and a number of small white plastic bags in a press in the kitchen. The tinfoil contained traces of heroin.

The five-gram bag of heroin was picked up near the fireplace and there was another three-gram bag left open on the floor. The total amount of heroin found in the flat was small, but it was good-quality 'gear'. The purity level was between 45 and 47 per cent. There was enough to make between 200 and 250 Qs, about £3,000 to £5,000 worth. Again the value of the seizure had dropped to around £2,500 by the time Felloni was sentenced a year later.[1]

One of the search team, Garda Seamus Boland, found a small black leather pouch hidden under the fridge. In it there was a small electronic weighing scales. He also found a small white plastic McDonald's teaspoon. Dublin drug dealers use the McDonald's teaspoon for measuring heroin. One spoonful is the equivalent of one fix and when Gardaí find these spoons in a raid they immediately suspect heroin dealing. Tony had been caught preparing £10 and £20 deals.

The amount and variety of the cash in the flat was further evidence that he was dealing at street level. The money was in different denominations and varied between notes and coins. There was £1,197.74 in mixed cash and £170 in coin in a bag in two presses in the living room. There was £1,650 on the kitchen table. In an upstairs bedroom there was another £1,330. In all, there was over £4,300 in cash hidden all over the flat. Tony was searched and he had another £145 on him. Luigi also had £440 cash hidden in one of his runners.

Tony was arrested and taken to Store Street Garda Station, where he was questioned about the drugs and money, on and off, over a three-hour period. As usual he said nothing so he was charged at ten past midnight and brought before the District Court the following

Monday morning, 31 July. The subsequent series of events followed a familiar pattern. He was remanded in custody, but was later granted bail. He went back selling heroin on the streets, and the complaints about his activities started to flood in again. Operation Pizza was still up and running, and Tony Felloni was still the target.

Over the next three months he was again put under surveillance. He tried to keep a lower profile but still attracted attention selling heroin. He put the word out he was no longer a big supplier. He claimed he had become what was known in the Dublin heroin trade as a 'lay-on', a dealer who bought his heroin in the city and sold it on in street deals at a smaller profit. 'I don't cut it up myself any more,' he told his customers.

The Drug Unit had heard the rumours that Tony Felloni was no longer 'a major player' but thought it more likely he had other reasons for putting the story around. He probably hoped that as a small-time dealer, he'd be left alone to deal in peace. The perception that he had scaled down his operation, that he sold only to feed his own habit, could also serve as a mitigating factor in his upcoming trial. The Drug Unit didn't believe the story.

They gathered evidence that Tony was now working with his children Regina and Luigi. They operated a network of couriers, mules and street dealers. He also bought heroin on the Dublin market because he got it at a very good price. Tony paid around £45 a gram when the going rate was between £80 and £120 a gram. He bought in bulk, as much as 100 grams at a time, and after street sales made over £15,000 profit.[2]

The Gardaí heard again from community activists, from residents, from local representatives, and even from drug addicts: 'Tony Felloni is still selling gear.' The complaints had reached the chief superintendent's office in Fitzgibbon Street station. The Drug Unit was watching Felloni but as usual he was proving difficult to catch. He now handled smaller amounts at a time and moved it on at a faster rate. The flat was raided a number of times. The detectives knew the heroin was there, but no matter how often they searched they couldn't find it. It stayed that way until 28 October.

Tony left the flat at lunchtime that day and walked downtown to buy heroin. He picked up a quarter-ounce for around £300, enough to make seventy deals worth £1,400. On his way he went by Store Street station to see if the Drug Unit's cars were there. He was happy when he saw them parked outside. The detectives were in; he worried when they were out. Six hours later he had every reason to worry. At 8.00 p.m. the front door of 73 Lower Dominick Street went in again. This time two sergeants and three Gardaí from the Divisional Drug Unit barrelled in behind it.

Tony was sitting on an armchair near the kitchen door. Regina was sitting across from him on the couch. Luigi's girlfriend, Paula Lynch, who was one of Tony's drug mules, was sitting on a chair over by the wall. Tony's father was also in the flat.

'What do you want? What are you doing?' Ronaldo Felloni roared at the Gardaí. 'There's no drugs here, you'll find no drugs here!' The old man kept complaining and obstructing the search, and had to be taken aside and held in another room.

The sergeant in charge of the raid, John O'Driscoll, headed immediately for Tony, who was sitting beside the fire. He went straight for his hands and before Tony could fully get up he slapped a pair of handcuffs on him and sat him back down. Drug Squad Gardaí know always to go for a person's hands first, to stop them or watch them getting rid of drugs. When dance halls or raves are raided, experienced Gardaí know to look at the hands and watch the hash and ecstasy being thrown on the floor. Inexperienced Gardaí will miss it. They look at the faces.

Regina had been counting a large pile of cash on the sofa. She dropped the money, jumped to her feet, grabbed a glass ashtray and tried to smash it over John O'Driscoll's head. He ducked, she missed and she was grabbed and held by the other Gardaí coming in from behind. Her father's daughter, Regina hated the police and often had to be restrained during searches. She fought and cursed and generally behaved like a woman possessed. Throughout all this mayhem, sixteen-year-old Paula Lynch sat calmly on the couch smoking a hand-rolled cigarette. This was taken from her and sent for analysis.

The Gardaí spread out and began to search the flat. One of them went into the sitting room and took out cash, in bundles of notes and coins, from the drawers of the presses. Another gathered up the money Regina was counting and put it into an evidence bag. More than £7,000 was found in the flat this time, over £4,800 Irish and £2,200 sterling. Twenty minutes later Angela Willis shouted to the others to come into the kitchen. The mystery as to where Tony had been hiding his heroin had finally been solved.

There were two shaving brushes beside the sink. Shaving brushes, Willis thought, are usually kept in a bathroom. When she picked them up and examined them, she noticed something different about them. She saw that each one was divided into two parts. The top parts with the brushes were heavier and loose. She unscrewed one of them and discovered several small packets of brown powder wrapped in plastic and hidden in the hollowed-out interior. She found more heroin in the other one and a small plastic McDonald's spoon on the sink. Tony had hidden half a gram in two bags in one of the shaving brushes, and a gram and a half in eight bags in the other. It appeared to be part of the deal he had bought that day; he had already sold some of it but hadn't divided up the remainder in time. The heroin had a street value of between £500 and £1,000.

Willie Johnson and Angela Willis asked Tony about the drugs, fully expecting the usual 'Nothing to say' or 'I want my solicitor.' To their amazement he started to talk. 'The two shaving brushes found on the kitchen sink here tonight are mine,' he said. 'There is heroin in each of the brushes. I am taking responsibility for it. I put it there earlier tonight. It does not belong to anyone else here. A great deal of it is for myself but the rest is for others whom I won't name.'

This was a remarkable statement for Tony Felloni to make. It was the first time in nearly thirty years that he made a full, frank and immediate admission to a crime. He signed a memo of his statement, and later confirmed the admission by signing a second statement back in the station—all this before he was even taken to court.

It is difficult to know why Tony Felloni finally decided to admit the obvious. It was more than likely a combination of factors. For one thing, he knew he was caught again red-handed and at this stage there was really no point in saying nothing. The Drug Unit also adopted a non-confrontational style of interviewing, which Tony tended to respond better to. And the fact that Regina was in the flat at the time led Gardaí to believe that he made the statement, taking full responsibility, to protect her. It wasn't the first time he had stood up for his daughter when he was caught with heroin. When a detective said to him in Kinsealy eight months earlier, 'Regina's a bit young to be in this business, Tony,' he got very angry. 'Look,' he said, 'she has nothing to do with this.'

Once again Tony was arrested and taken to Store Street Garda Station, where he spoke to a solicitor and was seen by a doctor. He confessed that the heroin was his for supply. The money was 'gear money', money he owed for heroin and money he earned from selling it. But Tony Felloni was not a squealer. He admitted only his own part in dealing and would not say anything about anybody else. He signed the statement at around 1.30 a.m. He was charged with possession of heroin for supply an hour later.

He was held in a cell until the next sitting of the District Court, at 10.30 a.m. on Monday, 30 October. He was again remanded in custody, only to succeed once again in securing bail in the High Court. Tony Felloni had now been arrested and charged four times in this jurisdiction with serious drug offences and all four times he was granted bail. There were seven reasons which the Gardaí could give in court for opposing bail: the seriousness of the offence, the nature of the evidence, the likely sentence on conviction, the fact that he was caught red-handed, whether or not he had skipped bail before, the possibility that he might dispose of evidence, and the possibility that he might interfere with witnesses. The fact, however, that he had committed this offence while on bail, or the fact that he was likely to commit the exact same offence if he was released on bail again, could not be used against him in court. There was a public outcry when people became aware that he had committed three of his offences while on bail. The case of Tony Felloni was the catalyst that led to the bail referendum of November 1996. 'King Scum' changed the Constitution.

Felloni was a free man again. The Gardaí were frustrated, the north inner-city community was furious while the media could only stand by and watch. Journalists were well aware of the case, but the law prevented newspapers and broadcasters from reporting it until it came to trial. Felloni had been charged four times, but he had not been convicted. The case was sub judice.

The sub judice laws did not apply to the Dáil, however, and the local TD had absolute privilege. Tony Gregory could raise the matter in the House without fear of being sued or accused of prejudicing the case. His efforts to name Felloni publicly as one of the city's biggest drug dealers may have been thwarted by Dáil bureaucracy eleven years before, but this time he severely criticised the bail system and named Tony Felloni in the process. 'It allows drug dealers such as Felloni back on the streets time and time again,' he said, 'even though he's already facing drug charges.' The case had become a political issue.

The first time Tony was granted bail on these charges was in September 1994. He signed a bond of £10,000 and his mother lodged £20,000 in court. The second time, four months later, he signed another £10,000 bond, and a separate bond, for £30,000, was signed on his behalf.

Felloni was also granted bail the third and the fourth time he was arrested and charged, in spite of strenuous Garda objections. It was only when evidence came to light that he might not turn up for his trial that Sergeant John O'Driscoll was able to act. O'Driscoll heard from one of his contacts in early 1996 that Felloni was about to leave for South Africa. He had paid £10,000 for a false passport on the black market, and it was due to be ready in the next few weeks. He had enough money to get out and start a new life in a country that had no extradition agreement with Ireland.

Tony Felloni was due up again in court on 9 February, but O'Driscoll didn't believe he would turn up. He arrested him as he signed on at Store Street as a condition of his bail on 24 January and brought him before the District Court. O'Driscoll wanted Felloni's bail revoked, but Tony's solicitor questioned him closely about his informant. The sergeant was very worried about identifying his source, but under cross-examination he was forced to reveal that his information came from a person with a criminal record. He wasn't happy about that, but Tony's bail was revoked.

Felloni appealed the decision to the High Court, where O'Driscoll was again quizzed on the source of his information. He was specifically asked about his informant's criminal convictions. He became extremely worried that if he gave details of these, his informant would be identified. He stated in court his firm belief that if it became known who had given him the information, that person's life could be in danger. It was only then that the questioning ended.

Tony took the stand and denied he was preparing to leave the country. He was then asked about a woman who had come forward at another hearing to secure bail for Luigi. She had perjured herself and spent two days in jail for contempt of court. Tony replied that he had met the woman for the first time after the hearing. The judge immediately stopped him, saying he was obviously telling lies. Tony couldn't have met her after the hearing—she had been taken away to jail. His application was refused and he was remanded in custody. He was never again granted bail.

Tony Felloni pleaded guilty to all four charges of possession and supply of heroin on 20 March. He was sentenced exactly three months later. He had two barristers to defend him in court—paid for, of course, by the taxpayer through the Free Legal Aid scheme. The first to speak, Brendan Grogan, pleaded for 'mercy' because of Tony's age and ill health. He pointed to a report prepared by an Eastern Health Board consultant psychiatrist which he said 'makes rather depressing reading—the degeneration from a young boy to a middle-aged man'. Dr Brian McCaffrey concluded that after spending so much of his life in prison, Tony had become somewhat institutionalised. Grogan asked the judge to consider when deciding on a sentence that 'it does not leave Mr Felloni at his age, looking down a long dark tunnel without any light at the end of it'.

The defence also asked for leniency on the grounds that Tony himself used heroin.

'He comes before the court as a person who is, without contradiction, addicted to heroin. He is also a person who unquestionably is a victim of heroin,' his other barrister, Eamon Leahy, told the court. 'His addiction is neither recent nor slight and it is quite clear from the reports from St James's Hospital that his addiction has cast a significant shadow over his health. That is coupled with the fact that his addiction in the past has caused the break-up of his marriage and undoubtedly has given rise on numerous occasions to the loss of his liberty.'

But the judge in the Dublin Circuit Criminal Court remained unmoved by the eloquence of the pleas. Judge Cyril Kelly had heard similar hard-luck stories before but he was much more influenced by what he saw day in day out from the bench in his court: the horror and destruction caused by heroin; the young people whose lives had been ruined and who had turned to crime to feed their habits. He didn't even look at Felloni as he passed sentence on him. 'I have no doubt from the evidence, the indictments and the pleas of guilty before me', he said, 'that he has become one of the prime movers of the drug trade in this city.'

On Thursday, 20 June 1996 Tony Felloni made Irish criminal justice history when he was sent to prison for twenty years—the longest custodial sentence in the history of the state for drug dealing. The length of the sentence has since been equalled only once, in the case of Patrick Eugene Holland, sentenced to twenty years for trafficking in cannabis, although this was reduced to twelve years on appeal. Holland, however, is the man Gardaí believe killed the *Sunday Independent* crime reporter Veronica Guerin, who was shot dead six days after Tony was sent to prison.[3]

Tony Felloni appeared relieved that it was finally all over. He made no attempt to cover his face as he walked out of the court handcuffed between two prison officers, oblivious to the RTÉ camera and the newspaper photographers. He would serve a minimum of fourteen years. His abuse of the bail system contributed to the severity of the sentence, the judge saying that he had taken into consideration the fact that 'after his release on bail he continued his evil trade'.

The reaction among community and anti-drug organisations was unanimous, euphoric and immediate. Residents' associations in the north inner city hailed the sentence as a 'historic decision'. The Inner-City Organisations Network, a coalition of community groups, said it was 'delighted'.

Politicians from all parties rushed out statements to the press. The Minister for Justice, Nora Owen, said the sentence served as a warning to drug traffickers that 'the full rigours of the law would be brought against them'. The opposition Fianna Fáil spokesman on justice, John O'Donoghue, said the case highlighted the fact that the bail laws in Ireland were 'archaic and the most liberal in the world'. Another government deputy, Eric Byrne of Democratic Left, promised that the government was working to widen the grounds for refusing bail.

The Felloni case had clearly demonstrated that the possibility an offender might commit another crime while on bail did not legally allow a court to deny him bail. The government set out to change that situation by means of a constitutional amendment. It wanted to bring in new legislation to 'allow a court to refuse bail to a person charged with a serious offence where it is reasonably considered necessary to prevent the commission of a serious offence by that person'. There would have to be a vote on the issue. It would be up to the electorate to decide, in a referendum, whether or not the government could change the Constitution.

For the next five months, both sides of an emotive argument were thrashed out in public. The majority of politicians in both the government and the opposition parties urged a 'Yes' vote, arguing that the change was needed 'in the fight against armed, organised criminals and those involved in the drugs trade'. The amendment would, they said, 'tip the balance against those who would commit serious criminal acts on bail' and 'restore protection to the innocent victims of such crimes'.

On the 'No' side, the Right to Bail Campaign claimed that this was merely a populist, cosmetic exercise, with the government wanting to appear tough on crime in the light of the upcoming general election. The campaigners argued that to deny a person bail was a fundamental breach of the principle of justice that suspects are 'innocent until proven guilty'. Everyone, they said, is entitled to their liberty until their trial. They also maintained there was no evidence that people on bail were committing a large amount of serious crime.

One vocal anti-amendment commentator, the RTÉ broadcaster and *Irish Times* columnist Vincent Browne, specifically examined the case of Tony Felloni, which he believed was no argument for changing the bail laws. 'Had the courts and prosecutions systems been operated with even elementary efficiency,' he pointed out, 'Felloni would have been sentenced long before he was charged with the second offence. The problem with Felloni was not that he was granted bail but that his trial was delayed too long.'

The advocates on both sides were silenced on 28 November 1996. The electorate voted by almost three to one to change the bail laws, but only 29 per cent had turned out to vote. The bill that was published four months later to give legislative effect to the referendum result was hailed by the then rainbow coalition government as 'clearly one of the most important anti-crime measures introduced since the foundation of the state'.

The irony is that two years later this 'urgent and vital' law and order mechanism had still not been signed into law. The new Fianna

Fáil/Progressive Democrat coalition, which in opposition not only supported but demanded the amendment, in government said it could not implement the legislation, as there was no room in the jails for the extra people that would have to be locked up.

The jailing of Tony Felloni did not mark the end of Operation Pizza. Luigi and Regina, whom he had brought in to his heroin dealing network, were both awaiting sentence on possession and supply charges. As one judge put it, this 'malign, evil and destructive influence set them on the road to drug addiction, crime and prison'.

1. Eight grams of 45 per cent pure heroin cut down at least once to street purity level of 15 to 20 per cent doubled the amount to sixteen grams. With ten to fifteen Qs in each gram, there were at least 160 street deals to be made from the seizure. At £25 each these would make £4,000 on the street.

By the time Tony was sentenced in 1996, 160 deals at between £15 and £20 made the seizure worth between £2,400 and £3,200. Alternatively, if the heroin was cut three times to 15 per cent purity to make 240 cheap £10 deals, the seizure was still worth around £2,400. The street value had dropped by at least £800, 20 per cent, in less than a year.

2. Tony bought 100 grams at £45 a gram for £4,500. For each gram, he made up between ten and fifteen Qs costing between £10 and £20. Ten £20 deals from one gram of heroin made £200 for him. He therefore made £20,000 from the 100 grams he bought for £4,500, a profit of £15,500.

3. Patrick Eugene 'Dutchy' Holland was sent to prison for twenty years by the Special Criminal Court on 28 November 1997, but he successfully appealed the severity of his sentence. On Monday, 15 June 1998, three judges in the Court of Criminal Appeal said there was a certain unfortunate aspect to Holland's original trial, in that references were made during it to murder and other charges. They took into account the fact that Holland was fifty-eight years old and reduced the sentence by eight years, from twenty to twelve.

12 Dysfunctional Children Make Dysfunctional Adults 1970–98

'I never had a normal girl's childhood, I was just used by my father to distribute heroin,' Ann Felloni said in the Dublin Circuit Criminal Court in November 1997, just before she was led away in handcuffs. She joined most of the others in her family when she was sent to prison for three and a half years after she was convicted of stabbing another woman. Mario and Luigi are beside her in the main prison in Mountjoy, Regina is in the women's prison in Limerick, Ronaldo is in Wheatfield Prison in Clondalkin and Tony is in the maximum-security prison at Portlaoise.

Her mother is still regularly in and out of jail, either as a visitor or as an inmate. She was in the Mountjoy women's prison for a week in February 1998. Ann's younger sister Lena, a homeless, heroin-addicted single mother, was also sent to prison for four months on 29 May 1998 for handling stolen property, picking pockets and common assault. She was out by July and had moved back into a women's refuge. Tony Felloni's youngest daughter is his only child who has not been in prison and does not have a criminal record. Ellavita Felloni is four years old.

The happiest memories of childhood the Fellonis have are of the times when they were with their grandparents. Ann remembers it as a stable, strict and secure early childhood. While Tony and Anne were in and out of prison, Mario, Ann, Luigi and Lena spent a few happy years on and off in their 'Nana's' flat in Gardiner Street.

Their grandfather 'Dan Joe' got them up, washed and fed them in the morning. He walked them to the nearby primary school, proudly parading his clutch of golden-haired toddlers in bright new clothes into the infant class. An easygoing man, he was never that worried if they were late. 'We were his pride and joy, snow-white hair, with the little clothes on us,' Ann remembers. 'My Ma always robbed the best of clothes for us.' Her mother agrees. 'My childer always had the best of clothes, whether they were bought or robbed out of Brown Thomas.'

Dan Joe would collect the children from school in the afternoon, stopping off on the way back to allow them time to play in the park. In the winter they would gather sticks with him for the fire. Then it was home and in for the night. The children changed, their pinafores and school clothes were taken away. Granny Mary washed and pressed them and the next day they looked as if they had just come out of the wrapping paper.

Lena spent the first eleven years of her life, from 1974 to 1985, being shunted back and forth between her parents and grandparents. Dan Joe and Mary moved from Gardiner Street to the flat in Dominick Street, a home Lena remembers as her only source of stability and normality as a child. When Tony was sent to prison for ten years in 1986, Lena left home for good and went to live with her grandmother. 'My Nana was always there for me, I wouldn't be in this predicament today if she was here for me,' Lena says. 'She was my rock.'

Ann Felloni was about five years old when her idyllic childhood ended overnight. Her mother had a row with Dan Joe and Mary so she took the children back and stopped them from seeing their grandparents for a time. The children lived with Tony and Anne as long as the two of them were out of jail, but Ann remembers being put into the orphanage.

The four Fellonis, who had all slept together in one room in Granny's, were separated at Goldenbridge. Boys and girls slept in different dormitories. But three-year-old Luigi missed his mother so much that he was allowed to sleep beside Ann. His younger sister Lena was in the cot beside them.

Mario slept with the rest of the boys on the other side of the orphanage. He and Ann made numerous unimaginative and childish attempts to escape. The plan usually entailed waiting and watching from the top of the winding stairs. When the front door was opened the opportunity was there to 'run for it'. Brother and sister would charge out the door, only to be caught halfway down the avenue and hauled back in tears, howling in protest and kicking the legs off the nuns.

'I always remember my Granny coming in and taking us home,' Ann says. 'Her love and affection made up for what my Ma and Da would do.'

One of Lena's earliest memories of her father is of seeing him behind bars when she was around seven or eight. Her grandmother would bring her over to England to see him in prison in the early eighties when he was serving his first sentence for trying to buy heroin.

It is perhaps not surprising that Tony and Anne Felloni did not place too much importance on their children's education considering they were never too concerned about school themselves. Ann went to at least four different primary schools and one secondary school before she left early. Like her older brother, she ended up in a juvenile detention centre.

Mario Felloni was a wild, violent and very disturbed child. He idolised his father but felt betrayed by him in later life. On a community outing to Kerry when he was still a child, he stood up on the seat of the bus as it passed by Portlaoise Prison. 'My Dad is in there!' he roared. 'Up the Provos!' The adult volunteers spent the weekend trying to calm him down and the bus had to take another route back to Dublin.

In 1982, when he was twelve years old, Mario was sent to St Joseph's Industrial School in Clonmel, Co. Tipperary for four years, after being caught stealing and not attending school. He escaped and the following year he was handed down one of the most bizarre sentences in a district court after he was found guilty of common assault and two counts of malicious damage. The judge in Swords sentenced him to two years, six months, three weeks and five days. He was locked up in Trinity House detention centre for juvenile offenders.

Fourteen months later he was back in court, this time in Balbriggan, and was sentenced to another two years for common assault, malicious damage and escaping from custody. He escaped again, and two months later on 24 April 1985 he was given another five months after he was caught in Cork. Two months later he was caught after he had again escaped from Trinity House and was sentenced to another two years at Balbriggan District Court for stealing a car and assault with intent to rob.

Mario was now fifteen years of age and the Department of Education's detention centres could no longer control him. He was put into the care of the Department of Justice and sent to the juvenile prison at St Patrick's Institution. He was convicted four more times in the next three years of a number of assaults, malicious damage, resisting arrest and failing to turn up in court. He graduated to the Mountjoy adult prison at eighteen years of age.

His younger brother Ronaldo, now nearly twenty years of age, never had much of a chance either. He was locked up on and off from the time he was six years old. He spent time in St Michael's Children's Centre in Finglas, in St Joseph's Industrial School in Clonmel and in Oberstown Boys' Centre in Lusk, Co. Dublin, until he was old enough to be sent to prison. During one six-month period in Oberstown he escaped four times. He was in St Patrick's Institution at sixteen years of age, and from there he followed his brother into Mountjoy Jail. He has convictions for assault, stealing (larceny) and selling heroin. Today he's locked up in Wheatfield Prison.

Of all the children, Lena Felloni managed to stay in school the longest—because, she says, she was living with her granny. She completed her Intermediate Certificate and left school at sixteen with four honours and three passes. Over the next two years she held down a number of jobs. She worked in the records department in Temple Street Hospital and in an Abrakebabra fast food restaurant, and she sold encyclopedias door to door. She also did three FÁS courses. But that was before she discovered drugs.

Ann, the eldest daughter, had a good relationship with her father during 1985 and 1986. Tony was 'a hammer man', a man with an eye for the ladies, to say the least. He was fond of his young female drug couriers and managed to sleep with many of them. Ann always knew when he was meeting one of them. He would dress up—clean shirt, tie, jacket and aftershave. At fourteen, his daughter would blow-dry his permed hair and think, 'He won't be home tonight!' To the questions next morning of 'Tony, where were you?', 'Da, where were you?', the answer was always brief and to the point: 'Out!'

His wife, Anne, threw him out of the house in Palmerston Place a few times when she discovered he was having affairs. He once stayed in the Royal Dublin Hotel for two nights before moving back to his mother's. His daughter Ann followed him over there. 'Isn't it great?' he would say as the two of them sat in Mary Felloni's. 'Isn't it great we can sit down and watch the telly and we don't have to listen to her?' Ann would agree. 'Da, c'mon, don't go back, we're not going back, we'll stay here.' But Tony would shrug his shoulders and sigh, 'Ah, we have to go back, babyer.'

Counting money, packaging heroin and police raids can all seem like a lot of fun to a child just out of primary school. But it was part of Ann Felloni's unnatural childhood which marked the beginning of many of her problems in later life. She suffered serious burns when she was about twelve years old. She was sitting with her back to the fire to dry her hair after a wash, wearing a nightdress her mother had stolen for her. She was telling the younger children a story, not realising that part of the nylon dress was in the fire. When the others tried to warn her, she silenced them and went on with the story. It was only when the material began to melt on to her skin that she started to scream. The children were alone. One of the neighbours came in and wrapped her in a carpet. She still has the scars today.

The others also had an unstable childhood and experienced the social and family problems which led to juvenile delinquency and criminality in later life. Mario was in a detention centre, Lena was with her grandparents, and Regina spent much of her childhood with her aunt. When they were with their parents in Palmerston Place, the Felloni children lived with the reality of addicts calling at all hours, community activists marching on the house and the possibility of a Garda raid at any time.

When Anne Felloni senior was critically ill with hepatitis, Tony hid some heroin in her hospital bed and in the bedside locker. 'I was in a semi-coma at this stage,' she remembers, 'and he was coming to the hospital once too often, twice and three times a day.' The packages were flattened out and pushed under the mattress. They were put in after the nurses made the bed and removed before the next morning. Husband and daughter Ann would sit one on each side of the bed, not saying much, occasionally glancing at one another.

Tony told the nurses that nobody was to be allowed see his wife unless they phoned and checked with him first. If she passed away, he knew he'd be contacted. His daughter Ann says it was a case of 'Fuck the oul wan, get the gear.' 'I remember one time I found it down the end of the bed and I wouldn't give it to him,' his wife remembers. 'He kept roaring give it to me and I says no, you're not getting it.' There was about two ounces of heroin, worth over £10,000. In the end he took it off her.

Three bags of heroin had just been delivered to the house one evening when the phone rang. The voice on the line warned, 'The cops are watching, there's gonna be a raid.'

'Oh Jesus!'

Bang! Down went the door and in came the Drug Squad.

'Oh Jesus, hide the stuff, hide the stuff quick.'

The house at Palmerston Place was being renovated, so one bag of heroin was flung into a cement mixer in the kitchen. Another was fired under the television, but with the Gardaí now streaming in the door, the last one was hastily shoved under the phone.

Mario, the wild boy, was taken into the bedroom. In spite of the kicks and punches he threw at 'the uniforms', he was kept in there as the search began. The smaller children were crying, but Tony Felloni's eldest daughter remained calm and clear-headed.

Ann walked into the living room, a precocious, bossy fourteen-year-old girl. There was one Garda there.

'Was this room searched?' she asked.

'Yeah.'

'Well, come on, get up and get out.' She walked over to the television, bent down to pick something up off the floor, and behind the Garda's back picked up the heroin. She pushed it down her front. One down, she thought, two to go.

The girl walked out to the hall. One of the detectives was on the phone, going 'Yeah, yeah.' There was a glass partition in front of him and he was watching the progress of the search in the other room. He wasn't looking at the phone and didn't see the package of heroin underneath it.

Ann was sitting on the stairs watching him, thinking he was going to look down at any minute. But he didn't. He replaced the handset without watching what he was doing and went in to join the search. The second package of heroin was safely tucked away. Mario was still making a racket in the bedroom. His mother ran in and hit one of the Gardaí over the head with a packet of firelighters.

The guards kept searching, the Fellonis kept shouting abuse, Ann knew she had to get what she had out of the house.

'I want to go to the baths, I want to go to the baths!' she started screaming at the Gardaí. She rounded up the rest of the children. 'Quick, all of yis – are your towels ready? Right!'

Luigi, Lena and Regina were all standing in front of the detective in charge: 'We wanna go to the baths.'

'No,' he replied, 'there's no one moving out of this house.'

The crying started. 'Ma, I want a fiver to go to the baths.'

Chaos ensued. Children crying, mother screaming, 'I'll kill you if you don't shut up!'

The detective relented. 'Let them go to the baths.'

The Fellonis trooped off down to Seán MacDermott Street, two packets of heroin with them.

'Mario,' Ann whispered, 'I have the stuff.'

'Gimme it,' he said to her, 'I'll get in the water.'

'Go way, you stupid cunt, you can't get in the water with that.'

'How do you know?'

'Shut up.'

The heroin stayed wrapped in a towel. The Fellonis had a swim and stopped off on their way home for chips.

The family had a dog which the children named 'Elwood Blues' after a character in the *Blues Brothers* film. One day the animal got sick and had to be taken to the vet. The vet prescribed a powdered medicine, which was to be put into Elwood Blues' meals every day. The powder was left in a jar in the kitchen.

Late one evening when Tony had sold his entire stash of heroin, one of his clients phoned and pleaded for more.

'The gear is all gone,' Tony told her on the phone.

'Jesus, Tony, I have a leather suit for you.' Heroin addicts short of cash will barter stolen goods for the drug. The woman persisted and arrived down at the door of Palmerston Place. 'Please, Tony, I'm dying sick.'

'Jaysus, Mary, I haven't got any.'

'Ahh, Tony, I need it. Go on.'

The dog powder was brown so Tony improvised. He put a small amount into a clear plastic bag.

'Well,' he said, 'if it doesn't kill Elwood Blues, it won't kill her.'

They were expecting to see Mary back complaining first thing in the morning. Instead when they woke up the house was surrounded by junkies.

'We heard you have deadly gear,' the woman on the doorstep told a bewildered Tony Felloni.

Mary was also there. 'That gear was lovely, where did you get it?'

Felloni stood there, scratching his head. 'I don't believe this,' he said.

It was one of two experiences the Fellonis had with dogs, drugs and vets but the other one did not have such a happy ending for the dog. When the family lived in Bridgefoot Street one of the neighbours came to the door.

'Look, Anne,' she said to Tony's wife, 'we were out all night robbing, we broke into a vet's and we stroked this dog. Can I have a few bob and you can hold the dog?'

'Right,' says Anne.

'We'll bring you back something nice, and the money,' the woman told her, 'but don't let anything happen the dog.' Apparently, the dog was a rare breed and valuable.

The children played happily with the dog until it bit Ronaldo. The toddler started to bawl. Anne walked over with a syringe in her hand. 'Bomfh!' her daughter says, 'Injection, the dog lies down.' Silence!

'Ma?' Ann said a few minutes later. 'The dog's lying down and it's not moving.'

'Ronaldo,' her mother shouted over to the baby. 'What did you do to the dog?'

The neighbour arrived back at the flat later.

'Sit down there, Bernie, I've something to tell you,' Anne said. 'The dog is dead.'

The woman started roaring crying. 'I told my Ma I'd give her the dog. How did it die?'

'I don't know. The thing was there walking around one minute and I looked in the corner and it was gone the next!'

The mystery had to be solved, so they all got into a taxi and took the dog over to the vet, who carried out a post-mortem. He discovered the dog had died from a heroin overdose. Bernie bawled.

The vet called the Gardaí. The Fellonis headed for the door. Two days later, one of Anne's friends arrived over with a picture of the animal in the paper. 'The fucking dog was wanted, dead or alive,' remembers Ann. 'There was only a few of them in the country at the time.'

It is perhaps little wonder with their father dealing heroin and their mother using it that five of the six Felloni children ended up on the drug. Ann says, 'I used to watch my Ma, my Ma smoked heroin at the time.' She remembers looking at her mother using a soup spoon to put heroin on tinfoil. Ann was on heroin at thirteen years of age.

'All the windows were locked, you know, I used to be out of my head on the fumes of it alone. Then one day I started messing with it myself.' It wasn't long before Ann Felloni was herself a heroin addict. She moved out in her late teens and into a flat in Summerhill with her boyfriend. They had two children and she started dealing. She bought heroin in England and posted it home to safe houses which she couldn't be linked to. 'I got into it big-time, I was running my own business, but I never got caught for drugs. I haven't got a previous for an Anadin.'

The experiences of her childhood began to affect her seriously when she turned fifteen. Over the next six years she received twenty-three criminal convictions, mainly for stealing, assault and criminal damage, an average of four sentences a year in spite of time served in prison. The fact that the prisons were so overcrowded meant she was able to avail of the temporary release system, and there was little incentive for her to stop committing crimes. She travelled the country on crime sprees, robbing houses in Cork, shops in Galway; stealing purses and handbags to fund her habit.

Ann Felloni was now by her own admission more or less out of control. A chronic heroin addict, she was diagnosed HIV-positive in 1989. She threatened and attacked anyone, including Gardaí, who got in her way. She would not hesitate to use a knife or a blade if she felt she had to. Ann has a crescent-shaped scar, four or five inches long, that loops around her left ear. It is about ten years old now but the outline of the stitches is still clearly visible. She claims she got it in a fight with her mother who, she says, slashed her with a Stanley knife. Her mother denies it.

Ann had recently given birth to her first daughter and was out having a drink with her mother in a bar on Dorset Street. 'I was after getting a nice few quid out robbing,' she said, 'so I bought a new brown denim suit and got my hair done for the night.' A row broke out, however, when another man put his arm around Ann's mother in the bar. Tony Felloni was in jail and his daughter didn't like it.

'Get your hands off my Ma,' Ann said to him.

'You shut up, you,' her mother replied. 'What about your dirty fucking father? You don't say anything about him.'

'Well, at least he never done it in front of our fucking face.'

So it began and on it continued and both got angrier until daughter turned to mother and said, 'Right, you and me, outside, have a go. Me and you now.'

The two women started fighting on the street outside. Ann overpowered her mother as they wrestled each other to the pavement. She punched and scratched her face and bit one of her fingers, then sat on her and pinned her to the ground. 'Relax,' she ordered her. When she thought her mother had taken her beating she got up and straightened herself out.

'Now Ma, you're drunk,' she said as she started to walk away. 'Come down to me and we'll talk about it tomorrow.' Ten years later she still says it was 'the biggest mistake I made'. She did not see her mother coming up behind her. She didn't hear her either, because Anne took off her shoes and crept up in her stocking feet.

Anne Felloni remembers the fight differently. She says her daughter came into the pub that night but her boyfriend ordered her out again. Anne says she intervened when she saw him hitting her later that evening. 'She was getting beaten up, so I jumped him, but when I was on top of him she jumped me.' Anne says she still has a scar on her arm after that fight.

Ann junior didn't even feel the side of her face open up, but her hair began to fill with blood. She ran to a nearby friend's flat, where they stuck a pillow on the wound and called an ambulance. She passed out there and woke up in the casualty ward. Her new suit was in shreds after having been cut off. All Ann kept thinking about was her newborn baby, 'She has to be fed, she has to be fed.'

Tony's mother arrived at the hospital and started crying hysterically. Mary Felloni phoned her son in prison to tell him what had happened.

'How bad is she?' he asked.

'Son, I don't know, she's all bandaged up.'

When she was discharged from hospital a few days later, Ann went home with a head like a mummy. She took the bandages off at a friend's house. As the girl squirmed and squinted, Ann was afraid to look.

'Marcella, is my face scarred?'

'No, Ann, it's not on your face.'

It took her three days to wash the congealed blood out of her hair. She'll have the scar for life.

Ann also fell out with her father soon after he came out of prison in 1993. The child he had left behind in 1986 was now a 22-year-old heroin addict.

'Come here!' he shouted at his daughter across the courtyard of Dominick Street flats one day. 'Come here, I want to talk to you.'

'Do you now?' she roared back. 'Well, it's an awful pity cos I'm going to have a turn-on so what do you want?'

'You're a drug addict now,' he said to her. 'While I was in prison a certain amount of money went missing and you took it, didn't you?'

'Yeah,' she replied.

'The money and jewellery I had for you, you won't get,' he told her.

'Yeah, well, I don't want it.'

Felloni's temper rose. His face clouded over and he began to grit his teeth.

'Don't grind your teeth at me,' she snapped at him. 'I'm not my Ma.'

'Ann, what happened you when I went to prison?' he asked.

'I idolised you but when you went inside you forgot about me.'

The loss of her father throughout her teenage years deeply affected Ann Felloni. When he came out of jail in 1993, Tony Felloni and Regina became closest of all.

Neither Tony nor Anne Felloni can be blamed for introducing their second daughter to heroin, but the fact that one was using while the other was selling it did not help. Lena began using around 1992 when she was eighteen years old. A good-looking, well-educated young girl, the only Felloni to hold down a legitimate job, Lena fell in with a junkie from Ballyfermot. They moved in together to a Corporation flat in Seville Place in the north inner city and he turned her into a heroin addict. She started smoking, moved on to injecting, and developed a habit which cost her £100 a day.

After three years of heroin, hash, cocaine and prescription drugs, Lena Felloni went on a programme at the National Drug Treatment Centre in Dublin. She had tried total detoxification before but couldn't handle it. By the end of 1995, however, she was three months pregnant. This increased her determination to try to get off drugs. She stabilised on the heroin substitute Physeptone for the duration of the pregnancy and her first child was born on 17 July 1996. The baby boy was born a heroin addict and had to be weaned off drugs in hospital. He has since been taken into care.

Mario Felloni is now in the medical unit in Mountjoy Jail. He is at the second stage of HIV infection and is being prescribed Physeptone along with a variety of drugs to slow down the spread of the disease. He is serving a ten-year sentence for an armed robbery he carried out in England. There was a good laugh among the north-city criminal fraternity the night his picture appeared on the BBC's *Crimewatch UK* programme before the London Metropolitan Police caught up with him. He was sent to Her Majesty's prison at Wormwood Scrubs on 7 April 1993.

Mario had a very tough time in the English prison system. He was a Category A prisoner, top-security and was moved around a lot. He changed prisons four times in three and a half years. He served time in 'the Scrubs', Swaleside, Whitemoor and Full Sutton prisons. He was so badly beaten up on one occasion that technically he died in the back of an ambulance; he stopped breathing and had to be revived. He was being taken to hospital but there was no police escort. The ambulance wasn't allowed leave the prison without one and he lay in it until the squad cars and motorbikes arrived.

Anne Felloni tirelessly petitioned the Minister for Justice for Mario's repatriation. Exactly one week before Christmas 1996, Nora Owen granted her request and her eldest son was transferred home to Mountjoy on compassionate grounds. He is due for release in October 1999.

His youngest brother, Ronaldo, is not due out of prison until two years after him. He got into a hackney cab in Dublin and put a knife to the driver's throat. He ordered her to take the car down a cul-de-sac, where she handed over her day's takings. He then kicked her out, drove off, crashed the car after a mile and a half and ran away. He got £15, £5 of it in sterling.

From the description of her attacker the woman gave, it wasn't long before the Gardaí picked Ronaldo up. He had committed the offence while on temporary release. He pleaded guilty in the Circuit Criminal Court and on 15 May 1997 he was sentenced to five years' imprisonment. The case particularly saddened Judge Joseph Mathews.

'I feel a true sense of compassion for you, for what I know of the sad saga of your life,' the judge said to him. He was speaking from personal experience. As a barrister twenty-five years earlier, he had defended Tony Felloni when he was up on an assault charge after breaking Anne's jaw. 'That was many years before you were born,' he told Ronaldo, 'and it is strange that I should now be the judge sitting here today with you in front of me.' The generational nature of crime was clearly illustrated.

Lena is the only Felloni who is old enough to be in jail and isn't. She was in Mountjoy for a few weeks in May and June 1998, serving time for outstanding charges. But life on the outside is extremely difficult for her. She lived on the streets for a time before she put her baby into care and moved into a women's refuge. She lived there for over a year, sleeping in a bunk bed and sharing the room with three other women. Many of the residents were heroin addicts. They would shoot up in the bedrooms and the bathrooms unknown to the staff. Lena is trying to stay off drugs, find a place to live and get her baby back. She is on a methadone maintenance programme and says she is managing to stay clean in spite of the environment she lives in.

'You're sitting there and everyone else is goofing off around you,' Lena says. 'I know I can't go near gear for my baby's sake, I have to be very strong.' She had applied for accommodation before her baby was born, putting her name down on the Corporation's housing list on 3 April 1996. When there is a shortage of housing all over the city, drug addicts don't get priority. She has written to Dublin Corporation, the newspapers, RTÉ and the Taoiseach, Bertie Ahern. 'Bertie wrote back saying he's made enquiries on my behalf,' she says. She has also tried private landlords but 'once they hear the name Felloni they just don't want to know'.

Ann's three children are also in care; their mother remains in prison. She contracted hepatitis in 1993 and is now suffering from asymptomatic HIV. 'I cannot have teeth extracted because it would be too dangerous due to cancer cells in my jaw,' she says. 'I got the virus off the father of my first two children.' She claimed social welfare benefits and says she spent £6,000 her grandmother left her in her will. But throughout her life, robbery has provided her with thrills, employment and income.

Noel Harty won't forget the Saturday evening in July 1995 when he first met a drug-crazed Ann Felloni. She and another thief were on a joyriding and robbing spree. They stole a car in Cork but were caught in Kilkenny speeding back to Dublin. Noel Harty was the sergeant in charge of the traffic corps. He followed them, stopped them and managed to get Ann into the back of the squad car. Her partner in crime sped away. Ann roared abuse at the sergeant, and he had to get out of the squad car to radio in. That's when Ann took control of the car.

She locked the doors and tried to get away but the car was stuck and the front wheels started spinning. Noel Harty tried to stop her but Ann drove forward. The sergeant's leg went under the front wheel. As it spun it sheared off layers of skin from his knee to his ankle. It kept spinning for about a minute. Ann turned off the engine only when a shot was fired over her head. Three men just happened to be out shooting nearby. They saw the Garda under the car and one of them fired off a round. Ann Felloni was released on bail. She was later caught robbing in Galway and Dublin. Noel Harty was seven months out of work. He had to get skin grafts on his leg. Ann Felloni got a four-year suspended sentence. Noel Harty is scarred for life.

Throughout 1997 Ann was in court in Dublin, Galway and Tipperary on charges relating to a spate of robberies and attacks over the previous two years. On 12 March she got two and a half years at Clonmel Circuit Court for an assault on a Garda in which a knife was used. The following month she was back in court in Galway after she pleaded guilty to handling over £1,000 worth of CDs, tapes, clothes and jewellery. She was caught with the stolen goods when the Gardaí raided an apartment complex at the Corrib Village. The judge added another eighteen months to the sentence she was serving and blamed the system of temporary release for allowing Ann out of jail to commit more crime.

Six months later another three months were added on at Dublin District Court after she was caught trying to steal a purse in Temple Bar. Her series of court appearances finished with her twenty-eighth conviction on 28 November 1997. She pleaded guilty to assaulting Martina Talbot and causing her actual bodily harm.

Ann admitted stabbing Martina Talbot when she came across her on Ormond Quay because she suspected her of stealing her clothes. 'I had a knife with me, a steak knife which I opened and just lashed out. I didn't know I stabbed her until I saw blood on her hand.' The court heard that Talbot spent the night in intensive care and a week in hospital before she signed herself out. She was left with a three-inch scar on her chest, and minor cuts which didn't need to be stitched. 'I just lost the head,' Ann said. 'I was out of my mind on gear at the time.' She said she tried to apologise to Martina afterwards. She later found her missing clothes.

The prosecuting Garda said that Ann had very advanced Aids and her prospects of living long were not that good. Her lawyer Jeremy Maher said heroin had dictated the way she lived for most of her life, from the time she was a child. Judge Raymond Groarke felt it would be inhuman not to take her personal difficulties into consideration. He sent her to prison for three and a half years. She is due for release in the year 2000.

The name Felloni is synonymous with drugs, disadvantage and crime in Ireland today. It is a name that Tony Felloni officially bought himself into nearly thirty years ago and it is now a name some of his children want to buy out of. Lena Felloni says she's still being victimised because of it: 'People don't know me, yet they have me labelled.' Ann takes some comfort from the fact that her children, Tony's grandchildren, are all in care: 'Once my kids are all right I'll be happy. They won't have to carry the name Felloni.'

As she was taken off to jail on Friday, 28 November 1997, Ann Felloni smiled at the camera and gave the sign of peace. She was, as her lawyer said, just a 'tool in her father's drugs organisation when other girls her age were going to school'. Ann may have worked with him as a child, but she had no role to play in the operation he set up in 1993 when he came out of prison. That poisoned chalice had already been passed down to the younger generation. Luigi and Regina were their father's next lieutenants.

13 *Rose Molloney 1973–98*

It was just after 7.00 p.m. on 2 April 1996 when Rose Molloney put her key in the door and opened flat 4, on the first landing, at 25 Hollybank Road. It is a red-bricked, three-storey Georgian-style house just two miles from the city centre in a mature residential area off Drumcondra Road in Dublin. The rents are high, but the neighbourhood is quiet and the comfort and convenience are worth it.

Rose had leased the bedsit about eight months before, having spotted an advertisement for it in the paper. She took the room for a year, at a monthly rent of £140. For this she got one small room, with a door leading off it to a small toilet and shower unit. There was a fold-up settee, which opened up into a bed, a small sink, a kettle and a cooker in the corner. The flat was poky but Rose didn't mind. She didn't sleep there very often, on average once a month.

Rose Molloney was a private person who didn't speak to her neighbours. She worked in town but didn't tell anyone what she did. She knew that as long as she kept paying the rent, no one would be too interested in finding out about her. Her mobile phone had just cost her £350, and she had to pay an extra £300 deposit in case she didn't pay the bill. She hadn't told many people she had rented the flat. When she came home that bright spring evening she had a lot of work to do.

There were two coffee jars, a large and a small one, hidden in the attic above the shower unit in the flat. Both were full of heroin, over 40 per cent pure, which had to be divided up. The large jar contained three one-ounce bags, which were for sale, and a smaller one which she kept for herself. She worked from the larger bags, cutting up the heroin into quarter-ounces, which she then stored in the small coffee jar. So far, she had made up eleven quarter-ounces in small plastic bags. These she would sell for around £550 each. Rose was in the wholesale heroin market.[1]

Rose used a small, black, digital scales to be sure of her measurements. She always kept a ready supply of plastic bags under the cushions on the bed for packaging the heroin. The rest she kept up in the attic. There was tinfoil in the flat and there was also £1,000 in cash, which Rose said belonged to her mother. There were clothes, money and newspapers scattered around, and there was some food in the fridge. Rose wasn't one for housework but then she didn't have to be.

She didn't have to live in the cramped little bedsit on Hollybank Road. She and her grandfather had bought a house together, she said, at Mellowes Road in Finglas and she had moved in two weeks ago. She was living there with her boyfriend. It was a comfortable, three-bedroom semi-detached home, with front and back gardens, and a porch at the main door. It still needed a bit of work and Rose had left £975 aside to pay a man for doing the windows. Rose had 'no idea' how much the renovations had cost. Come to think of it, she didn't know how much the house cost either. It was, after all, paid for in cash. There was no mortgage on 127 Mellowes Road.

Rose Molloney was twenty years of age. She was driving a two-year-old Nissan Micra car, bought for £6,000 two months before. She wasn't sure of the details but then that never worried her. If she was stopped at a Garda checkpoint, all the documents were in the glove compartment. Unfortunately for Rose Molloney she ran into the Gardaí a lot sooner than she had hoped, because when she opened the door to the bedsit on that warm April evening, she was greeted by the sight of Seamus Boland and Darragh O'Toole turning the place upside down.

It was hardly surprising that Rose got caught up in Operation Pizza, the Garda operation to target the Felloni family. Rose Molloney was Regina Felloni. The two Gardaí found an ESB bill in the name of 'Rose Molloney', and a lease agreement which Regina had signed Rose Melloni, changing only the first letter, F, in her surname.

As soon as she walked in she was grabbed by the wrists. Her keys and mobile phone were taken from her. She sat handcuffed as the search continued. The Gardaí pulled back the cushions to reveal the plastic bags. They picked up a paper bag with a pair of surgical gloves in it, and in the chest of drawers they found a bundle of money tied up in an elastic band.

She watched as Seamie Boland climbed into the attic and came down with the coffee jars, the scales and more plastic bags. When she was asked if she knew what was in the jars she calmly replied, 'Yeah, heroin. It's mine. I accept it.' She even signed a memo in the Garda's notebook to that effect. The street value of the heroin was almost £30,000.

Regina was arrested and dropped off at Store Street Garda Station as the search team headed for 127 Mellowes Road. Regina's boyfriend answered the door. He was shown the warrant. 'Eh, I'm only visiting,' he said. The Gardaí didn't believe him. They walked in and searched the house. There were a number of letters and other documents in Regina's name. Some were addressed to her at Mellowes Road, others to the flat in Dominick Street.

The Gardaí found the £975 for the windows in a sideboard in the kitchen. They also found a piece of a plastic bag with the corner torn out of it—the corner is often used for wrapping heroin. There was a piece of rolled scorched tinfoil in the living room. Heroin is smoked through tinfoil. Regina had been smoking heroin and snorting cocaine for the previous two years.

Regina Felloni had never been involved in drugs until her father came out of prison in 1993. Born on 20 December 1975, she was raised by her aunt, Evelyn Carroll, in a Corporation flat in Bridgefoot Street, where the Fellonis lived before they moved into Palmerston Place. Evelyn looked after Regina while her mother was drinking, taking drugs, shoplifting and fighting; her father was away robbing, selling drugs or locked up in prison.

Regina is remembered as a happy, mannerly, approachable child. She was quiet and shy but generally did her best in class. However, she changed in her early teens. She started playing truant and getting involved in juvenile crime. She was up before the Children's Court for shoplifting, fighting and missing school.

Regina, like her father, is missing part of her left middle finger. She lost it at sixteen years of age, when she tried to close the door of Evelyn's flat by putting her fingers behind it and pulling it fast. She didn't get her hand out of the way in time and the door slammed shut on her finger. Regina took out a personal injury claim against Dublin Corporation, alleging that the door was in a dangerous and defective condition. She lost.

By the time she was seventeen, Regina had four convictions for shoplifting and common assault. She doubled her convictions over the next three years and each time she appeared in court she was sent to prison. She was sentenced to four, six, eight and six months respectively for shoplifting and stealing. The chronic overcrowding problem in Mountjoy, however, meant she was never in jail for long before she was eligible for temporary release.

Regina became interested in finding out about her father while he was in prison serving his second sentence for heroin. She started skipping school and going down to see him, but didn't tell her brothers or sisters. The two became very close and after he came out of prison, she got involved in his heroin business. In the process she developed her own £100-a-day habit.

Regina was running a nice little wholesale heroin operation of her own but insisted she was being forced to sell heroin by a ruthless and dangerous moneylender. 'I owe a chap money and you don't mess with this chap,' she told the Gardaí the night she was caught in Hollybank Road. 'I had to sell gear for him or me family'd be involved. The chap is in prison at the moment. I have fellas watching me.' She said she had been selling heroin for about four months and admitted taking precautions against getting caught, such as using surgical gloves 'to keep me fingerprints off the stuff'. But she repeated that she had no other choice. 'I owe money and it's the only way I could get it or they'd stab me . . .' she insisted, 'I can't say any more.'[2]

Regina signed a statement confirming her story, but the Gardaí didn't believe it. There was no evidence she was being leaned on. She was charged with possession of heroin with intent to supply and brought before the Dublin District Court, where she was remanded in custody.

She applied for bail but a young woman who came forward on her behalf was questioned so rigorously by the Gardaí at the first bail hearing that she never turned up for the second one. Regina remained in prison until she was sentenced. But the family business had started falling apart long before Regina was taken out of it. Tony was in jail and Luigi had been caught twice, the first time nine months before his younger sister.

It happened in the Dominick Street flat in June 1995. On the previous day Tony and Regina had gone out and left Luigi in charge. He had been up and down like a yo-yo all afternoon, answering the door. Between one and four thirty he had served nineteen addicts. The routine was different depending on the customer and each one knew the score. The money was always handed over to Luigi first and he went back into the flat to count it, shutting the door. Courtesy was never a consideration, in this business the customer was never right. Luigi was back out in less than a minute with whatever amount of heroin was paid for. Sometimes the exchange was made at the door, sometimes on the balcony or down at the stairs.

The following day was even busier; the dealing began earlier. The first caller arrived just after eleven that morning, and over the next three hours nine more addicts called to the door. All were shifty, nervous and in an agitated state. Sometimes Luigi would say a few words to them, but mostly when selling at the door he just opened it a small crack and stuck his hand out. He took the money and handed over the heroin.

All the activity around number 73 was hard to miss. The Drug Unit saw it all because the flat was under surveillance. So when at 2.00 p.m. on 22 June 1995 a weary Luigi closed the door after taking money from another junkie, he reopened it two minutes later only to be met by Seamus Boland. The bewildered addict had been snatched from the door. The Drug Squad Garda stood in his place.

The door was shoved in and Luigi's hands were grabbed and held. The hallway was small and blocked by a washing machine. Luigi fought, trying to get his hand up to his mouth to swallow the heroin. He struggled for a couple of minutes but just couldn't manage it. Giving up, he opened his fist and let a £20 deal fall to the floor. Luigi was handcuffed and brought back into the flat. The rest of the Gardaí began to search.

The living room was full of Fellonis—Tony, Regina and Tony's parents. The elderly couple had been sitting quietly in the flat while junkies banged on the door all morning. At seventy-nine years of age, Mary was very frail; she died three weeks later. Ronaldo was in his eighties but was as usual full of fight, roaring at the Gardaí that they would find nothing.

Nine more addicts called to the door. The phone rang constantly. 'Tony, would it be all right to drop down for a half?'[3] a woman phoned and asked. 'Yeah,' Seamie Boland replied. Twenty minutes later she knocked on the door and walked straight into the raid. 'I'm looking for a half, how much for a half?' As soon as she was arrested she started to cry. She had £60 in her pocket, the price of a half. Another known addict was arrested with £40 in his pocket. The other seven were searched and had on them between £20 and £60 each.

Three thousand pounds in cash was found in the bedroom. Another £2,100 in £5, £10 and £20 notes was scattered around in a drawer in the cabinet. There was a neat bundle of over £1,000 sterling beside that. In another press there was nearly £200 sterling and an Irish £20 note in a brown envelope. In all there was over £6,500 in Irish and sterling, along with £2,000 in traveller's cheques.[4]

Tony said the traveller's cheques were for Regina, who was going on holidays. The sterling was for his mother, who he said was travelling to the North to see relations at the weekend. No explanation was given for the rest of the cash, or for the surgical gloves, the small plastic McDonald's spoons, the digital scales, the large number of white plastic bags and the small amount of hash that was also found in the flat.

Luigi was arrested and charged with possession of both cannabis and heroin with intent to supply. He followed his father's example by refusing to co-operate in custody. He too had learned 'Nothing to say.' In reply to the charges he just said 'No.' Six months later while he was out on bail—like father like son—he was caught again selling heroin.

Luigi was known as a likeable rogue. He always seemed to be in good form, and he didn't appear to have a cruel or vindictive side. Born on 13 June 1973, he spent much of his childhood with his maternal grandmother in a small Corporation house on the south side of the city. Not surprisingly, he didn't do very well in school and didn't bother going in that often.

The secondary school he intermittently attended had a reputation for being one of the toughest in Dublin. Luigi had no books and no uniform. He did little work in class and less outside it. He was regularly suspended for swearing at the teachers and one year came back after his summer holidays proudly wearing a 'Fuck Off' T-shirt.

The young Luigi usually took extended holidays, not returning until well into the new term. He left school early and secured his first criminal conviction at fourteen years of age, when he was fined £10 in the Children's Court for stealing. A week after his sixteenth birthday he was sent to prison for the first time. He was sentenced to ten months in St Patrick's Institution, again for stealing.

He was sent back to St Pat's five times over the next four years for fighting, robbing, trespassing, and breaking and entering. He served sentences ranging from twelve months to two years. At twenty he graduated to Mountjoy, after he was convicted of burglary in the Circuit Criminal Court. He was sentenced to three years' imprisonment but was out in less than a year and a half. It was then he started selling heroin for Tony. The last time he had been involved in his father's business he was eleven years of age.

The first time Luigi was charged with a drug offence was that afternoon in June 1995 he was caught selling from the Dominick Street flat. Luigi was a heroin addict. He earned what he needed by selling for his father. Bail was set in the District Court at Luigi's own bond of £500 and an independent surety of £5,000. Four months later there was a hearing, in most cases a formality, so the court could approve the person prepared to go bail for him. The Divisional Drug Unit had other ideas.

On 18 October a young woman entered the witness box in the Dublin District Court number 4 and said she was prepared to go bail for Luigi Felloni. Tony was in court for the hearing. The woman said her name was Natasha Harte and that she lived at 171 Lower Dorset Street flats. She presented an AIB deposit book with a balance of £5,889.21, more than enough to cover Luigi's bail. The Divisional Drug Unit was not happy.

Garda Peter Oates put a series of questions to 'Natasha Harte', ostensibly to ascertain whether she had ever been disqualified as a bailsperson or whether she had already pledged the money in the account to cover another person's bail. The woman became hesitant and Tony could see she was wavering. He left the court before the final question. Peter Oates looked her straight in the eyes and asked her, 'Who are you?'

There was silence in court before the woman broke down crying. She admitted that her name was in fact Natasha Butler and she lived at 109 Pinebrook Grove in Artane. Defence counsel was on its feet straight away explaining to the court that it had had no knowledge the woman in the dock was not who she had claimed to be. The judge was furious. Natasha Butler was sent to prison for two days for contempt of court.

When the real Natasha Harte was interviewed by Gardaí she told them the book was hers but she had not seen it for a couple of months. However, the balance on the book when it was lost was nil. Forged entries had been made to bring the balance to over £5,000. The money was never in the account in the first place. When the Gardaí questioned Natasha Butler, she admitted she had been given the book by Tony Felloni and told to go bail for his son as Natasha Harte.

Unfortunately for Natasha, the Divisional Drug Unit now had a policy of investigating every person who was prepared to go bail for the Fellonis. They also opposed any attempt by the family to secure bail by means of a cash lodgment. It is more difficult for drug dealers to put forward people with an independent surety because they know those people can be questioned about their finances in court. It is much safer and easier for them if the judge allows them bail by means of a cash lodgment, either in court or at the jail. Drug dealers have access to ready cash and no questions are asked about the money.

The failed scam did not prevent the family from applying for bail again and this time Luigi succeeded in getting out of jail. He immediately went back to work for Tony. He bought heroin in England, and arranged to have it brought into Ireland. He sold it from the flat, and also from Buckingham Street, Dorset Street and in front of the church in Seán MacDermott Street. It was time for the Drug Unit to pay another visit to Luigi.

On 11 January 1996 the flat in Dominick Street was raided again. This time Luigi and 'Dan Joe' were the only two there. 'No drugs here, there's no drugs here,' the two of them sang in unison as the Gardaí swarmed into the living room. 'Dan Joe' read the warrant before being taken into the bathroom to be searched. Luigi didn't bother. 'No drugs here,' he sang again to the Garda searching him. He changed his tune when a batch of heroin fell out of his Y-fronts.

Standing there red-faced in his underpants, Luigi Felloni admitted everything. 'It's gear,' he said. 'By that I mean heroin. There's six half-grams in it. I take full responsibility for it. I want to say that no one knew what I had. It's worth about £300 and I was going to sell it.' The search also turned up the predictable 'bureau de change' of Irish and foreign currency in the upstairs bedroom. There was over £180 sterling, £725 punts, 211,000 pesetas, US$17, and a £50 note, which appeared to be fake.[5] A number of white plastic bags were taken away for analysis, and once again Luigi was charged with possession of heroin and possession for supply. He was later released again on bail.

The day after his father was jailed for twenty years, Luigi was due in the same court before the same judge for sentencing. He never turned up, in spite of the fact that he had been seen around the north city a few days before. The prosecuting Garda, Danny Rice, said he had been warned his case was due up for Friday, 21 June. Judge Cyril Kelly issued a bench warrant for his arrest and five days later Luigi was brought before him. He was remanded in custody until his sentence hearing on 10 October.

Luigi pleaded guilty not only to the offences he was charged with after the raids on the flat, but to possession at Dublin Airport of over £20,000 worth of heroin for supply. The heroin had been taken from one of the family's mules more than a year before. Luigi's lawyer claimed he had begun to attend Narcotics Anonymous and was getting counselling at Coolmine Therapeutic Centre. Niall Durnin said that Luigi hoped to go there some time in the future, having had a complete change of heart since going into custody. He was now, his lawyer told the court, trying to deal with his heroin addiction. Tony Felloni, he said, dominated his son and recruited him into the drug trade; Luigi, the court heard, was afraid of his father and made no money from drugs.

The judge read the probation report and ordered that Luigi be kept away from his father in a separate prison: 'I see no point in putting him in prison with his father and just throwing away the key.' He blamed Tony Felloni for the fact that his son was before him at all because, he said, Felloni introduced Luigi to heroin when he was only fourteen years of age. 'He is', he went on, 'a victim of a violent childhood in a dysfunctional criminal family.' He jailed Luigi for six years, but ordered that he be transferred to Coolmine in March 2000 after he had served three and a half years.

Regina, on the other hand, continued to use heroin in prison right up to her sentence hearing. She tested positive for opiates in one test and was unable to provide samples for testing on two other occasions. The hearing on 16 December 1996 was adjourned for a day because of this. The judge wanted another test carried out on her because he wanted to know whether or not she was still using drugs in prison. Regina refused to be tested before returning to court the next day.

She claimed in her defence that Tony had beaten her up, forced her to do what he wanted and turned her into a drug addict. The judge accepted that Tony might have originally forced her into drug dealing. She may come from 'an unenviable background', he said, 'but now this child is an adult. She has reached the age of full responsibility.' The Gardaí also believed she was responsible enough to run her own heroin operation from the flat at Hollybank Road. In spite of her denials, Regina Felloni was sent to prison for six years and nine months on 17 December 1996, three days before her twenty-first birthday. All three Fellonis had been jailed in the same court by the same judge.

Perhaps the most significant aspect of the case was the fact that the court noticed just how much money this young, unemployed drug addict was banking—she had at least £50,000 in one account. Judge Cyril Kelly criticised banks and building societies for facilitating heroin dealing by ignoring obvious realities. He was also highly critical of the state, which appeared to be benefiting from the money. 'It seems extraordinary that the state is taking tax back for monies lodged in these accounts from what clearly may be illegal money— DIRT tax, withholding tax—in any event. DIRT may probably be the appropriate word.' The £50,000, however, turned out to be only the tip of the iceberg. The Fellonis had a lot more accounts and a lot more money.

---

1. A quarter-ounce of heroin is about seven grams. Regina sold them for £550 but they were worth more than five times cost price when they were cut down. Seven grams at 40 per cent purity meant around fourteen grams at street purity of 20 per cent. Fixes of 20 per cent purity sold for at least £20. Fourteen grams at between ten and fifteen Qs a gram would make a minimum of 140 £20 street deals. The pusher stood to make £2,800.

2. Transcript of interview with Regina Felloni at Store Street Garda Station. 11.30 p.m., 2 April 1996.

Q. Did you bring the heroin into the flat, Regina?

A. Yeah, I brought it in.

Q. When?

A. About two months ago.

Q. How much heroin is in the jars?

A. I don't know, to tell the truth.

Q. How much was there originally?

A. I don't know.

Q. Did you make the smaller packs? The quarter-ounces?

A. Yeah.

Q. Why had you surgical gloves in the flat, Regina?

A. To keep me fingerprints off the stuff.

Q. How long have you been selling heroin?

A. About the last four months.

Q. Why?

A. Because I'm under pressure and I owe money and it's the only way I could get it or they'd stab me.

Q. Do you want to say who they are?

A. No, I better not. I'd only make it worse for myself.

Q. Is there anything else you'd like to tell us?

A. I was under pressure. I owe a chap money and you don't mess with this chap. I had to sell gear for him or me family'd be involved. The chap is in prison at the moment. I have fellas watching me. I can't say any more.

Q. Do you want to say anything else?

A. No.

3. A half a gram, four or five street deals depending on the heroin purity.

4. Money seized in raid on 73 Lower Dominick Street, 22 June 1995

a. IR£2,188 found in a drawer

b. IR£3,030 found in the bedroom

c. IR£20 found in a cabinet

d. £195 sterling found in a cabinet

e. £1,140 sterling found in an envelope in a drawer

f. £2,000 in traveller's cheques

TOTAL £8,573 in Irish and sterling cash and traveller's cheques

5. Money seized in raid on 73 Lower Dominick Street, 11 January 1996

a. IR£725

b. £189.80 sterling

c. US$17

d. 46,000 pesetas (cash)

e. 165,000 pesetas in traveller's cheques

f. £50 note (fake)

All found in an upstairs bedroom

TOTAL £2,022.38: £914.80 in Irish and sterling, pesetas worth £1,097.58 and US dollars worth £10 (on 11 January 1996)

14 *Pawns and Corpses 1994–98*

Josephine Heary and Luigi Felloni took a taxi to Dublin Airport on Monday morning, 22 May 1995. Josephine was seventeen years of age. She was living in a flat in Ballymun and was five months pregnant at the time. On their way out to the airport Luigi handed her a bundle of cash, Irish money, and told her to change it into sterling. 'You're a tenner short of £2,500,' the woman at the Bureau de Change told her. She had £40 of her own and she changed that too. The couple flew to London just after midday.

Josephine Heary had met Tony Felloni for the first time a month before. She was out for a drink with a friend in the Parnell Mooney in Dublin city centre when Tony came up to them. Her friend knew him and she introduced him to Josephine. Tony joined them for a while, then made his excuses and left.

'He's a big drugs dealer,' her friend whispered as he walked away, 'and he's looking for girls to bring gear in from England for him.' Josephine did not believe her at first. Tony Felloni looked so old and he never said a word about drugs. 'It's easy money,' the girl insisted. 'There's no way you'll ever get caught.'

A few days later Josephine bumped into Tony again. He chatted away to her. 'When's your baby due?' he asked. 'What do you do for a living?' He was, she remembered, all charm; 'normal' and 'nice'. It wasn't until the third or fourth time she met him that he spoke to her about his drug business. He asked if she would be interested in bringing drugs in from England. 'There's good money in it for you,' he told her. 'I'll give you £300 when you bring them back to me.'

He offered her an incentive-linked system of payment, promising her £100 for every package she could carry. Josephine Heary was pregnant and broke. Tony Felloni was offering her a chance to make 'easy money'. The more heroin she could bring in, the more money she could take home. She could risk carrying the drugs in her clothes if she liked, but Tony said there was less chance of her getting caught if she concealed the drugs internally. Heary was hooked.

Two weeks later Tony met her again. He wrote down his telephone number on a small piece of paper and gave it to her. 'If you need anything,' he said, 'just ring, but whatever you do, don't carry my number around with you.' After that, any time he met her he was always smooth, soothing and reassuring: 'You have my phone number if you need anything. No matter how big or small, just ring me.' When she asked him what she would do if she got caught, he ignored the question and fobbed her off. 'Don't be talking about that, you won't get caught,' he replied. 'Just don't tell anyone and you won't get caught.'

On Sunday, 21 May, Tony called up to Josephine Heary's flat. It was 6.00 p.m. 'Come on with me to Dublin Airport,' he said to her. 'You're going to London with Luigi tomorrow to get me some drugs.' Tony told Josephine there would be three packets to take back and she would be paid £100 for each of them. She would carry the drugs, he told her. Luigi would make the arrangements and watch her back. Tony didn't tell her she'd be bringing back heroin and Josephine didn't ask.

He dropped her off outside the airport terminal, gave her £200 and told her to go in and buy an Aer Lingus return ticket. She would be flying out at twelve fifteen and coming back at ten past ten that night. Josephine paid £128 for the ticket and was told she could collect it the next day. Tony drove her home, told her Luigi would call for her the following morning and not to say anything about this to anyone. She had to give him back the £72 change.

Josephine Heary had never met Luigi Felloni until he picked her up in the taxi. When they got to the airport they followed Tony's orders. They split up, they didn't speak to each other and they didn't sit near each other either in the terminal or on the plane.

They met up again in London at around 1.30 p.m. and took the tube to King's Cross Station. After a twenty-minute walk they stopped at the door of a house which Luigi said belonged to a friend of his. He took about £1,000 of the £2,500 she had changed into sterling at the airport and told her to mind the rest. Josephine went into the house while he disappeared to buy the heroin.

Luigi was gone for around an hour. Josephine spent the time watching television with his friend. When he came back, she recalls, he was all in a fuss. He went into a room and wrapped the heroin into two small packets, which he put into condoms. He gave them to Josephine, telling her to hurry as they had to catch the train to the airport. Josephine went into the toilet and put the two packets into her vagina. They took a taxi and train back to Heathrow.

Their orders for the return journey were the same as the way out. They checked in at different times, they sat in different seats on the plane and they did not speak to each other throughout the flight. They were supposed to get a taxi together when they got off the plane. Instead they made the journey into the centre of Dublin handcuffed in the back of a squad car. Customs officers and Gardaí met them when the plane landed.

Josephine was stopped and searched by Customs officers and the money Luigi had told her to mind, £1,300 sterling, was found in her case. They also found the piece of paper that Tony had given her with his phone number. If she rang it now he wouldn't be much help. She was taken to a room where she handed over the two condoms. There was over sixty grams of high-quality heroin in them, 63 per cent pure, with an estimated street value of over £20,000.[1]

When he was stopped at the airport, Luigi said he was coming back from London after visiting Mario in Highdown Prison in Surrey. No, he said, he didn't know Josephine Heary even though he had walked through the terminal with her. His father's name was Anthony, not Tony, and no, he didn't know his own home phone number. 'There's no number on the phone. I'm no good with numbers,' he said. But his story didn't really stand up and both he and Josephine Heary were arrested and taken away.

When Tony heard his son had been taken into custody he went down to Store Street Garda Station and demanded to see him. He had no faith in Luigi's ability to withstand a tricky question and answer session and was furious when he heard he'd said anything at all. There were to be no more stupid yarns. Tony made sure before he left the station that from then on Luigi would keep his mouth shut. His son was to act the way he and the others had been trained to act.

After that Luigi either stayed totally silent or responded to questions with 'Nothing to say.' But by then it was too late. He was still convicted of trafficking in heroin.

Luigi had already claimed that the Fellonis were able to put nine couriers with over twenty-nine ounces of heroin through Dublin Airport on one day alone. He said he paid £1,000 an ounce for good-quality heroin in England. If true—and Gardaí don't know whether it is or not—it is an indication of the scale of Tony Felloni's operation. Those twenty-nine ounces could have been sold off on the Dublin market for three times the cost, giving Tony Felloni a profit of £50,000 in one day.[2]

On another occasion, Luigi boasted, he had gone to London to buy heroin, was £5,000 short of the asking price and had given the supplier six pistols to make up the difference. This claim was treated with a lot more scepticism. The Fellonis were never known to handle guns. Only one of them, Justin, was ever convicted of a firearms offence, and that was over twenty years before. Justin, who died in 1996, never worked in his brother's drug business.

Tony hand-picked his drug mules and couriers. He preferred to use mules because they were prepared to carry drugs internally, in spite of the health risks, and so had a better chance of getting past Customs and Gardaí. He usually only sent them out and back one at a time, so that he could keep track of how much heroin was coming in. He had been manipulating vulnerable and naive young women for over thirty years, and he knew when to charm them and when to bully them.

Josephine Heary was typical of the type of woman he employed. She was young, impressionable, 'an innocent abroad'. She lived in a Corporation flat in Ballymun and she had no job or other source of income, being too young for state benefits. When Tony met her she was worried about how she was going to provide for her unborn baby. It was the baby that in the end saved her from a lengthy prison sentence.

Josephine Heary was sentenced to three years for importing heroin for Tony Felloni, but the judge was lenient and ruled she should spend only the first three months in prison. 'She had to be punished,' Judge Cyril Kelly said. 'She should have known the damage caused by drugs and that her child was to be brought up in a situation where she was introducing them; but it would not benefit the state to leave her baby motherless.'

Heary had been particularly useful for Tony's purposes because she had never been in trouble before in her life. She had no previous convictions and therefore was not known to the Gardaí. It was difficult to single out people like her as drug couriers among the thousands of transit passengers every day. Gardaí or Customs officers had no reason to stop her. She was ideal for 'King Scum's' heroin importation operation, as were Stewart Lynch, Paula Lynch and Emma Mooney.

Emma Mooney was twenty-one years of age when she was jailed for four years. A chronic heroin addict, she needed £100 a day to feed her habit. She also needed money to bail her boyfriend out of jail. On 31 January 1995 a man approached her on Seán MacDermott Street in the north inner city. He offered her £300 to bring in heroin from Liverpool. Tony Felloni had criminal connections and business interests on Merseyside as well as in London. Mooney agreed. She had made drug runs for other dealers before.

The next day she flew to Liverpool, collected the heroin in the city, hid the packages inside her and flew back to Dublin that evening. She didn't realise she was being watched and she was arrested at the airport as part of an operation set up to target another north Dublin criminal gang. She was carrying £80,000 worth of Tony Felloni's heroin. She took the rap and never told the Gardaí who the man she met was. She didn't have to, they already knew.

Emma Mooney completely changed in prison. She came off heroin and went back to school. After a year and a half her sentence was reviewed and she convinced the judge she had been rehabilitated. She had changed from a desperate junkie to a confident, educated and attractive young woman. Determined to make something of her life, she was studying to become a gym instructor. Emma Mooney was freed on probation to live with her mother. On 15 January 1998 she walked out of Mountjoy Jail, leaving behind Tony Felloni's other victims, his sons, his daughters, his clients and his couriers.

One of those couriers, Paula Lynch, was caught during Operation Pizza. Like the other young girls, she was ideal fodder for Tony Felloni because of her background, her age and her addiction to heroin. Born and reared in Coolock on Dublin's north side, she first used drugs when she was twelve. She started smoking 'pot' before moving on to 'acid' (LSD) and ecstasy. She began hanging around with drug addicts in the north inner city and was smoking heroin at fourteen years of age. Two years later she was injecting and 'skin popping', the practice where addicts inject heroin into their muscles rather than their veins; the effect, however, is not as immediate. It was in these circumstances that she met Luigi Felloni and his father.

As Luigi's girlfriend, Paula Lynch was a frequent visitor to the Felloni family home in Dominick Street. Tony immediately spotted her potential as a heroin courier. He taught her how to handle drugs and told her how to behave during Garda interviews. 'Remember three words,' he told her, '"Nothing to say!"' Paula Lynch was often in the flat during the Operation Pizza raids.

In the spring of 1996 the Gardaí got a tip-off that the Fellonis had a clearing house for cutting and distributing drugs in Glasnevin, three miles north of the city centre. The top flat at 66 Botanic Road was put under surveillance and it wasn't long before addicts and dealers associated with the family were seen coming and going. The Gardaí watched the house for two weeks before moving in.

The top flat at number 66 was a labyrinth of doors in a small space. The front door opened into a small hallway. The door on the left led to a toilet and shower, the door on the right into the living room. In the living room there was another door on the left which led into the kitchen and one on the right which led into the bedroom.

There was nobody home when the Divisional Drug Unit raided the flat on 13 April 1996. The doors were closed, but both the light and the television in the living room had been left on. Whoever was living there hadn't gone far. There was a large number of plastic bags and a mobile phone on the shelf by the TV. The blazing fire completed the familiar picture of a heroin distribution den. Paula Lynch had rented the flat with another man three weeks earlier, at £85 a week. They were using it to cut and smoke heroin.

Just then the police radio crackled. The Gardaí inside were told that a man had gone in the main front door and was heading up the stairs. All three ran into the bedroom and closed the door behind them just in time to hear the front door open. There was the click of the door being locked after it was closed. The outside door was now secured. The man walked into the living room and locked that door behind him too. He had sealed off the entry route behind him, or so he thought, so he threw the keys down on the coffee table and relaxed. He 'got the shock of his life' when Seamie Boland and two other Gardaí walked in on him. He had never even thought of locking the bedroom door.

Nineteen-year-old Stewart Lynch grew up in Blessington Street, in Phibsborough in Dublin. He came from a good home but fell in with a bad crowd when he met up with the Fellonis. He ended up with a heroin habit that cost him £100 a day. It was then that the convictions started to build up—one for malicious damage, another one for drugs, for which he was bound over to the peace for two years. His family didn't even know he was a drug addict until the night he was arrested in the Botanic Road flat.

Stewart found himself working for the Fellonis to pay for his drug habit. He was the runner, the courier and the bottom of the pile. For delivering batches of heroin around the city, he was paid two, maybe three street deals, £40 or £50 worth, only half of what he needed to keep him going for the day. He was a necessary link in the distribution chain but he, like the others, was dispensable. His value to the Fellonis lay in the fact that he wasn't known to the Gardaí before they arrested him.

Stewart was handcuffed and put sitting on the sofa. There was a bag of heroin with 115 street deals on the coffee table in front of him. Each deal was made from a small tied corner of a small plastic bag. The brown powder in each one was high-quality heroin, 56 per cent pure.[3] He had just begun to divide it up when he was caught. Stewart didn't own the heroin nor did he live in the flat. The man who did arrived five minutes later. The woman with him gave her name as Gráinne Errity. Paula Lynch gave a false name and a false date of birth.

Paula Lynch and the other man, 'the tenant', were arrested at the main door and brought upstairs as the flat was being searched. Two wooden panels beneath the cooker were unscrewed and a digital scales was found hidden there, along with rolls of money and cash in bags. There was almost £1,000 in Irish and £170 sterling.

The 'tenant' was shown a pair of surgical gloves and asked what they were for.

'I was going to get streaks in my hair,' he replied.

Two McDonald's teaspoons were found in the kitchen, another one was picked up off the mantelpiece.

'What do you use them for?' he was asked.

'Stirring tea.'

'What do you use the plastic bags for?'

'Meats,' he said, 'cold meats.'

Also found in the flat was a book of evidence for the drug trafficking case against Luigi Felloni and Josephine Heary. The file contained Garda and witness statements, transcripts of interviews, and copies of search warrants. There were also separate copies of High Court documents relating to the freezing of all Tony's, Luigi's and Regina's assets. The order had been made only a week before. The file was seized and all three people, the tenant, Stewart Lynch and 'Gráinne Errity', were arrested and taken to Store Street Garda Station.

Down at the station things got a little more complicated. Paula Lynch finally admitted who she was but she was nervous and appeared to be worried about something. She told the Gardaí she was pregnant, but they suspected she was hiding heroin internally. They had no power to carry out an internal search. They kept telling the sixteen-year-old how dangerous this was. They spoke to her mother, who spoke to her, and only after persistent pleading did Paula finally agree to be examined by a doctor. He delivered, not a baby, but two round white plastic packs of heroin from her vagina. Each one weighed around an ounce; together they had a street value of around £14,000.

The doctor could see there was still a package inside her but neither he nor the Gardaí were prepared to take any more chances. The teenage heroin addict was taken to the Rotunda Hospital, where the third bag was removed from her vagina. It contained twenty-seven grams of 54 per cent pure heroin. If there had been the slightest leak from any of the packages, Paula Lynch would have died.

The following month she was released on bail after she pleaded guilty to having the heroin for supply. She was ordered to stay away from Luigi and to live with her mother while awaiting sentence. But Paula decided she knew best. She left school and began staying out all night. Then after just three days she stopped her drug treatment at the Coolmine centre and started taking drugs again. Her urine samples proved positive on a number of occasions, and the month before her sentence hearing she turned up to give urine only twice.

Paula Lynch was jailed for four and a half years for carrying over £16,000 worth of heroin for the Fellonis.[4] The judge described her as 'a very silly young woman who had rebuffed the chances given to her by the court earlier this year. By acting as a courier for a major drugs player, he said, she was helping to spread her problem to other young people, with the devastating effects we are all too aware of. She is vulnerable and must be put into custody. She will now spend the next two Christmases in detention.'

Stewart Lynch, no relation to Paula, also admitted his role as the delivery boy in the Fellonis' business, but that was where the similarity with Paula ended. Stewart was not the owner of the heroin and had never made any money from dealing for the Fellonis. They had been feeding his addiction and they made that addiction work for them. Lynch pleaded guilty to possession with intent to supply and was granted bail until his trial. It was to be another two years before the case came to court.

In the meantime his aunt managed to get him a place on a drug rehabilitation programme in Cuan Mhuire in Co. Kildare. He entered in September of 1996 and didn't come out until four months later. He then went on another drug programme at Coolmine, and took counselling sessions at Teach Mhuire in Co. Wicklow. He has been drug-free ever since and gives regular urine samples to prove it.

Stewart Lynch looked nervous and remorseful as he stood six foot tall, dressed entirely in black, at the Dublin Circuit Criminal Court on 26 February 1998. He was the last of the Felloni drug couriers to be sentenced. His attitude had completely changed since his arrest. He had used the intervening period to straighten out his life and said he would never get involved in anything like drugs again.

Lynch was given a five-year suspended sentence and he walked out of court 29 a free man. His father, grandfather and aunt thanked the lawyers and the Gardaí outside. Stewart Lynch asked for a chance and he got one.

So too did Paula Lynch, who spent two years in prison and changed from an arrogant teenager to an educated young woman. She came off drugs in Mountjoy; forty-seven urinalyses since January 1997 confirmed that, every one of them was clean. She got a very good result in Leaving Certificate English when she sat the exam in prison, and took home economics the following year. Paula now had a plan for her future; she had left her past and her previous boyfriend behind. The remainder of her sentence was suspended on April Fool's Day 1998.

There won't be a second chance for the Connington children. Every second Sunday, their parents, Frankie and Mary Connington, leave their Corporation flat in Dominick Street just across the road from where Tony Felloni lived. They walk the hundred or so yards to the junction with Parnell Street, turn left and walk along it to the bus stop on the far side of O'Connell Street. They have to take it slowly though. Frankie is sixty-two, Mary is sixty-four and suffers from high blood pressure and arthritis. But this is a pilgrimage they have to make.

The 40 bus goes on to Finglas but the Conningtons get off on the Old Finglas Road, just past St Vincent's, the Christian Brothers' school. As they walk across the road, the painful memories begin to flood back. They make their way to the garden of remembrance in Glasnevin Cemetery to pray for four of their five children, all heroin addicts, all dead. Elizabeth, Frankie, Roderick, Leslie—none of them reached the age of thirty-five.

'Look at the two of us here like two old fools, we're on our own now. Four children dead, one over in England,' Frankie says. 'I support her and she supports me, we've only got each other to keep us going. We've lost the lot because of drugs.' Mary puts a single red rose at the letters in stone, Leslie Connington, 4.3.1995, Francis Connington 14.7.93. She does this every time she visits the garden.

All four followed the same path that leads inexorably from heroin addiction to crime to prison to HIV and Aids; it is the path that almost always ends in premature death. 'I couldn't talk to them, they wouldn't listen,' Mary says. 'One by one the drugs took them away.'

The family moved into a Corporation flat in Dominick Street eighteen years ago. Their only daughter, Elizabeth, was on heroin within a year. It was the mood swings that first alerted Mary to the changes in her. She then began asking her mother for money for clothes but she never came back with any new ones. When Mary told her husband of her suspicions, he told her she must be imagining things.

'What are you doing, Elizabeth?' Mary asked her one day. 'What's going on?'

'You know, Ma, it's something I can't do without.'

Elizabeth was the first to die, in the autumn of 1992. Serving a sentence for addiction-induced robbery, one evening she was taken from Mountjoy Jail with a blood clot in her leg. There were complications, however; Mary thinks the clot travelled up to her heart. Elizabeth died in Beaumont Hospital. She was twenty-eight years old. She spent the last eleven years of her life miserably, pathetically and uncontrollably addicted to heroin.

Over the next two and a half years Mary and Frank buried three more of their children. Roderick contracted HIV and began to wither away. His brother Alex, who was working in England, came over and brought him back there with him to get some treatment. Seven months after his sister passed away, Roddy died in London of an Aids-related illness. It was May 1993. He was cremated and his ashes were sent back to his parents in Dublin. He was thirty years old. His parents say he spent over £12,000 on heroin.

Mary thought her oldest son, Frankie junior, had escaped. He was married and living with his wife and three children in Coolock. But when his marriage fell apart, so did his life. When he turned on to heroin it took his life. Like his brother before him, he died in England. He overdosed on a cocktail of pills, drink and methadone.

It was with a depressing sense of inevitability that the Conningtons realised their youngest son, Leslie, could also die young. 'What in the name of God is going on here?' his mother said to him. He too was a chronic heroin addict; he too had the HIV virus. He was attacking people and robbing shops and petrol stations to get the money to feed his habit. He, like the others, didn't have to go far from his home in Dominick Street flats to buy his heroin. Everyone knew the Fellonis were dealing.

Mary remembers the day he died. 'He wasn't out of the house for long. I used to watch him going over there to get his gear. You were at work, Frankie,' she says to her husband. He has worked as a welder for more than twenty years. Neither of them has ever been in trouble in their lives and they're still searching for an explanation as to why their children died. 'Why did I lose so much, because I loved them?' Mary still finds it difficult to talk about Leslie's death over three years ago. At twenty-seven years of age he overdosed in his own home. It was she who found him dead in the bedroom.

'Give us a try at that to see what it does,' Jem Dixon said to his brother. He was watching Noel and a friend inject heroin into their veins. Little did he know that fifteen years later, he and five of his immediate family would be dead because of it. 'I was hooked almost immediately,' he said.[5] He continued to use heroin right up to his death.

Jem Dixon passed away on Christmas Eve 1995. He was a 42-year-old heroin addict who died from an Aids-related illness, a shell of the man he once was. Half of one of his legs was amputated after he injected into the wrong vein with a dirty needle. Gangrene set in. He also lost his index finger from using dirty needles. Resigned to dying young, he was one of four Dixons in a family of eight to die prematurely.

His sister Ellen was also a heroin addict. She died three years earlier, also from an Aids-related illness. Her husband, Thomas, is dead too, while their two children, Thomas and Linda, went on heroin in their teens. The following month Ellen and Jem's brother Michael 'Snake' Dixon died from an Aids-related illness. He was thirty-one years old. His wife, June Maleady, also died of an overdose, aged twenty-five. Their two-year-old child was found lying in her arms. Four months after Michael, Noel Dixon, thirty-two years old, died after being hit on the head with a hammer in a row over drugs.

The Dixons and the Conningtons are among hundreds of parents who have lost their children to heroin in Dublin. The Eastern Health Board estimates there are at least 10,000 people on heroin in Dublin and the surrounding area. As to many parents of those addicts, drug addiction remains a mystery to the Conningtons.

'I often asked Elizabeth what it's like to be on drugs. "Ma," she said, "you're in a different world." Well, my only daughter is in a different world today.'

The couple sit alone in their three-bedroom Dominick Street flat. The pictures of their dead children are framed around them on the living room walls. The Conningtons are still grieving. 'We're still going through it, you never forget.' Their only surviving son, Alex, is still living in England. He had left the country after serving a seven-year sentence for burning down a prison officer's home.

When asked about Tony Felloni, the Conningtons don't want to get involved. They know he sold heroin to some of their children but they also know he wasn't the only one. 'I've no love for him, or any of the drug pushers. They're killing children, that's all they're doing. Twenty years is not enough for any of them.'

The state cannot save their children now, but the Conningtons do believe it should remove the financial incentives for criminals to deal drugs. 'All the money they made, all their millions, I want to see it all taken off them,' Frankie Connington says. As far as Tony Felloni is concerned, 'The house, the lot he shouldn't be left with a penny.'

1. Sixty grams of heroin at 63 per cent pure diluted would give a minimum of 120 grams of street-level heroin. This would make a minimum of 1,200 Qs, which would sell at between £10 and £20 each. Twelve hundred £20 street deals would give the haul a street value of £24,000. With the glut of heroin on the streets at the time the estimate was reduced to £20,000 to allow for some of it to be sold off at the cheaper rate.

2. Tony Felloni could sell the heroin to other Dublin suppliers for around £3,000 an ounce, giving him a total of £87,000. If you take away his initial cost of £29,000 and £8,000 for taxis, flights and other courier expenses, he was still left with a profit of £50,000.

A supplier who bought an ounce of heroin off Tony Felloni for £3,000 still stood to make a lot of money. One ounce was about twenty-eight grams, cut down made about fifty-six grams, and each gram made between ten and fifteen street deals or Qs. The minimum of 560 Qs would sell at between £10 and £20 each. Even if all were sold at the cheapest rate of £10, the supplier would almost double his money at £5,600 making a profit of £2,600. It was more likely he made a lot more.

3. Even though this heroin was 56 per cent pure Stewart Lynch had already started dividing it up into street deals, ready for sale. If he had known it was of such high quality, he could have cut it down to half the purity and doubled his profits, but he had no way of knowing. Lynch and other pusher addicts would have had no access to laboratory facilities. The only way he could test it would be to give it to a junkie who would bang it up and tell him it was good. But good heroin starts at over 20 per cent. A dealer cannot distinguish between 20 per cent pure and 56 per cent pure just because a junkie tells him it is good or indeed it's very good. The only thing a junkie can tell him for certain is that it is not muck.

4. The two bags taken out of Paula Lynch in the station contained 27.59 grams and 27.605 grams respectively. The bag taken out of her in hospital contained 27.253 grams. She therefore had a total of 82.448 grams of 54 per cent pure heroin concealed in her vagina. At between ten and fifteen Qs a gram, the haul was worth at least 824 street deals at £20 each, giving a total value of £16,480.

The Gardaí valued the haul at between £15,000 and £20,000. By rights they should have doubled that value because at 54 per cent pure the heroin could have been cut. However, because Paula Lynch was arrested at the same time as Stewart Lynch and his 56 per cent heroin was valued without having been cut down, the Divisional Drug Unit thought it was only fair to do the same. Besides they treated both addicts leniently in view of their ages, their levels of addiction and the fact that they were at the bottom end of the distribution chain.

5. In an interview with Paul Williams in the *Sunday World*.

15 *Fellonious Assets*
1976–97

On 13 September 1996 Sergeant John O'Driscoll walked into the Irish Permanent Building Society at 56 St Stephen's Green, one of the most prestigious business addresses in Dublin. There he met one of the managers, Mr David Kelly, and served him with a section 23 order under the 1994 Criminal Justice Act. The financial records of a Mr Anthony Carroll were handed over to him. Anthony Carroll's money was really that of the convicted heroin dealer Tony Felloni. John O'Driscoll had in his hands documentary evidence that the Fellonis had money. Armed with pen, paper and a calculator, he set out to establish just how much.

One of the first bank accounts the Fellonis opened was at the Bank of Ireland in Cavendish Row in Dublin in Regina's name, on 12 January 1976. It has not been established definitively who actually opened the account but it definitely wasn't Regina Felloni; she was only three weeks old at the time. Between 1977 and 1993 there were just six transactions on the account, but over the next three years it became 'extremely active'. By then Regina was eighteen years old and had started selling heroin with her father. Both of them used the account. Three years later when they were both sent to prison there was nearly £70,000 in the Bank of Ireland account.[1]

Tony Felloni opened an account in his own name in the Irish Permanent Building Society in 1984. He arrived back in Ireland in March of that year after serving his sentence in Britain for conspiracy to supply heroin. He had no work, he hadn't had a job for over twenty years and he had no visible means of support. Nevertheless he began putting money in the building society account, on average once a fortnight. By the end of 1984 he had made twenty-five lodgments.

197

A year and a half later his first Dublin heroin operation was busted and Felloni was sent to prison for ten years. While he was in jail, however, the money continued to go into his account. There were a number of lodgments in 1988, 1989 and 1991. By the end of 1992 there was over £153,000 in the Irish Permanent account.[2]

Two weeks later Felloni was let out of Mountjoy on temporary release. On 5 March 1993 he granted power of attorney in respect of the account to a solicitor, W. & E.T. Bradshaw. He gave his address as 11 Palmerston Place in spite of the fact that the house had been sold three years earlier.

Between January and July of 1993, while Tony was acclimatising himself once again to life on the outside, preparing for his release from prison, there was a series of withdrawals from the Irish Permanent account. All the money was eventually taken out, the final £51,000 on 13 July. This was the last recorded transaction on that building society account. Two days later, with remission for good behaviour, Tony was fully released from Mountjoy. He still had his own Allied Irish Banks account and he also had access to other accounts in his children's names.

Regina had three more accounts in addition to the one that she used with her father. She had a building society account with the ICS on Westmoreland Street in Dublin, which she opened on 6 January 1994. Over the next two and a half years more than fifty-six lodgments were made to the account. Some were in sterling, others were in very small amounts. Regina sometimes put coins into the bank, but 'look after the pennies and the pounds will look after themselves'; within two years there was over £18,500 in the ICS account. No money was ever withdrawn.[1]

Her second bank account was in the AIB on Upper O'Connell Street in Dublin. It was opened on 11 July in 1994. Within three years there was over £24,000 in this account. Regina also opened a Post Office savings account with a deposit of over £620 on 23 November 1995. She made three more lodgments to that account, bringing the total to over £1,620.[1]

Luigi was nowhere near as wealthy as his father or sister. He had less than £1,000 in an Irish Permanent Building Society account in Liffey Street, and just over £200 in the Bank of Ireland on Cavendish

Row, where Regina's account was opened twenty years before. He was also awarded over £2,000 arising out of a road traffic accident claim.[3]

Between them, these three Fellonis had eight bank, building society and post office accounts in Ireland. All were located within a mile of each other in Dublin city centre, convenient to the north inner city, where the family sold heroin. At one stage, Tony had deposits of at least £153,000 with a further £10,000 in cash. Regina had over £113,000 in four separate accounts and her father also used at least one of them.

The Gardaí also discovered substantial amounts of money when they raided the Fellonis' houses and flats over the years. The Store Street Drug Unit found over £1,000 cash in Irish and sterling in Palmerston Place in 1986. The national and the divisional Drug Units found over £10,000 cash in Irish and sterling when they targeted Tony from 1994 to 1996. 'From whence does he get the £4,922.74, the £4,990, the £2,240 sterling?' the judge at Tony's trial wondered aloud. 'He is unemployed, he has never worked, has had a variety of cars and has not lived an ostentatious lifestyle.'

When Luigi was arrested twice in the Dominick Street flat, a total of nearly £7,500 was found in cash, £2,000 in traveller's cheques along with 211,000 pesetas and US$17. When Regina was charged, over £1,000 was found in the flat at Hollybank Road and another £975 in Finglas. Over £1,100 in Irish and sterling was also found in the clearing house at Botanic Road. The Fellonis, as John O'Driscoll swore in an affidavit, 'handled enormous sums' when they were selling drugs.[4]

The Fellonis also had considerable assets. Nearly two weeks before Christmas 1995, they bought a house at Mellowes Road in Finglas for £46,500 cash. Regina told the Gardaí that she and her grandfather Ronaldo were the joint owners. When the Gardaí raided it they found a brand new £4,000 suite of furniture there, bought in Arnott's just the week before. Regina also owned a car, a Nissan Micra worth around £6,000.

Nobody knows where Tony, Regina and Luigi got all this money. The Gardaí believe it came from drug dealing but the Fellonis have strongly denied that. Although they were major drug dealers they may well have obtained wealth from other sources. It is still a mystery as to how the Fellonis accumulated so much wealth, but it's a mystery which is due to be settled when the court case continues in October 1998.

The north-central Divisional Drug Unit had identified considerable assets belonging to three unemployed heroin dealers at a time when a move to confiscate the assets of criminals was a relatively new approach in the fight against crime. It was only in the early part of the 1990s that some Irish politicians began to take the view that such a strategy would remove much of the incentive to get involved in criminal activity.

The principle of going after a criminal through his money is not new. In the 1920s the US government succeeded in jailing the Chicago gangster Al Capone after it examined his finances and convicted him of tax evasion. Successive governments here were slow to come around to the belief that senior Gardaí had held for years—that a criminal upon conviction should lose his ill-gotten gains along with his liberty. But all that changed irrevocably on 26 June 1996.

The murder of the crime journalist Veronica Guerin evoked a wave of unprecedented public outrage at perceived government unwillingness and inability to tackle the worsening crime problem. The men suspected of murdering her were part of a multi-million-pound criminal drugs gang which had been importing vast amounts of cannabis into the state for years.

The gang leader was a millionaire who lived in a country house in Co. Meath. He bought another house for his son, he owned three cars, he took holidays in the Caribbean and considered himself untouchable. His wife ran an equestrian centre and provided horses during shooting for the Tom Cruise film *Far and Away*. She strove for respectability by becoming part of the 'horsey set'. The other gang members drove luxury cars and lived in city centre apartments and comfortable suburban homes. New draconian laws were demanded. The rainbow coalition government acted swiftly.

The following month the Criminal Assets Bureau was set up with the aim of identifying and confiscating a criminal's wealth. The Act under which it was established allows the Bureau to get a High Court order to freeze for seven years the actual or suspected assets of a criminal or a suspected criminal. If the suspect cannot prove that their wealth was accrued by legitimate means, then it is taken from them and handed over to the state. The onus of proof is on the person targeted by the CAB, and those targeted do not even need to have a criminal conviction. If, for example, a person buys a house with a mixture of criminal and legitimate money, the CAB can still seize that house because it was part-purchased with the proceeds of crime.

This policy of 'seize and freeze' was a momentous development in Irish criminal justice history. It had a dramatic and immediate impact on organised crime here. The CAB began to operate on a kind of 'shoot first, ask questions later' basis. It froze millions of pounds worth of assets. It sent out tax bills and social welfare repayment demands for millions of pounds to Irish criminals at home and abroad. It confiscated and sold off houses, boats, cars, horses, anything it suspected was bought or acquired through money earned illegally.

The CAB, however, was not established until the last day of July of 1996, nearly six weeks after Tony Felloni was sent to jail. The north-central Drug Unit had by that time already taken steps to confiscate his money. In April of that year John O'Driscoll decided to proceed under the provisions of the 1994 Criminal Justice Act. This had never been done before. The move to seize Tony Felloni's assets inevitably drew in Regina and Luigi. The Gardaí hoped to bestow on the Fellonis the dubious honour of being the first people to lose their money under the Act.

The 1994 Criminal Justice Act was enacted to combat money laundering. It enables the state to pursue through the courts all money and property it believes has been acquired illegally, with the ultimate aim of confiscation. It is the courts that must decide how many of the assets have been procured illegally, and the state can move to seize only after the Gardaí have secured a conviction.

The process is therefore far more circuitous and complicated than if the CAB had gone after the Fellonis. The Bureau could simply have moved in, frozen all the assets, and sold off the Nissan Micra and the house in Finglas. John O'Driscoll had to prove in court his contention that the Fellonis earned their money selling drugs. Only then could he take any of it from them. If the CAB had been on the case it would have been the other way round. The Fellonis would have had to prove in court they didn't earn their money from selling heroin. Only then would they have been allowed to keep it. The Criminal Assets Bureau could also have moved on the Fellonis regardless of whether or not they were convicted in the courts.

Using the Criminal Justice Act was by far the more difficult option, and the one more likely to fail, but it was the only option John O'Driscoll had at the time. The Criminal Assets Bureau did not exist. After it had been established, however, O'Driscoll was able to co-operate with the Bureau and it was able to help him in his investigation to track down the money. Six months after the CAB was set up, Gardaí investigating the Fellonis' assets were able to carry out a search under the Criminal Assets Bureau Act. They found documents which confirmed that Regina had bought the house in Mellowes Road for £46,500 in cash.

It wasn't until Regina's arrest on 2 April 1996 that the Divisional Drug Unit could even begin to go after the Fellonis' money. The last of the three to be arrested, Regina, like her father and brother, had been caught red-handed. The Gardaí were confident of securing a conviction against her because when arrested she admitted the offence. They supplied the Director of Public Prosecutions with details, records, statements and evidence of transcripts. Eamon Barnes, the DPP, reviewed the evidence and was satisfied that the three Fellonis, Tony, Luigi and Regina, had all benefited to some extent from drug trafficking. He directed that an application be made to the High Court under section 24 of the Criminal Justice Act freezing all their realisable assets. Once the money was secured, the Gardaí would be ready to confiscate it after the sentence hearings.

The Gardaí had to move fast, though, because Tony had already started moving the money. He passed some of it on to Regina to bank for him after he was refused bail and kept in prison from January 1996. At that stage Regina had not been charged with a drugs offence, she was still free and Tony knew that John O'Driscoll could not apply for an order to freeze her assets. She could therefore look after both her own and her father's money. Three months later, however, Tony began to reassess his options. He had good reason to be worried after 2 April.

John O'Driscoll didn't give him long to ponder his dilemma. He went into the High Court two days later and swore that he believed the Fellonis had earned their money from selling heroin. 'My concern', he told the judge, 'is that these moneys will be moved or withdrawn from the accounts in which they are lodged at present.' The state asked the High Court to freeze the assets of all three Fellonis.

The Gardaí knew that Tony Felloni had been spreading the money around while still effectively retaining control of it. John O'Driscoll had confidential information that he had been talking about moving more of the money immediately after Regina's arrest. This was now a matter of urgency for the Gardaí. They had to freeze the assets—particularly the bank and building society accounts—before anyone could withdraw the money from them. If that happened, the Gardaí might never find it again. One phone call from Mountjoy Jail and Tony or Regina could have their money transferred out of the country.

None of the three Fellonis had been sentenced by April, but John O'Driscoll knew he had secured Tony's conviction because he had already pleaded guilty. Luigi and Regina had already admitted in custody to having heroin for supply. That was why O'Driscoll felt he could ask the court to freeze the money. But one of the first things the judge wanted to know from him was how he found out about the money in the first place.

'I have evidence that he has a belief in relation to Allied Irish Banks but I have no foundation for that,' Mr Justice Paul Carney said to the barrister for the state, Shane Murphy, in the High Court when the sergeant was still in the dock. 'Was he inspired with this knowledge or how did he come about it?' O'Driscoll told the judge he found documents relating to bank accounts, in particular an AIB account in Tony's name, during a search of 73 Lower Dominick Street. He said he also knew about Luigi and Regina's Bank of Ireland accounts. On 4 April 1996 Mr Justice Paul Carney issued the orders in the High Court freezing all Tony's, Regina's and Luigi's assets—realisable properties, money and accounts. Luigi was doubly unlucky. He had put £700 into his Irish Permanent account only the day before. Over the next eight months all three were convicted and sent to prison, one by one.

The Gardaí had identified assets totalling around £200,000, a figure that may appear relatively small for a family that sold vast amounts of heroin in Dublin over a ten-year period. But they had only identified them. They still had a long way to go to prove their claim that the assets were the proceeds of drug dealing. The Fellonis said they weren't. Tony Felloni might have been expected to have squirrelled away a lot more because of his renowned meanness and his relatively frugal lifestyle. He neither spent lavishly nor took foreign holidays. He didn't buy expensive cars nor did he live in palatial mansions. He didn't seem to be able to enjoy himself spending any of it—he appeared to take pleasure in money for its own sake. 'Money was his God,' his daughter Ann said.

Heroin distribution networks are expensive to run. Tony, Regina and Luigi lost over £24,000 in cash, traveller's cheques and foreign currency and nearly a quarter of a million pounds worth of heroin during Operation Pizza alone. They also lost hundreds of thousands of pounds worth of heroin when their couriers were intercepted. Tony's English suppliers still had to be paid for the drugs before they would sell him any more.

There were other costs in running a heroin operation such as courier payments, transport costs, pay-offs, mobile phone bills and accommodation expenses. The bedsit Regina rented in Hollybank Road in Drumcondra cost £140 a month. She had it for eight months. Bail money had to be forfeited if any members of the family breached the conditions of their release. The three Fellonis also dipped into the merchandise and dented the profits. Regina and Luigi developed expensive drug habits while Tony became addicted after he began smoking heroin.

In reality the Fellonis appear to have made relatively little out of the dangerous business of selling heroin. Even if the £200,000 identified as theirs when they were jailed is indeed the proceeds of selling heroin, this is minuscule when compared to the money turned over by the Veronica Guerin murder gang, which imported and distributed £17 million worth of cannabis into Ireland between 1992 and 1996. This gang made the Fellonis look like amateurs. It was structured and disciplined and it ran like a business. Each individual had a specific role. One handled the guns, another the cash, another one or two imported and distributed the drugs. The gang leader oversaw the entire operation but had very few dealings with individual members. His lieutenant was responsible for the nuts and bolts of the day-to-day drug running business. In marked contrast, Tony Felloni tried to do everything himself. One minute he was dealing with serious criminals on the wholesale heroin market, the next minute he was selling £10 and £20 bags to junkies at his door.

The Veronica Guerin murder gang also operated in the less dangerous and more socially acceptable world of cannabis distribution. They cornered the market and made it more lucrative. There is less of a stigma attached to the drug and the market is broader across the social classes, including as it does students and professionals. Unlike heroin, it does not wipe out entire communities or generations of young people. Cannabis has not been responsible for hundreds of deaths in Dublin and it does not bring Concerned Parents groups out onto the streets. The gang worked away quietly for years while Felloni brought everyone down on his head.

The state, however, remained determined to take all the Fellonis' money, no matter how little they appeared to have earned in comparison to other criminals. If people, particularly people in the north inner city, were to have any confidence in the Gardaí, the justice system and the apparatus of the state, it was important that the Fellonis come out of jail broke. It was especially important for people whose lives had been destroyed by the family, who had lost loved ones as a result of their heroin dealing. Tony, Regina and Luigi were to have no nest egg waiting for them upon their release.

The case itself was hugely symbolic. As one prison governor put it, 'If they don't get the Fellonis' money they can throw their hat at it!' It was not just money, it was the principle and the precedent. The Criminal Justice Act, the law set up to tackle money laundering, had to be seen to work. The message had to be sent out loud and clear that times had changed for criminals.

The Fellonis were the first criminals against whom proceedings of this nature had been instigated. Their assets were the first to be frozen under the Act in April of 1996. But they fought the case because they said their earnings weren't drug money, so in the end the first person to lose their assets over a year later under the 1994 Criminal Justice Act was a 28-year-old Dublin drug dealer.

Alan Lynch from Mourne Road in Crumlin was what the judge at his trial in May 1997 called 'a graduate of the University of Crime' in prison. Lynch got into supplying heroin when he came out of prison after serving a seven-year sentence for robbery. He went on to control a large number of the heroin suppliers in Dolphin's Barn in the south inner city. A lone operator, who didn't sell on the streets himself,

Lynch was not an addict feeding his habit—he was in the business 'to make money'.

He was first caught after Gardaí raided his apartment in November 1995 and found £20,000 worth of heroin and over £7,000 in cash. He was arrested again a year later after he was spotted getting into his car carrying a double-barrelled shotgun wrapped in a bag. Two Gardaí walked over to him but he drove the car at them and they had to jump for safety into the nearby bushes. In the meantime his girlfriend had also been arrested after she withdrew £8,000 from a bank account.

Lynch and his girlfriend were both convicted and the £15,000 that Lynch earned from drug dealing was the first to be successfully seized by the state under the 1994 Criminal Justice Act. His girlfriend now holds the honour of being the first person in the history of the state to be charged with and convicted of the new offence of handling drugs money. Since that time there have been a number of uncontested seizures of assets under the 1994 Act, including the confiscation of over £90,000 in Irish and sterling from Charles Bowden, the country's first so-called 'supergrass'. Bowden admitted that the money was the proceeds of drug trafficking. The Fellonis will have to be content with their place in legal history as the first contested case under the Act.

As far as the state was concerned the case was cut and dried. The Fellonis were drug dealers who had made their money out of the misery of others. Under no circumstances were they going to be allowed to enjoy the financial rewards of their trade. The Fellonis, on the other hand, knew that by fighting the case they had nothing to lose. They had plenty of time, they were all in jail, and why should they let the state take their money when it wasn't earned selling drugs? It became abundantly clear on the day the case opened in the Dublin Circuit Criminal Court on 2 July 1997 that the Fellonis were going to fight to hold on to what they had.

The family's legal team consisted of a solicitor, Jim Orange, and two barristers, his son Garnet Orange and Blaise O'Carroll. O'Carroll told the court that they would fight the state's attempt to seize the money 'every step of the way'. The provisions of the 1994 Act, he said, seemed 'quite draconian' as a person's livelihood could be wiped out. He would, he said, be requiring strict proofs of all details concerning the Fellonis. He said he would want every single conviction proved and would be asking the judge, Kieran O'Connor, to determine whether the proceedings were criminal or civil. He also said that on behalf of his clients he intended to pursue the case right up to the Supreme Court to test the constitutionality of the Act if necessary. The lawyers also indicated that they might be prepared to take the case to Europe.

The Fellonis had never been too worried about the law or the Constitution but all this was music to Tony's ears. This was a day out, and an enjoyable diversion from the dreary routine of Portlaoise Prison. Sitting on a bench in the corner of the court, Tony was in great form as he listened to the prosecution and defence statements. He chatted away amicably to both Luigi and Regina. He cracked jokes with his daughter, who smiled back at him on a number of occasions. Regina also appeared content with the proceedings. She even whistled a tune during one of the short breaks in the hearing.

Anne Felloni was also in court that day and she spoke to all three, including her husband. She too was interested in the money, and attended all the hearings that Tony, Regina and Luigi were brought up for. The court sittings afforded her an opportunity to see and speak to her children; she remains particularly close to Luigi. If her husband and children succeeded in holding on to all or indeed some of the money, then Anne wanted her share. She was not divorced or legally separated from Tony Felloni. 'If he gets anything,' she said, 'I'll do him for maintenance for that child' (Ellavita). As long as she remained his wife, Anne knew her case for a share of 'the realisable assets' would be that much stronger.

There was, however, one very important issue to be decided before the case itself could proceed: who was going to pay the Fellonis' lawyers? The legal team had anticipated this problem quite early on. The Fellonis wanted to be sure their lawyers would be paid for their services, and they wanted a resolution of this question before going ahead with the substantive case as to whether or not the state could actually take their assets. It was another six months before the point was decided.

The cost of defending the case was estimated at over £31,000. The Fellonis had told their lawyers they could take their fees from the money frozen by the High Court. They applied to the High Court for a variation of the freezing order so that money could be released to pay their lawyers to fight the state. On 2 May 1997 they received their first setback, when Mr Justice Frederick Morris refused to allow this to happen.

The judge did not close this door completely, however. He refused their application because he wanted all other avenues of potential payment explored first. In other words, if the Fellonis failed elsewhere to have their legal bills paid, they could always come back to the High Court and apply again for some of the frozen moneys to be released.

The Fellonis then decided to apply for free legal aid and get the state to pay their bills. Judge Cyril Kelly in the Circuit Criminal Court had already made an order granting the family legal aid to fight the criminal case, but in July of 1997 their solicitor Jim Orange received a letter from the Department of Justice telling him their fees would not be paid by the state. The Department told him that the 1962 Criminal Justice Legal Aid Act 'provides for the granting of legal aid for persons charged with a criminal offence. As your clients have not been charged . . . the Act does not apply.' It was the second time the Fellonis had been refused a means to ensure their lawyers would get paid.

The irony of the situation was that in spite of all the money the Fellonis had, they actually did have a case for legal aid. The High Court had frozen all their realisable property, including all their money, known or unknown. Tony, Regina or Luigi couldn't legally touch a penny in any account they had anywhere. This meant they were left with no money with which to pay for a legal defence. Every citizen is entitled to a defence under the law, and if they can't afford one then the state is obliged to pay for one. If the Fellonis were to be continually refused access to their money, as well as access to criminal legal aid, they could quite legitimately argue that the state was depriving them of their constitutional right to legal representation.

There was a third option for the Fellonis: to apply for civil legal aid. It was not, however, an option which either the family or their lawyers felt was open to them. It had still not been established whether or not the court proceedings were civil or criminal, but if civil legal aid was applicable and granted, then the Fellonis' solicitor, Jim Orange, would most likely have to give up the case. It would be taken over by a Law Centre solicitor who would instruct new counsel and start again from scratch. Orange argued that his being taken off the case at this stage would result in 'a lack of continuity which would adversely affect the defendants', i.e. the Fellonis.

Tony was, as he put it, 'very anxious' that Orange 'should continue to represent me throughout the remainder of these proceedings'. He said he did not apply for civil legal aid because it would require having to instruct a different solicitor and counsel. 'I feel that having regard to the nature of these proceedings,' he swore in an affidavit, 'I should continue with the solicitor and counsel who have acted on [my] behalf since the commencement of these proceedings on 4 April 1996.'

With all other options exhausted, the Fellonis went back to the High Court to try for a second time to have money released from the frozen assets to pay their lawyers' fees. The High Court again refused the application, but at that hearing on 18 December 1997—over a year and a half after the case began—Mr Justice Peter Shanley finally clarified most of the issues involved.

First of all, he ruled that the Fellonis were entitled to criminal legal aid. Judge Cyril Kelly's order granting the family a certificate for legal aid during the criminal trial remained in place regardless of whether or not the Department of Justice thought the family was eligible. If the Department believed otherwise, he said, it could appeal the decision: 'The order is valid and enforceable unless appealed or quashed.'

The High Court also ruled the confiscation of the Fellonis' assets was part of the criminal case for drug trafficking against them. It was a continuation of the case that had put all three in jail in the first place. The criminal case against the Fellonis would therefore be concluded only when the Circuit Criminal Court had settled the dispute over their assets. As such the family were still entitled to criminal legal aid.

Mr Justice Shanley also left it open to the Fellonis to apply for civil legal aid if such a need arose in the future. He conceded they may not have Jim Orange, the solicitor they wanted, but he pointed out they could have the barrister that had part-argued their case. In the event, he said, there would be 'no serious injustice to the Fellonis'.

It seemed the way had finally been cleared for the real issue to be decided: whether or not the state could seize all, some or none of the Fellonis' assets. The Fellonis had succeeded in retaining the legal team of their choice and ensuring that their fees would be paid by the taxpayer. The Gardaí were also content with the judgment because they were anxious to press on with the case. Then a bombshell was dropped.

In the last few minutes of one of the hearings to decide the issue of who would pay the Fellonis' lawyers, counsel for the Director of Public Prosecutions, Shane Murphy, stood up. He calmly told the judge that the Fellonis had double the number of bank accounts and almost twice as much money as the state had previously thought. During all the legal argument over who would or wouldn't pay the lawyers' bills, Sergeant John O'Driscoll had quietly ploughed ahead with his investigation. He followed the money trail overseas.

1. Accounts held by Regina Felloni

a. Allied Irish Bank, O'Connell Street, A/C 24904032.... Balance £24,368.07

b. Bank of Ireland, Cavendish Row, A/C 23842219... .... Balance £68,995.65

c. ICS Building Society, 25 Westmoreland Street, A/C 28892098... Balance £18,510.88

d. Post Office Savings Bank, A/C E871370.....Balance £1,629.95

2. Accounts held by Tony Felloni

a. Irish Permanent Building Society, 56/59 St Stephen's Green, A/C 2321680514....Highest recorded balance £153,703.99

b. Allied Irish Banks, Upper O'Connell Street, A/C 25679021....Gardaí believe this was opened only so that Tony could buy a mobile phone. There was a stipulation at the time that a person should have a current account to own a mobile phone.

3. Accounts held by Luigi Felloni

a. Irish Permanent Building Society, Liffey Street, A/C 50257308.....Balance £710.42

b. Bank of Ireland, Cavendish Row, A/C 57899360... ......Balance £226.73

Luigi was involved in a road accident before he was sent to prison. He claimed for damages and was given a cheque for £2,078. It took ten days for the bank to clear the cheque, so in the meantime he borrowed £300 and gave his sister another £300. But when the three Fellonis' assets were frozen in April 1996, the prison governor held on to the remainder of the money from the claim, around £1,481. Luigi went to the High Court and won the case. On 1 May 1998 Mr Justice Shanley ordered he was to get his money back. The judge said that the money was obviously not covered by the freezing order because that order related to money the Fellonis received from drug trafficking.

4. Cash seized from raids on Tony, Luigi and Regina during Operation Pizza

a. Tony	£12,152.74 (£4,922.74, £4,990, and £2,240 sterling)
b. Luigi	£10,595.38 (see endnotes 4 and 5, Chapter 13)
c. Regina	£1,975 (£1,000 cash, £975 for windows)
TOTAL	£24,723.35

16 *The CAB Moves In* *1993–98*

'It seems strange to me', the judge said, 'that a girl just out of her juvenile years, no work background, can lodge expansive sums of money in financial institutions.' It was 4 July 1996, the day Regina Felloni pleaded guilty to heroin dealing. Judge Cyril Kelly, addressing the Circuit Criminal Court, asked the obvious question. How could a twenty-year-old unemployed heroin addict lodge so much money to banks and building societies without them asking any questions?

'The financial institutions have a duty to our society as well,' he said. 'A young girl with in one account at least £50,000; the financial institutions cannot turn a blind eye or ignore obvious realities. They are facilitating this as much as the person next door who does not complain.' This £50,000 was only a fraction of Regina's wealth. Nine months later, on 21 March 1997, a man walked into Swords Garda Station in north county Dublin and handed in a bundle of documents. He would not give his name or any information about himself. He simply said he had found the documents, handed them over to the Gardaí and left.

The documents included six sterling bank drafts made payable to Regina Felloni. Two of the drafts were dated 8 January 1995, two more 29 December of that year. The final two were dated 10 January 1996. Three were issued at the Bank of Ireland in Dorset Street in Dublin, the others at the Allied Irish Bank at 37–8 Upper O'Connell Street. The total value of all six bank drafts was nearly £20,000 in sterling.[1]

The discovery of the bank drafts marked a dramatic new turn in the investigation into the Fellonis' wealth. The drafts proved the family had more money than the Gardaí had originally thought. The

Gardaí now had to establish just how much more. The drafts also indicated that the money was being held outside the country, most likely in Britain and/or Northern Ireland. Over the next six months, Sergeant John O'Driscoll followed the trail of the Fellonis' money between Dublin, London, Liverpool and Belfast.

Tony Felloni opened the first account in his own name outside the state on 6 August 1993, just after his release from prison. He opened the account at the Donegall Square East Branch of the Abbey National Bank in Belfast, and deposited £20 sterling. It was the first recorded transaction Tony, Regina or Luigi had made since Tony withdrew over £150,000 in July from the Irish Permanent account he held in Dublin. That account was in the name of Anthony Carroll. On 3 September, a month after it was opened, £25,000 sterling was put in to the Belfast account. Six weeks later another £25,000 was lodged. By 24 April 1997 there was nearly £60,000 sterling in the account.[2]

Regina was also busy in the banks. On 2 June 1994 she went to Liverpool and opened an account in the Midland Bank. The north-central Drug Unit believed that the Fellonis bought some of their heroin from dealers in Liverpool. Regina put down two addresses when she opened the account. One was the flat at 73 Lower Dominick Street in Dublin; the other was at 5 Argyle Road, Anfield, in Liverpool.

Tony also used this account. He lodged money to it a number of times from the Bank of Ireland in Phibsborough and the AIB at Upper O'Connell Street, where Regina had an account. The Fellonis continued to deposit in and withdraw from the Liverpool account until they were sent to prison in 1996. When the account was examined in August of the following year it contained over £20,000 sterling.[1]

The Fellonis opened four more bank accounts in Belfast in September of 1995. Regina opened three of them; the fourth was a joint account held in her own and Tony's names. This was a market yield account, opened with an investment of £6,200 at the First Trust Bank on 22 September. The money was invested in the account for five years. It is still on deposit in the bank in accordance with Regina and Tony's instructions.[2] On the same day Regina opened another account in the Abbey National. Six lodgments were made to it

213

between September of 1995 and the first week in January 1996. There is now over £22,000 sterling in that account.[1]

Exactly one week later Regina Felloni was back in Belfast and opened accounts in the Northern and Ulster Banks. The Gardaí became aware of the existence of the Northern Bank account only when a bankbook was handed in with the other documents to Swords Garda Station. Regina opened the account with a £700 sterling cash deposit. Only one more transaction was ever carried out, a lodgment of over £3,000 sterling in December of 1995.[1]

The fourth account opened in Belfast that September was in the Ulster Bank around the corner with £300 sterling. Three months later almost £2,000 was lodged to it, on the same day that the £3,000 was put into the Northern Bank. Regina gave the bank her address as 73 Lower Dominick Street and admitted on the form that she was unemployed. But she declared only one other bank account, the one at the First Trust in Belfast.[1]

John O'Driscoll now knew that Tony and Regina Felloni had six UK bank accounts between them. All were outside the state's jurisdiction. O'Driscoll contacted the Financial Investigation Unit of the City of London Police, and the RUC Drug Unit in Belfast. The three police forces pooled their information, and production orders were served on the banks in England and Northern Ireland to establish just how much money the Fellonis had.

On 27 May 1997, John O'Driscoll flew to London, where the Abbey National Bank has its head office. He got documents relating to Tony and Regina's accounts in the branch in Belfast. He also received information on the account held at the Midland Bank in Liverpool. The following month he drove to Belfast, where RUC Detective Constable Neil Woods gave him documents relating to the final three Belfast accounts. When John O'Driscoll put all this information together his suspicions were confirmed. The Fellonis had over £115,000 in the Belfast and Liverpool banks.[3]

The Director of Public Prosecutions wrote to the British authorities about the accounts. On 16 October 1997 applications were made on behalf of the Irish government to the High Court in Belfast for restraint orders freezing the accounts in the North. A week later a similar application was made to the High Court in London. The money in all six accounts was frozen. It was the first time assets in Northern Ireland were restrained in a case that was being prosecuted in the Republic of Ireland.

The discovery of the accounts in Belfast and Liverpool was, the Gardaí believed, further evidence of the scale of the Fellonis' drug trafficking operation. It was easier to do business there with sterling accounts. They felt the money was hidden in these accounts not only to avoid detection, but to enable the Fellonis to enhance their connections with drug dealers in Britain. The Fellonis denied this. They said the money was not from the sale of drugs.

The new accounts also meant that the Gardaí had to revise upwards their estimate of the assets they believed were available to the Fellonis. With fourteen accounts, a house and a car, the value of the assets the state was trying to seize was now over £360,000. That figure continued to increase as the money accrued interest in the banks and the value of the house soared on the Dublin property market. The Gardaí even got offers from people seeking to buy it. Only the value of the Nissan Micra dropped.

The details of the new accounts only came out in the High Court in December of 1997, as the Fellonis were trying to free up some of the frozen money to cover their legal fees. John O'Driscoll claimed in court that the Fellonis had 'made untrue averments' when they swore they had no assets other than those he had identified by April of 1996: 'I say the defence have failed to indicate the true nature and extent of their realisable assets.'

The Fellonis denied this. They claimed they had not disclosed the existence of the six UK accounts before because the restraint order covered all their accounts and assets, known or unknown. Regina claimed she had not been untruthful because even though she didn't mention the accounts, she had been thinking about them! The additional assets, she said, were 'within my contemplation when I swore my earlier affidavit'. Tony argued that he had taken literally the clause in the restraining order applying it to all his realisable property. Mr Justice Peter Shanley said he did not propose to determine whether or not the Fellonis were telling the truth but this, he said, was an 'excuse' he found 'hard to believe'.

One of the most significant developments in the case that day was the fact that the Fellonis actually admitted they owned the accounts. Six months earlier their counsel had said the state would have to prove 'everything' in the case. The Gardaí took this literally and were dreading the possibility that they would have to prove the accounts actually belonged to the Fellonis. This would mean taking detailed twenty- or thirty-page statements from witnesses in Liverpool, London and Belfast. Some of those witnesses would almost certainly have had to travel to Dublin to give evidence in court and many may have been reluctant to do so. Every individual financial transaction would have been open to intense scrutiny under cross-examination in court. This nightmare scenario disappeared once the Fellonis accepted ownership of the accounts.

In light of the fact that he had only recently found out about the Belfast and Liverpool accounts, John O'Driscoll did not rule out finding even more money. 'I cannot discount the possibility that there are other bank accounts over which the defendants or either of them have control,' he told the High Court, 'or funds to which they have access, which I have yet to uncover.'

But if the state thought it could now, after almost two years of court appearances, finally get down to the issue of trying to seize the money in the courts, it was badly mistaken. In January of 1998, the Fellonis' legal team said they were thinking of challenging the constitutionality of the 1994 Criminal Justice Act, the money laundering legislation which gave the state the power to seize the assets. Within a month they had decided to go ahead.

The Fellonis' lawyers claimed that the powers of confiscation which the law allowed the state presented what they called 'the appalling vista' that a person's assets could be totally taken away retrospectively. Senior counsel Blaise O'Carroll said the Fellonis were entitled to know which particular bank transactions, as well as lodgments to their accounts, the state claimed represented money from drug dealing.

This would be one of the main planks of the Fellonis' defence in their attempt to hang on to at least some of their assets. They said that some of the money was from savings, the sale of property and personal injury compensation awards. They argued that the DPP could not make a round claim that all the family's money was from selling heroin and therefore seize the lot.

'It is incorrect to say all [my] assets are the proceeds of drug trafficking,' Tony swore in a High Court affidavit. 'I have monies in accounts coming from a variety of sources and going back many years.' His affidavit did not specify precisely where the money came from. His lawyers said they would need an accountant to help them with the case; the family insisted their assets were lawful until the courts decided otherwise.

'It is with some considerable reluctance that I make this ruling,' Mr Justice Barr said in the High Court on 16 February 1998 as he gave the Fellonis leave to challenge the constitutionality of the Criminal Justice Act. Quite apart from the Fellonis, he said, an unemployed person could be enjoying a lifestyle indicative of great wealth and could have a million pounds in the bank. 'If such a person was convicted of being a drugs baron,' he asked, 'why should he be in a special position to protect his million pounds if it was clear that it was the product of unlawful activities?'

'It would be unpalatable to many people', he went on, 'that a drugs baron who got a ten-year sentence for dealing in heroin would come out and retire on a million pounds in respect of which he had not been charged.' But the judge also stressed that someone convicted of an offence had the right to come into court and explain where the remainder of his or her assets came from.

Senior counsel for the Fellonis, Blaise O'Carroll, had argued first of all that this was a penal sanction contrary to the Constitution and the European Convention on Human Rights. Secondly, he said, the DPP should have to state precisely which assets were the benefits of drug trafficking. And thirdly, he claimed there was a precedent where the Supreme Court had found that the onus was not on a convicted person to show where his assets come from.

Tony Felloni was worried about three aspects of the seizure under the 1994 Act: the fact that it confiscated not just some but all of his assets; the fact that it could take into account transactions which took place before the law was even enacted; and the fact that the state needed to prove the case only to a civil and not to the more difficult criminal standard of proof. This, he claimed, was a violation of his own, Regina's and Luigi's civil rights.

Mr Justice Barr described the issue as 'one of great public importance' and said he would recommend the Attorney General's legal aid scheme so that the Fellonis would not have to act without the benefit of a solicitor and counsel. Now the taxpayer would be picking up the tab for the Fellonis' constitutional challenge as well as their ongoing criminal case.[4]

The Gardaí were not unduly perturbed by the family's decision to challenge the constitutionality of the 1994 Criminal Justice Act. If they hadn't decided to do it, someone else would have. If the Fellonis won the case and the legislation was found to be flawed, then it was up to the government to tighten it up. If on the other hand the legislation was deemed constitutional then it would make it far easier for other Gardaí in other cases to seize the assets of convicted criminals.

And so the game of legal poker continued, both sides playing for the Fellonis' money and property. In taking the constitutional case, the Fellonis were now exploring a second legal avenue to prevent the state winning the game. They had played an ace but the Gardaí had another ace up their sleeve. They too had a second legal avenue to explore.

In a small, newly furnished office in a five-storey building somewhere in Dublin, the Criminal Assets Bureau was examining Tony Felloni's tax files. Felloni didn't know about it until the CAB was ready to go to court. The Bureau had already become marginally involved in Felloni's affairs when powers granted under the 1996 Criminal Assets Bureau Act were used to search Regina and her grandfather's house in Finglas. Now, however, the Bureau decided to become directly involved.

There were three areas of Felloni's financial affairs open to the Bureau for investigation. It could investigate the money he earned from drug dealing, it could investigate the money he claimed in social welfare benefits from the state, and it could investigate the money he was supposed to have paid in tax.

The first area was already being investigated by Sergeant John O'Driscoll. He had secured High Court orders freezing all the Fellonis' asssets, and the Bureau was happy to allow him to proceed with his objective of seizing these assets. The CAB had also decided against investigating Felloni's social welfare benefits. The amount of money he collected in benefits was relatively small and more than likely Felloni was entitled to them anyway. In many ways following this up would have been a waste of the Bureau's time, particularly when there was a far more productive pit to mine. The CAB settled on the third option: it decided to examine Felloni's tax affairs.

When CAB officials opened Tony Felloni's tax files they discovered that the Revenue Commissioners had already investigated him but had little success recovering any money. Anne Felloni says the Revenue Commissioners were aware of Tony's wealth in the early 1970s. When they looked for money from him, she says he told them to 'Fuck off!'

Felloni's money was again brought to the attention of the Revenue Commissioners in the 1980s, this time by the Gardaí. They believed something was going on when they regularly saw this unemployed man in the Bank of Ireland at Foster Place and in the Irish Permanent in O'Connell Street. Felloni became annoyed when individual Gardaí recognised him and went over to talk to him.

On 12 December 1984 Felloni's home was raided. The Gardaí found financial records which related to four building society accounts. There was over £1,700 in an account in the First National Building Society; over £4,800 in the Irish Permanent on the North Circular Road; another £3,700 in the EBS; and £166 in the Irish Permanent on O'Connell Street. In total, Felloni had over £10,400 in the accounts. The information was passed on to the Revenue Commissioners but the Gardaí heard nothing back.

The Revenue Commissioners took an interest in him again after he was sentenced to ten years in 1986. Felloni wrote to them from prison, pleading poverty and asking why they were picking on him. An attempt was made to seize some of his money for an unpaid tax bill. The Commissioners tried to use an attachment order whereby money could be taken from his account to cover unpaid taxes, but most of the money was moved out of the account before the taxman got to it.

The Revenue Commissioners were never renowned for a determination or willingness to pursue hot money. Tax officials were reluctant even to attempt to get money from major criminals, and with good reason. The General burned out one official's car and shot another official from the Department of Social Welfare. Brian Purcell, a higher executive officer, was shot in May 1989 after he explained at an appeal hearing why Martin Cahill had lost his benefits. Ordinary citizens were a safer bet for the Revenue Commissioners. The CAB didn't see it that way, but then the CAB has the protection of anonymity.

Members of the Criminal Assets Bureau are guaranteed anonymity under the law. Only the man in charge of it, Chief Superintendent Fachtna Murphy, and the Bureau's legal adviser, Barry Galvin, can be identified. It is an offence to name any other official of the Criminal Assets Bureau. The public doesn't even know where the CAB offices are. The tax officials who work in the Bureau can therefore pursue criminals like Felloni with vigour, safe in the knowledge that their identities are protected. The CAB took over Felloni's tax files from the Revenue Commissioners in January of 1997. The Commissioners had already calculated how much tax Felloni owed over the seven years between 1978 and 1985. By the summer of 1997 the CAB was ready to go to court.

On 30 July the summary summons of the case between Anthony Felloni and the Criminal Assets Bureau was issued in the High Court. The court presented Felloni with a hefty tax bill, the CAB saying that he owed over a quarter of a million pounds to the Revenue Commissioners. The Commissioners arrived at the figure by totalling up Felloni's unpaid tax and interest payments over a seven-year period. The tax he owed ranged from over £7,000 for the year ending April 1979 to a maximum of over £16,000 for the year ending April 1983. He was billed over £12,000 for unpaid tax in both 1984 and 1985. The assessment ended that year because in 1986 Felloni was sent to prison.

It is, however, the interest payments on the outstanding tax bills that really bring the figure up. The interest on the £9,000 tax owed by April 1980 was over £21,000. The following year the interest bill was over £26,000. It increased to over £31,000 for 1982, up to a maximum of £36,000 for 1983. Interest payments on the total tax bill over the seven years amounted to more than £180,000, two-thirds of the entire bill. Felloni was invited to contest the assessment but he never did. On 29 April 1998 the Bureau secured a High Court judgment against Felloni and the tax bill stood. There wasn't even a hearing. The court ordered him to pay the £273,730.06 and another £116 in costs. The judgment was published in *Stubbs Gazette* the following week.

The Criminal Assets Bureau now had two options. It could ask the High Court to lift the order freezing Felloni's assets to enable the tax bill to be paid; or it could await the outcome of John O'Driscoll's move to seize Regina's and Luigi's, as well as Tony's, assets. If the Fellonis managed to hold on to some or indeed all of their money and property, the CAB's tax bill ensured that Tony would immediately lose his money. So in the game of legal poker, Felloni still had a hand to play, but no matter which way he played it he was almost certain to lose.

In addition there was no reason why the Revenue Commissioners, working with the Criminal Assets Bureau, could not serve a tax bill on Regina Felloni as well, particularly since it appeared that most of the family's money was held in accounts in her name. The option was also there for the Department of Social Welfare to seek repayment of benefits and dole money paid out to the Fellonis over the years, considering they had admitted they owned the money in the banks. There was also a third option, perhaps the simplest solution of all. If the seizure was found to be unconstitutional under the 1994 Act, the CAB could move in and freeze all the Fellonis' assets again. This time, however, the onus would be on Tony, Regina and Luigi to prove that the money was lawfully earned.

At the time of writing, both the constitutional case on the 1994 Act and the criminal case over the seizure of the assets still had to be heard. It may take years to settle the issue, particularly if the Fellonis' lawyers exhaust all legal channels here before taking the case to the courts in Europe. The tax bill was, however, an insurance policy against the possibility of Tony Felloni being seen to hold on to any of the money he earned, regardless of whether he earned it legally or illegally. In a pincer-like movement the state had advanced on Tony Felloni on two fronts. He was caught in a financial vice grip between John O'Driscoll's case on one side and the CAB's tax judgment on the other.

The Criminal Assets Bureau decided to wait and see if John O'Driscoll and Frank Cassidy got Felloni's money. It didn't go to court to collect the outstanding tax. The option remained open, however, because—like Tony Felloni—the Criminal Assets Bureau had plenty of time. Tony was now living in a single cell, number 24, on E wing in Portlaoise Prison beside some of the country's most notorious and dangerous criminals. For the next few years, Tony Felloni was going nowhere.

1. Accounts outside the state held by Regina Felloni
a. Midland Bank, Breck Road, Liverpool, A/C 91174932....Balance £20,797.16 sterling (Tony also lodged money to this account.)
b. Abbey National, Donegall Square East, Belfast, A/C X10655547....Balance £22,741.66 sterling
c. Northern Bank, 8 Donegall Square North, Belfast, A/C 53103471 ......Balance £3,720 sterling
d. Ulster Bank, 47 Donegall Place, Belfast, A/C 52412004.....Balance £2,204.44 sterling
e. Six sterling bank drafts, total value £19,397.41

2. Accounts outside the state held by Tony Felloni
a. Abbey National, Donegall Square East, Belfast, A/C X7727396.....Balance £59,413.09 sterling
b. First Trust Bank, Arthur Street, Belfast, A/C 2/F/2675/018....Opened with £6,200 (joint account, five-year investment)

3. Total in all six accounts £115,076.35. By the time they were actually frozen, the figure, with interest payments, had increased by over £430 to £115,513.39. The money is still earning interest.

4. Seizure of assets under 1994 Criminal Justice Act
Court hearings:
4.4.96   High Court order freezing assets of Tony, Regina and Luigi Felloni
            Mr Justice Paul Carney, High Court
20.6.96   Tony Felloni, twenty years
            Judge Cyril Kelly, Circuit Criminal Court
10.10.96   Luigi Felloni, six years
            Judge Cyril Kelly, Circuit Criminal Court
17.12.96   Regina Felloni, six years, nine months
            Judge Cyril Kelly, Circuit Criminal Court
2.5.97   Fellonis refused leave to take lawyers' fees from frozen assets
            Mr Justice Frederick Morris, High Court
2.7.97   Case opens to seize assets under 1994 Criminal Justice Act
            Judge Kieran O'Connor, Circuit Criminal Court
15.7.97   Department of Justice refuses legal aid for lawyers' fees
18.12.97   High Court refuses Fellonis leave to take lawyers' fees from frozen assets
            for a second time but rules Fellonis entitled to legal aid to fight the case
            Mr Justice Peter Shanley, High Court
16.1.98   Fellonis indicate intention to challenge constitutionality of 1994
            Criminal Justice Act
            Judge Kieran O'Connor, Circuit Criminal Court
16.2.98   Fellonis granted leave to pursue constitutional challenge and granted
            legal aid under Attorney General's scheme
            Mr Justice Robert Barr, High Court
Seizure of assets case due to go ahead on 19 October 1998, but may be further postponed. No date for constitutional challenge to 1994 Act.

17 *King Scum Has AIDS 1998–*

Tony Felloni settled into life in Portlaoise Prison. He was comfortable. He was well looked after there. Released from his cell at 8.15 a.m. each day, he got his breakfast, dinner, tea and supper handed to him. He was locked up every night at 8.00 p.m. He had taken a computer course, a big step for a man who had never even owned a mobile phone. He also learned how to cook. Felloni was one of many hardened criminals who wandered across the yard to domestic science classes every Tuesday and Thursday, books and folder in hand. The inmates got to keep the cakes they, or more usually their teacher, baked, and eat them back on the prison landing or give them out as presents.

But life wasn't all trouble-free. Tony had few visitors. For a while Regina was brought down under escort from Mountjoy Jail to see him at least one Sunday every month but since her release she never came to see him. He shared a landing with other more violent criminals, like Warren Dumbrell and Paul Ward, who were both serving sentences for holding prison officers hostage, and with gang leader and drug dealer John Gilligan. He kept his head down and did his time quietly.

And yet Tony Felloni needed prison. He had become so institutionalised that he couldn't manage on his own for more than two days. But most worrying of all was that he was now over sixty years old and had serious health problems. He was HIV-positive—a potentially fatal condition. His abuse of heroin, the substance which had defined his life for nearly twenty years, had finally taken its toll on him. He had shared too many dirty needles. The headline in the newspaper screamed, 'King Scum Has AIDS'.

In truth Tony was getting better medical and holistic care in prison than he would have on the outside. But that didn't stop him trying to get out. He decided to appeal his twenty-year sentence. It was his right and it wouldn't cost him anything. Once again it would be the taxpayer who was picking up the tab.

Felloni's senior counsel, Brendan Grogan, argued in the Court of Criminal Appeal that the judge who sentenced him in the Circuit Criminal Court, Cyril Kelly, didn't take a number of factors into account before he imposed what was the longest sentence for drug dealing at the time. Tony had pleaded guilty, he said, and should have been given more credit for the time and expense he had saved the state. He was fifty-three years of age at the time and therefore already at 'an advanced age'. The judge, he said, made the sentences for each charge consecutive and therefore didn't consider the overall effect of that.

Brendan Grogan also argued that the court should take pity on the drug dealer. Felloni, he said, was an addict as well as a dealer but he wasn't a very good one. He didn't seem to have done very well out of selling heroin. He lived in a local authority house, he drove a modest car and he hadn't managed to enjoy the benefits of the money he made. In addition, any money he did make was found by the Gardaí and seized by the state. Felloni, he said, had been given a virtual life sentence. There was no incentive for him to mend his ways. There was, as he put it, 'no light at the end of the tunnel'.

It was an eloquent plea but the facts of the case were damning. Senior counsel, Tom O'Connell, reminded the court that Cyril Kelly had no discretion because the law demanded that sentences for offences committed on bail be consecutive. Felloni, he said, was a serious and incorrigible criminal who went back and committed the very same offence even after serving ten years for it.

The probation and psychiatric reports did not support Tony's case. They pointed out that Felloni didn't deal in heroin to support his habit, therefore his addiction could not be seen as a mitigating factor. He admitted using drugs in prison and he gave no indication that he intended to stop. It was, the reports said, difficult to see him make the changes in order to become a law-abiding citizen. The consultant psychiatrist, Dr Brian McCaffrey, said he couldn't see him having a life outside prison.

It didn't take the three-judge Court of Criminal Appeal long to make up its mind. Mr Justice Hugh O'Flaherty pointed out that Felloni was a heroin dealer 'on a grand scale' and was back before the court on the same offences. The picture, he said, was one of 'unmitigated gloom without a chink of light'. The court dismissed his appeal and told him the twenty-year sentence stood. It did, however, grant him one concession. The sentence was backdated by three months to March of 1996 to start from the time he went into custody.

Tony could have perhaps rightly felt hard done by. Most long-sentence prisoners who appeal their sentences can hope to have a few years knocked off. Tony only got a reduction of three months and he was entitled to that because he was in jail for that time. The case of Patrick Eugene Holland was used against him in the argument for giving drug dealers long sentences. A fellow Portlaoise inmate, Holland also got twenty years and he was only dealing in cannabis. Felloni was dealing in heroin. Ironically when Holland's case came up for appeal he won it and his sentence was reduced by eight years. Drugs gang leader John Gilligan also had his sentence reduced by eight years. Felloni can, therefore, feel somewhat unlucky that he went to the appeal court before them.

It is also possible that were he to be sentenced today Tony Felloni would not have got twenty years in prison. The government has since toughened the law on sentencing for drug dealers. It says that those caught with more than €12,700 worth of drugs should go to jail for at least ten years. That is the mandatory minimum sentence. It has, however, in reality become the maximum sentence and it is rare now for serious drug dealers to get ten years or more.

The law allows judges to give sentences of less than ten years in serious drugs cases if there are mitigating circumstances. Co-operation with the Gardaí is one such mitigating factor as is an early plea of guilty. Drug dealers caught red-handed invariably plead guilty at the arraignment stage. That is the point in the court proceedings where they have to make a decision to either admit their guilt or fight the case. With overwhelming evidence against them, most realise it would be foolish to risk a fight and lose.

So even though that plea of guilty may come a year into the proceedings, it is still the earliest time at which a defendant can plead. Credit is therefore given at the sentence hearing. As regards co-operation, the Gardaí rarely state outright in court that a suspect was unco-operative unless they were downright obstructionist. Therefore the effect of the law has been in fact to turn the minimum sentence into a benchmark for judges and if there are any mitigating factors then the drug dealer invariably does not get ten years. In the current climate Felloni would perhaps only have got nine years.

At the time of his appeal in February 1999, Felloni was still serving the longest sentence for drug dealing ever handed down in an Irish court but it was a record he wouldn't hold on to for much longer. Four months later the Cork drug dealer, Edward 'Judd' Scanlon, was sentenced to twenty-two years for supplying ecstasy and cocaine. Two years later John Gilligan received twenty-eight years in the Special Criminal Court in 2001 for importing huge quantities of cannabis. He joined Tony on the E wing in Portlaoise Prison. Tony has never been granted temporary or compassionate release. When his father Ronaldo died in Blanchardstown Hospital Tony didn't get out for his funeral. He has applied to the parole board to be considered for early release.

Every one of Tony's six children still has problems with heroin addiction and each one of them has been in trouble since their release from prison. Two of the girls managed to get in trouble while still in prison serving their sentences. Three months after he lost his appeal, one of Tony's granddaughter's was making her first Holy Communion. Tony didn't know or care too much about it but his daughter Ann, the child's mother, did. Naturally she wanted to attend the ceremony even though she was in Mountjoy Jail. In May 1999 she was granted compassionate leave for the weekend. Her children were in foster care and she had been released a number of times before for similar reasons. She had in the past always returned but this time she didn't.

Ann was not seen as a threat to society. The prison authorities believed she would come back but, when she hadn't by the end of June, the Gardaí circulated her description and began searching for her. A week later she was arrested in Clondalkin and brought back to Mountjoy. She had been at large for seven weeks.

Two months later she ran away again. This time she was on the way to a counselling programme for heroin addiction when she gave her escort the slip. She was back within a week but a few months later the prison doctor told her she was pregnant with her fourth child.

The following year her younger sister did the very same thing but in a rather more dramatic and colourful fashion.

Regina was taking driving lessons as part of a pre-release programme. Once a week a prison officer escorted her from the prison to a nearby driving school for her one-hour lesson. Regina may have been high profile but security-wise she was low risk. She was due out at the beginning of May 2001 and the programme was part of her preparation for the outside world. She was one of over 200 inmates released each day either to take part in such a programme or on temporary release. However, on 31 July 2000 when she and the officer were on their way back from the lesson she asked him if she could go to the toilet. She went in to a fast food restaurant in Phibsborough at midday but didn't come back.

Regina was only on the run that day. She went back to the north inner city and started taking heroin. At around 8.00 p.m. that night a man passing by the Pope's Cross in the Phoenix Park noticed her unconscious, lying on the grass. He dialled 999 and an ambulance took her to the James Connolly Memorial Hospital in Blanchardstown. She was stoned. The prison was informed and two officers picked her up and drove her back to prison.

Regina's adventure could have added almost two years to her sentence. Instead she only got an extra fourteen days and lost some of her visiting and recreation privileges. She was at the time very upset over articles in the newspapers which linked her to the convicted murderer Catherine Nevin. Nevin was serving life for having her husband Tom shot dead in their pub Jack White's in Co. Wicklow. Regina and Catherine were friends for a time but they fell out. Regina was caught with a syringe and blamed Catherine for it.

Prison officers decided to search her cell as part of a routine drug search. Regina left but took her syringe with her. She gave it to Catherine Nevin to mind but pricked her as she was handing it over. Nevin became distraught over the possibility that she may have contracted HIV. She panicked and started screaming. Prison staff arrived and Regina's syringe was found. She blamed Nevin for the trouble she got into and took it out on her later. She attacked her, pulled her hair and slapped her around. The newspapers heard about the fight and ran the story which in turn caused Regina more pain.

The driving lesson escape elicited a not-unexpected silly-season response from the politicians. 'It defies rational understanding on how to run a prison service that a member of the Felloni family—while serving a sentence for serious offences—should be on temporary release to have driving lessons,' Alan Shatter, the Fine Gael spokesman on justice said. 'Zero tolerance has now become zero competence.' Labour's Róisín Shortall was a little more circumspect: 'There must be a full review of security procedures,' she said. The prison service ignored the howls of outrage and saw the incident for what it was—a pointless stunt by a distressed young woman.

Anyway Regina had more serious concerns than politicians, the prison authorities or the problems with her fellow inmates. She served the first part of her sentence in the old women's prison at Mountjoy, a wing off the juvenile prison St Patrick's Institution. She was one of the last people to speak to 19-year-old Patrick Dunne while he was alive during recreation time on 15 July 1997.

Regina knew Patrick well and that day she had a shouted conversation with him through the walls. He told her he wanted to get out and was going to do something to get to hospital. He told her he could escape from there. The plan, however, went tragically wrong. At 11.00 p.m. that night he was found hanging by a sheet from the sink taps in his single cell.

Regina was subsequently diagnosed with cancer in prison. When the old prison closed she was moved along with all the other women into the new state-of-the-art Dóchas Centre. This new women's prison at Mountjoy was a far more pleasant and civilised environment. The inmates lived in their own rooms, not in cells. They slept in beds, not in bunks or on the floor. They had quilts and their own television sets. It was a much more relaxed regime.

The prison authorities were also very sympathetic towards the seriously ill young woman. She was by no means a model prisoner but they still gave her 25 per cent remission on her sentence. Regina was released on 18 May 2001 and is now bringing up a baby girl on her own. Regina said Nicoletti Felloni was born in May 2002 and mother and baby are living with Regina's aunt Evelyn, the woman who reared her. Regina has only been in trouble once since she got out of prison. She was caught stealing toiletries from Dunnes Stores in Henry Street on 10 November 2001. Two months later she was convicted of shoplifting and fined €50 at the Dublin District Court.

Mario said he regularly visited Regina in prison but by the time she got out she could visit him because he was back in prison. It was ironic because two weeks after her day trip on heroin he told the *Evening Herald* she was silly to do what she did. Mario was released in 1998 on compassionate grounds before he had served his full sentence. He had HIV and hepatitis C and went on a methadone programme for his heroin addiction. He said he left Ireland in the 1980s and started robbing banks in England because his girlfriend died and he couldn't handle the pressure. 'I have seen people OD and die,' he said. 'My own girlfriend died beside me in the bed from a drugs overdose. I woke up one morning and felt her cold beside me.'

The 30-year-old had been living with his mother Anne since his release, first near Fatima Mansions, then in Inchicore. He used the interview to warn other young people about the dangers of taking drugs. He said prison had saved his life but heroin was killing him. But by that time he had already been involved in a series of silly and petty incidents that would put him back again in a cell in Mountjoy.

On 21 January 2001 Mario was charged with obstructing a Garda who was trying to search him for drugs at Cornmarket in the south inner city. He was convicted and sentenced to one month in Mountjoy on 20 July. He wasn't two days inside, however, when he attacked a prison officer and on 22 July he was charged with that. On 18 August he was up again before the Dublin District Court and told to sign on at Kevin Street station three times a day. On 10 December 2001 he was convicted of assault and given six months in jail. He served four and was released from Mountjoy on 24 April 2002.

His younger brother Ronaldo also continued his chaotic, drug-addicted criminal lifestyle. He was released early from a five-year sentence in 1999 for robbing a taxi driver of £15 but it wasn't long before he was in trouble again. A chronic drug addict, he had no money and nowhere to live. He went straight back to petty and sometimes violent crime.

Ronaldo mugged two German students on the 46A bus at Mounttown Road in Dun Laoghaire and stole their cash and credit cards. He also stole a purse from a woman who was sitting having a cup of tea in the Clarence Hotel. He took it off the table when she wasn't looking but she noticed him walking away and he was arrested and charged. He committed that offence while on temporary release.

He was caught shoplifting and given six months in August 1999. Two months later he was caught shoplifting again as well as picking the pockets of shoppers in Grafton Street. He got nine months for that. And he was also caught twice selling drugs in June and November of 1999. On one of these occasions he was arrested selling heroin in McDonald's in O'Connell Street.

It was clear that Ronaldo was no master criminal. In spite of his attempt at a one-man crime wave he almost always got caught. Nineteen-ninety-nine was a particularly bad year for him. He was released early that year and was back in jail by Christmas. He was sentenced for ten more offences. It brought his criminal record to over twenty. The advent of the millennium wasn't much better for him. On 13 May 2000 he was sent to prison for three years for the attack on the German tourists.

Like his two other unfortunate brothers Luigi couldn't stay out of trouble either. Six days before Christmas 2000 he walked out of Mountjoy Jail a free man. He managed to steer clear of the law for a while but he gravitated back into the drug scene and the only life he knew. Seven months later he was caught with heroin on Corporation Street in the north inner city and convicted of possession of the drug and obstructing the Garda trying to search him. He was sentenced to two months in prison. He was also convicted of the same two offences again three months later, this time at Seán MacDermott Street. On 11 October 2001 he was given probation at the Dublin District Court.

The only Felloni who hadn't been in jail by the time her father was sent to prison for twenty years finally ended up there by the time he lost his appeal. On 19 September 1997 Lena was arrested for stealing and brought to the Bridewell Garda Station. While she was being brought to the holding cell she bit Garda Una Shanley and drew blood. Two and a half years later she pleaded guilty to the assault and was given a six-month suspended sentence at the Dublin Circuit Criminal Court. The judge took pity on the violent, single, drug-addicted mother. 'I hope you provide a better life for your child than your family provided for you,' Judge Pat McCartan told her. However, the following year she was up again before the courts, twice for shoplifting, first in May, then in October. She was sentenced to four months in prison on each occasion.

Even their fifty-three-year-old mother Anne who is bringing up Tony's youngest child still couldn't stay out of trouble. On 21 June

1999 she received her forty-sixth conviction at the Dublin District Court for her speciality—shoplifting. But Anne was clearly losing her touch. It was a pointless, petty and bizarre attempt at a crime which would be funny if it wasn't so sad, particularly for five-year-old Ellavita. Anne was caught trying to rob thirty-three pairs of women's knickers from Penneys on Mary Street on 21 November 1998. Security staff at the shop detained her until two Gardaí went down and picked her up. Garda James Brennan arrested and charged her and she was sentenced to eighty hours community service. It wasn't the first time she was convicted of stealing underwear. Over thirty years before Judge Robert Ó hUadhaigh sent her to prison for a year for the same offence. The excuse she gave him for stealing more than one pair was that she had a kidney problem. It obviously hadn't been cured.

Ann junior was also caught shoplifting after she was released from prison and sentenced to six months on 4 January 2000. Three months later the case of the traffic Garda from Waterford who was seriously injured when Ann drove the patrol car at him finally came to the High Court. Noel Harty had undergone skin grafts and tests for HIV and hepatitis C. He also suffered internal bleeding and post-traumatic stress and retired early from the Gardaí. Mr Justice Roderick Murphy summed up the incident in one word—frightening. On Monday 28 May 2001, six years later, Noel Harty was awarded over £80,000.

The state had to foot the compensation bill for Ann's criminal behaviour but it was determined to take as much money as it could from her father, brother and sister. They had made their money from drug dealing in spite of Tony's claims to the contrary. 'I am unemployed for long periods of time,' Tony wrote to the Revenue Commissioner as far back as 1991, 'like thousands of other misfortunes in this country.' It was true he didn't work but he wasn't broke and a week before Christmas 1998, Judge Raymond Groarke delivered the latest round of bad news. The three Fellonis were brought in handcuffs from their three separate jails to hear the verdict.

The judge found that Tony, Regina and Luigi were drug dealers who had benefited substantially from selling heroin. They were supposed to be living on social welfare but they had substantial criminal assets. 'Their financial dealings are such as cannot be explained by any straightforward employment,' the judge said. The

Fellonis didn't even try to present any evidence to contradict the Director of Public Prosecution's case. The truth was they couldn't.

The judge carried out assessments as to how much they had made from drug dealing and how much they could pay. He based his assessments on the amount of money in the bank accounts, tracker bonds, cash the Gardaí found during its searches of the Finglas house and the Fellonis' flats, and the value of the car and the house. In Tony's case the judge said he made £400,000 of which £80,000 was recoverable. Regina, he found, also made £400,000 but the state could get back £300,000 of that.

The judge believed Luigi made far more money dealing heroin than the state was able to link him to. After all, he told the Gardaí when he was arrested at Dublin Airport that he had gone to England with £50,000 cash to buy heroin. However, since the evidence wasn't put before him in court Mr Justice Raymond Groarke was, as he said, 'somewhat restricted' in what he could do. He found that Luigi had made £75,000 from drug dealing and ordered him to pay back £23,127.

The Gardaí and the lawyers for the state were delighted. After just two days they had comprehensively won the first contested case under the 1994 Criminal Justice Act, the so-called Money Laundering Act. The Fellonis didn't really put up a fight. Detective Inspector John O'Driscoll said afterwards the victory would send a message to the country's drug dealers that they would not be allowed profit from their acts. The judge also rejected an application for free legal aid in the event of an appeal. It was the end of the legal road on this one.

The Fellonis never bothered following up their challenge to the constitutionality of the 1994 Criminal Justice Act and there's no point in them doing that now either. John Gilligan has since tried it and lost. He was convicted in the Special Criminal Court and it assessed his earnings from drug dealing and ordered that €17.7 million be taken from him. He challenged that in the High Court which held that while the 1994 Act was constitutional, the confiscation order was not. The Special Criminal Court could not determine how much Gilligan made from drug dealing. The state is appealing that decision to the Supreme Court.

The next step along the Felloni money trail was the process of actually taking the money off them. Frank Cassidy, a solicitor from the Chief State Solicitors Office, who also worked closely with the

Criminal Assets Bureau, was appointed the receiver. His job was to gather and liquidate all the Fellonis' assets and put the money into one account. First he collected £12,394.66 from Tony—£4,917.74 from his Bank of Ireland account in Camden Street and the remainder in cash (punts and sterling). Then he took £14,191.84 from Luigi—£12,676.75 of this was in punts, sterling, traveller's cheques, pesetas and US dollars. The remaining £1,515.09 was taken from his Bank of Ireland, Irish Permanent and Post Office accounts.

But these figures were dwarfed by the amount seized from Regina—£206,605.67. In truth much of this was Tony's money which he got her to hide for him. The largest single figure that went to make up that total was received from the sale of her house in Finglas. Everything of value had been stripped from 127 Mellowes Road including the fireplace in the living room. Dublin Corporation had boarded it up with steel shutters. It had been abandoned and was in a derelict and dilapidated state. However, it was still put up for auction on 27 July 1999 and sold after competitive bidding for £70,500.77.

Regina's car, a 94-D Nissan Micra, was sold for £2,750. The sterling drafts realised £23,930.18, and £1,975 which was found during a search of the Finglas house was also handed over. The remaining £114,926.42 was taken from the AIB, the Bank of Ireland, the ICS Building Society and the Post Office. Solicitors, auctioneers and stamp duty on the sale of the house cost £6,476.70. By the end of 1999 Frank Cassidy had lodged the money from all three—£233,192.17—to the receiver's account.

Regina and Luigi had long ago given up but Tony made one last-ditch effort from Portlaoise Prison to hold on to the drug money. He tried to stop the High Court ordering the closure of the receiver's account and the handing over of the money to the state. On 14 February 2000 he claimed he was being denied his rights under the Irish Constitution and the European Convention on Human Rights. The confiscation, he said, was a criminal penalty, a double jeopardy and therefore he was being punished twice for the same offence.

He also had a go at the Criminal Assets Bureau for good measure. 'I say that all or part of the Proceeds of Crime Act 1996 and the Criminal Assets Bureau Act 1996 is unconstitutional and, as well, these Acts contravene the European Convention on Human Rights and Fundamental Freedoms,' he boldly declared. 'I further say it is unconstitutional because it is a criminal law made to look like a civil law.'

It was stirring stuff but alas for Tony it didn't work. Dublin Corporation was paid £8,445 that Regina owed it since it registered a judgment against her on 19 November 1996. The claim related to legal costs awarded against her after she lost a personal injury action she took against the Corporation. She claimed she hurt her finger in a defective door in her Auntie Evelyn's flat. On Tuesday 5 April 2000 the High Court ordered the money that was left, almost over £225,000, be paid to the Exchequer. It was the first time this had been done since the foundation of the state and the first such case under the 1994 Criminal Justice Act.

Ironically it was the taxpayer that enabled the Fellonis to fight the state at every stage of the confiscation battle. Tony, Regina and Luigi were all on free legal aid. Their barristers and solicitors were paid for by the state. By April 2003 the bill was over €53,000 of which €22,402.38 was paid to Tony's lawyers, €22,005.88 to Regina's and €8,998.26 to Luigi's.

However, John O'Driscoll and Frank Cassidy hadn't quite finished. They remembered that Tony's mother Mary had lodged £20,000 in cash as bail for him on 27 February 1994. Tony had always turned up for court and therefore once he was convicted, his mother was entitled to her money back. But Mary Felloni had since died and the money remained unclaimed with the County Registrar for over six years. The questions now were whose was it and what was to be done with it.

The answers to both were simple. The money was never Mary's. It was Tony's. The £20,000 had been taken in lots of £10,000, £2,000 and £8,000 from Regina's Bank of Ireland and AIB accounts. It was then lodged to Mary's account on 15 September 1994. Two weeks later she used it to bail her son out. The money was clearly the proceeds of drug trafficking and therefore liable for confiscation.

Frank Cassidy went to court and argued that point and won. On 30 May 2001 he was ordered to seize the cheque for £21,090.75 but it couldn't be handed over to the state until Regina was formally served with the documentation. She had been released from prison but she wasn't well and it was over a year before the Gardaí caught up with her. On 17 October 2002 the final cheque representing the last of the Fellonis' known Irish assets was lodged to the Department of

Finance account for €26,937.79. In seventeen months it had gained just €158.06 interest.

The state took €312,149.77 from the Fellonis but they still owe more. Tony owes over €85,841.07, Luigi over €11,346.58 while Regina owes over €129,309.28. The state is unlikely to pursue them for it. However, if the Gardaí find they have the money and can pay but won't pay, then the state can go after them under Section 19 of the Criminal Justice Act. This allows the DPP to ask the court to impose a consecutive sentence in default of payment. Tony and Luigi could get an extra twelve months each while Regina could get three years. The state is also still chasing the money in Northern Ireland and England. There's still at least another £115,500 sterling to be seized. The hunt for the Fellonis' drug money continues. It has now moved abroad….

Epilogue

The drug problem in Dublin was contained for a number of years after 1986, the year Tony Felloni was first jailed in Ireland for selling heroin. This was due to a number of factors including the enactment of tougher laws, the jailing of main dealers and the availability of better treatment facilities. But the problem was by no means eradicated and between 1990 and 1996 it got dramatically worse. The numbers seeking treatment for heroin addiction doubled in that seven-year period. Not only did the number of addicts increase but they got younger. Two out of every five had started using drugs before they were fifteen years old.

The Health Research Board found that by the end of 1996 there were 4,865 addicts receiving treatment for drug addiction in clinics all over the country. It was the first time 2,041 of them had presented themselves for help. The problem of heroin addiction had spread out from Dublin to the surrounding counties of Wicklow, Louth, Meath and Kildare, but addicts were also turning up in Cork, Limerick and Waterford.

The scale of the increase in heroin addiction was particularly remarkable in the north inner city and two months after Tony Felloni was sent to prison in 1996 the Concerned Parents movement re-emerged there before quickly spreading to other parts of the city. Again it was born out of the perceived inability of the government, the Gardaí, the Health Board and the local authorities to tackle the heroin epidemic which Felloni had done so much to create. The events of August and September 1996 were a replica of those of 1983/4.

Once again mass meetings were held in schools and community halls in the north and south inner city and also further afield in the suburbs of Tallaght and Clondalkin. Once again homes were marched on as part of the 'Deliver us from Evil' campaign and suspected drug dealers were ordered out of the areas. Hundreds of people gathered and bellowed 'PUSHER, PUSHER, PUSHER—OUT, OUT, OUT!' at their

236

front doors. Flats were boarded up and 'DRUG SHOP CLOSED' was painted on many of them. Once again there were allegations of violence, Garda intimidation and IRA infiltration. A group of men in Tallaght wearing black balaclavas posed with guns for newspaper photographs and vowed to shoot drug dealers.

That movement culminated on 27 September 1996 with 3,000 people marching from the north inner city through O'Connell Street and up to the Department of Justice on St Stephen's Green. In a bigger version of the February 1984 march, the residents and children carried similar banners, placards and a coffin. Again they demanded action on the drug crisis and bitterly criticised the government and the Minister for Justice, Nora Owen. A third city-wide anti-drugs march was held on 19 June 2002 but this one was smaller than the others and, although the campaigners again warned the drugs crisis was continuing to get worse, this time they were simply ignored.

Local task forces have been set up in the thirteen suburbs of Dublin and Cork deemed to be the worst drug-affected areas in the country and government funding has been allocated to tackle the problem at local level. But the problem of heroin in Ireland is continuing to get worse. It is no longer confined to the poorer areas of the capital. Heroin addiction has spread down the east coast as far as Arklow, inland into the south-east towns of Carlow, Portlaoise, Tullamore and Athlone. There is now a treatment centre for heroin addicts in Galway. The addiction has also moved north of the country into towns like Navan, Drogheda and Monaghan and is popping up in some of the most unexpected places like Kingscourt, Co. Cavan. Rural heroin has now become a frightening reality.

Another sinister development in the past four years has been the emergence of a new drug epidemic, with cocaine at its core. Once the drug of choice for the rich and famous, exclusively associated in its original form with wealth and glamour, it is now being pushed in the poorest areas of inner city Dublin, supplementing and sometimes replacing heroin as the intravenous drug of choice. In its annual report for 2001, the European Monitoring Centre for Drugs and Drug Addiction warned of a 'blurring of the traditional boundaries in the use of cocaine', specifically among 'socially excluded groups'. Crack cocaine is also being used in Dublin, particularly among the immigrant communities.

Cocaine abuse in this country has soared. Ireland now has the second highest percentage of young people—18- to 24-year-olds—in the European Union who have used cocaine in the last twelve months. It is a figure that is expected to rise. Cocaine is a more profitable drug from a dealer's point of view. It sells for a higher price and addicts need to buy more quantities, more often, because the highs don't last as long as they do on heroin. Not only is cocaine more expensive for a drug addict, it is also as addictive as heroin and more difficult to come off. Unlike heroin, for which there is methadone, there is no substitute treatment for cocaine.

Meanwhile heroin dealing has become more disparate as the main dealers like Felloni have been replaced by hundreds of smaller dealers who are harder to catch because they deal in smaller amounts. Many of the major dealers have fled the country but some are still running their businesses from Holland and the UK. Their places have been taken here at home by a younger, more violent and altogether more dangerous drug dealer than Tony Felloni ever was. The ex-pat drug barons now living abroad deal directly with European and Asian suppliers on the continent and arrange huge shipments for the young drug dealers who have succeeded them at home. Firearms, mostly pistols and sub-machine guns, are now included in the shipments as 'sweeteners'.

Today the supply of heroin, cocaine, cannabis and ecstasy in Ireland is controlled by heavily armed criminal gangs who often co-operate to bring in large shipments but feud murderously to protect their own markets or take over another's territory. Not surprisingly therefore the number of drug addicts continues to increase. The Eastern Health Board has estimated that the number of drug addicts in the capital increased from 8,000 in 1996 to 10,000 in 1998 to 15,000 in 2003, but there are no definitive figures either for Dublin or for the rest of the country. No one knows just how many drug addicts there are in Ireland today.

No one knows how many people have died from drug-related illnesses or heroin overdoses either, but every Christmas the people of the north inner city put up a Christmas tree in memory of the dead. Over 130 people are remembered with Mass cards, flowers, photographs, names on stars, stories and poems. Tony Felloni has, however, survived his own brush with heroin addiction. He is due out of prison in the year 2010.